The Sociolinguistic Competence of Immersion Students

SECOND LANGUAGE ACQUISITION
Series Editor: **Professor David Singleton**, *Trinity College, Dublin, Ireland*

This series brings together titles dealing with a variety of aspects of language acquisition and processing in situations where a language or languages other than the native language is involved. Second language is thus interpreted in its broadest possible sense. The volumes included in the series all offer in their different ways, on the one hand, exposition and discussion of empirical findings and, on the other, some degree of theoretical reflection. In this latter connection, no particular theoretical stance is privileged in the series; nor is any relevant perspective – sociolinguistic, psycholinguistic, neurolinguistic, etc. – deemed out of place. The intended readership of the series includes final-year undergraduates working on second language acquisition projects, postgraduate students involved in second language acquisition research, and researchers and teachers in general whose interests include a second language acquisition component.

Full details of all the books in this series and of all our other publications can be found on http://www.multilingual-matters.com, or by writing to Multilingual Matters, St Nicholas House, 31-34 High Street, Bristol BS1 2AW, UK.

SECOND LANGUAGE ACQUISITION
Series Editor: David Singleton, Trinity College, Dublin, Ireland

The Sociolinguistic Competence of Immersion Students

Raymond Mougeon, Terry Nadasdi
and Katherine Rehner

MULTILINGUAL MATTERS
Bristol • Buffalo • Toronto

Library of Congress Cataloging in Publication Data
A catalog record for this book is available from the Library of Congress.
Mougeon, Raymond.
The Sociolinguistic Competence of Immersion Students/Raymond Mougeon, Terry Nadasdi and Katherine Rehner.
Second Language Acquisition: 47
Includes bibliographical references.
1. Second language acquisition. 2 Immersion method (Language teaching)
I. Nadasdi, Terry. II. Rehner, Katherine. III. Title.
P118.2.M678 2010
306.44–dc22 2009033796

British Library Cataloguing in Publication Data
A catalogue entry for this book is available from the British Library.

ISBN-13: 978-1-84769-239-9 (hbk)
ISBN-13: 978-1-84769-238-2 (pbk)

Multilingual Matters
UK: St Nicholas House, 31-34 High Street, Bristol BS1 2AW, UK.
USA: UTP, 2250 Military Road, Tonawanda, NY 14150, USA.
Canada: UTP, 5201 Dufferin Street, North York, Ontario M3H 5T8, Canada.

Copyright © 2010 Raymond Mougeon, Terry Nadasdi and Katherine Rehner.

All rights reserved. No part of this work may be reproduced in any form or by any means without permission in writing from the publisher.

The policy of Multilingual Matters/Channel View Publications is to use papers that are natural, renewable and recyclable products, made from wood grown in sustainable forests. In the manufacturing process of our books, and to further support our policy, preference is given to printers that have FSC and PEFC Chain of Custody certification. The FSC and/or PEFC logos will appear on those books where full certification has been granted to the printer concerned.

Typeset by Techset Composition Ltd., Salisbury, UK.

Contents

Tables and Figures vii
Preface xi

1 Introduction 1
  Sociolinguistic Variation in First Language Speech
    Communities 2
  Variation in Second Language 4
  Research on the Learning of Sociolinguistic Variation
    by Second Language Learners 6

2 Methodology 23
  Research Goals 23
  Characteristics of the French Immersion Student
    Population under Study 26
  Speaker Sample 47
  Corpora Used as Comparative Norms 50
  Research Hypotheses 53
  Data Analysis 56

3 Variation in L1 Spoken French 58
  Introduction 58
  Grammatical Variation 59
  Lexical Variation 78
  Extra-Linguistic Constraints 80
  Linguistic Constraints 82
  Phonetic Variation 83
  Conclusion 90

4 Students' Learning of Variation 91
  Frequency and Treatment of Variants in the French
    Immersion Students' Educational Input 91
  Comparison of the Frequency and Treatment of Variants in
    Teachers' Classroom Discourse and the Teaching
    Materials 105

	Types and Frequency of Variants Used by the French Immersion Students	109
	Learning of the Linguistic and Stylistic Constraints of Sociolinguistic Variation	125
	Effect of Independent Variables on the Learning of Sociolinguistic Variation	131
5	The Potential Benefits of Increased FL1 Input in an Eductional Context	140
	Introduction	140
	Effects of Increased Exposure to FL1 Speakers in an Educational Context	143
	Conclusion	150
6	Conclusion	155
	Introduction	155
	Sociolinguistic Variation in the Educational Input of French Immersion Students	156
	Educational Implications of Results	164
	Limitations and Directions for Future Study	168

Appendices 170
   Appendix A: Semi-Directed Taped Interview Schedule – Including Reading Passages 170
   Appendix B: Student Questionnaire Survey 173
   Appendix C: Objectives of the Ontario Ministry of Education Concerning the Development of Sociolinguistic Competence by Secondary School French Immersion Students 187
   Appendix D: Results of the GoldVarb Analyses of the Sociolinguistic Variables Focused upon in the Current Research 188

Notes 208
References 214

Tables and Figures

Tables

2.1	Immersion students' sex, place of birth and grade	28
2.2	Immersion students' social class background: mother, father and combined	29
2.3	Languages spoken fluently by immersion students' parents	31
2.4	Languages spoken at home by immersion students' parents	32
2.5	Languages spoken at home by the immersion students	33
2.6	Languages spoken outside of the home by the immersion students	34
2.7	Use of French by the immersion students within and outside the home	37
2.8	Use of French by the immersion students in the school setting	37
2.9	Languages of media use by the immersion students	38
2.10	Time spent in Francophone environments by the immersion students	39
2.11	Time spent in Francophone environments by immersion students as a function of place	40
2.12	Time spent with a Francophone family by the immersion students	41
2.13	Time spent with a Francophone family by immersion students as a function of place	42
2.14	Values associated by the immersion students with the importance of the French language within the Canadian context, the learning of French and the French-Canadian culture	46
2.15	Chief characteristics of the 41 student sample	48
2.16	41 students' curricular and extra-curricular patterns of French language use	49
3.1	Effect of linguistic context on schwa use and non-use	86
3.2	Sociostylistic status of variants in L1 Canadian French	89
4.1	Marked informal variants in the French immersion teachers' classroom speech and in L1 Canadian French	92

4.2	Mildly marked informal variants in the French immersion teachers' classroom speech and in L1 Canadian French	93
4.3	Percentage of formal variants in the French immersion teachers' classroom speech and in L1 Canadian French	94
4.4	Percentage of hyper-formal variants in the French immersion teachers' classroom speech and in L1 Canadian French	94
4.5	Percentage of neutral variants in the French immersion teachers' classroom speech and in L1 Canadian French	95
4.6	Marked informal variants in the French Language Arts teaching materials (compared to L1 Canadian French)	97
4.7	Percentage of mildly marked informal variants in the French Language Arts teaching materials (compared to L1 Canadian French)	98
4.8	Percentage of formal variants in the French Language Arts teaching materials (compared to L1 Canadian French)	100
4.9	Percentage of hyper-formal variants in the French Language Arts teaching materials (compared to L1 Canadian French)	101
4.10	Frequency distribution of variants *alors*, *donc* and *(ça) fait que* in the pedagogical materials according to syntactic context	102
4.11	Percentage of neutral variants in the French Language Arts teaching materials (compared to L1 Canadian French)	103
4.12	Distribution (%) of marked and mildly marked informal variants in L1 Canadian French, immersion teachers' French, French Language Arts materials (dialogues) and French Language Arts materials (texts)	106
4.13	Distribution (%) of neutral, formal and hyper-formal variants in l1 Canadian French, immersion teachers' French, French Language Arts materials (dialogues) and French Language Arts materials (texts)	107
4.14	Frequency (%) of marked informal variants in the speech of immersion students compared to L1 Canadian French, French immersion teachers, written dialogues and texts	111
4.15	Frequency (%) of mildly marked informal variants in the speech of immersion students compared to L1 Canadian French, French immersion teachers, written dialogues and texts	112
4.16	Frequency (%) of forms that resemble marked and mildly marked informal variants in the speech of immersion students compared to L1 Canadian French, French immersion teachers, written dialogues and texts	114
4.17	Frequency of non-native variants in the speech of immersion students	117

4.18	Frequency (%) of formal and hyper-formal variants in the speech of immersion students compared to L1 Canadian French, French immersion teachers, written dialogues and texts	120
4.19	Frequency (%) of neutral variants in the speech of immersion students compared to L1 Canadian French, French immersion teachers, written dialogues, and texts	122
4.20	Linguistic constraints on the use of variants found in the speech of L1 speakers and French immersion students	126
4.21	Effect of stylistic parameters in the speech of French immersion students and L1 speakers of French	130
4.22	Effect of independent variables on variant choice in the speech of the French immersion students	132
5.1	Mildly marked informal variants for which beneficial effects are likely to obtain	144
5.2	Marked informal variants for which beneficial effects are likely to obtain	145
5.3	Formal variants for which beneficial effects are likely to obtain	146
5.4	Hyper-formal variants for which beneficial effects are likely to obtain	147
5.5	Variants for which negative effects are likely to obtain	149
5.6	Expected effects on French immersion students' speech of greater interactions with FL1 speakers in a school setting	151
6.1	Sociostylistic status of the variants and their frequency in the immersion students' speech and their educational input and in FL1 speech	157

Tables in Appendices

D1	Effects of linguistic and extra-linguistic constraints on *ne* use versus non-use of *ne*	188
D2	Effects of linguistic and extra-linguistic constraints on *seulement* versus *juste*	190
D3	Effects of extra-linguistic constraints on *alors* versus *donc*	191
D4	Effects of extra-linguistic constraints on *alors* and *donc* versus *so*	192
D5	Effects of linguistic constraints on the use of three variants denoting future time reference	193
D6	Effects of extra-linguistic constraints on the use of three variants denoting future time reference	194
D7	Use of *je vais* versus *je vas* as a function of length of stay in a Francophone environment	196

D8 Effects of linguistic and extra-linguistic constraints on *nous* versus *on* 196
D9 Effects of linguistic constraints on singular versus plural verb forms in the third person plural 197
D10 Effects of extra-linguistic constraints on singular versus plural verb forms in the third person plural 198
D11 Effects of linguistic constraints on auxiliaries *avoir* versus *être* 199
D12 Effects of extra-linguistic constraints on *avoir* versus *être* 199
D13 Effects of linguistic and extra-linguistic constraints on *chez* 1 versus à *la maison* 200
D14 Effects of linguistic and extra-linguistic constraints on *travail* versus *emploi* 202
D15 Effects of linguistic and extra-linguistic constraints on *vivre* versus *habiter* 203
D16 Effects of linguistic and extra-linguistic constraints on *auto* versus *voiture* 204
D17 Effects of linguistic constraints on schwa use versus non-use 205
D18 Effects of extra-linguistic constraints on schwa use versus schwa non-use 206
D19 Effects of morphophonetic context on /l/ use versus non-use 207
D20 Effects of style on /l/ non-use in the speech of the French immersion students and Mougeon and Beniak's North-Bay Franco-Ontarian students 207

Figures

5.1 Rates of /l/ non-use (%) in interviews versus reading passages by unrestricted speakers, restricted speakers, and French immersion students 147
5.2 Rates of schwa non-use (%) in interviews versus reading passages by unrestricted speakers, restricted speakers, and French immersion students 148

Preface

This book is designed for three kinds of readers. First, it will be of interest to graduate students who are interested in sociolinguistic variation within the field of second language acquisition. We hope this volume will provide a solid foundation and theoretical orientation for scholars wishing to examine variation in a wide variety of languages in different settings. The second target audience for this volume are teachers of French as a second language. It is rare indeed for faculties of education to provide second language teachers with information concerning the variable use of linguistic forms, their frequency of use and the linguistic/social factors that govern their usage. Our book not only provides French as a second language (FSL) teachers with such information, but also offers them opportunities to reflect on the factors that condition the learning of sociolinguistic variation by French immersion students. Finally, and perhaps most importantly, our research is intended for those responsible for curriculum development. Policy-makers need to be made aware of the variable use of language in order to develop pedagogical materials that promote the acquisition of such use by classroom learners.

The idea for the present volume began more than 10 years ago when we extended the sociolinguistic methodology we had used to investigate variation and change in the speech of Francophone bilingual students residing in minority communities to research on the learning of variation by French immersion students. During the writing of this book, we have been fortunate enough to have interacted with a number of individuals who, contemporaneously, pursued research projects similar to our own. These researchers have helped through their own research, through their interest in our work and through various exchanges at conferences. We would like to express our gratitude to them here: Julie Auger, Bob Bayley, Hélène Blondeau, Jean-Marc Dewaele, Naomi Nagy, Denis Preston, Vera Regan, Gillian Sankoff, Pierrette Thibault and Alain Thomas.

We would also like to express our thanks to our family members, Françoise Mougeon, Paula Kelly and John Ippolito for their support and encouragement. We gratefully acknowledge funding support received from the Social Sciences and Humanities Research Council of Canada and would also like to express our thanks to the French immersion teachers in the Greater Toronto Area, who allowed us to gather the student speech corpus on which our research is based. Finally, we would like to thank Roy Lyster and Dalila Ayoun for providing insightful comments that have greatly improved the quality of our manuscript.

The present volume builds largely on previous work of scholars such as Elaine Tarone, Doug Adamson, Denis Preston, Bob Bayley and Vera Regan who initially conducted research on the variable use of target and non-target forms by second language learners. In our own research, we have extended the study of variation to a large number of variables involving target-language forms whose sociolinguistic status differs. By raising awareness of the sociolinguistic challenges that second language learners face, we hope to pave the way to new developments in second language pedagogy that pay greater attention to sociolinguistic variation. By doing so, we can expect the next generation of French immersion students to make even greater progress acquiring a native-like mastery of French.

Chapter 1
Introduction[1]

More than three decades of research focused on the second language outcomes of French immersion programs has produced a wealth of studies documenting the successes and limitations of French immersion students' communicative proficiency [see notably Calvé (1991), Harley (1984), Lyster (2007) and Rebuffot (1993) for overviews]. For the most part, these studies have concentrated on grammatical competence, that is the receptive and productive knowledge of the target-language system, and to a lesser extent on discourse competence, that is the receptive and productive knowledge of coherent and cohesive target-language discourse. However, considerably less research has been devoted to French immersion students' sociolinguistic competence, that is the receptive and productive knowledge of sociolinguistic variants and of the linguistic, social and stylistic factors that govern their usage.

The goal of this volume is to bring together and discuss from both a theoretical and applied perspective the results of a research project that focuses on the acquisition of sociolinguistic competence by French immersion students.[2] In so doing, we hope to make a significant contribution to this understudied aspect of French immersion students' communicative competence. In the chapters that follow, sociolinguistic competence will be examined in relation to the learner's knowledge of sociolinguistic variation. More specifically, we will be assessing the extent to which French immersion students master a full repertoire of sociolinguistic variants, acquire their discursive frequency and observe the same linguistic and extra-linguistic constraints on variant choice adhered to by first language (L1) speakers of French. We will also assess the extent to which the French immersion students' learning of sociolinguistic variation is affected by a number of crucial independent variables (e.g. the learners' extra-curricular exposure to L1 French and the treatment of sociolinguistic variation in the educational input of the French immersion students). It should be pointed out at the outset that the present volume constitutes a unique and original contribution to research on the learning of sociolinguistic competence by advanced second language learners in an educational setting. To our knowledge, there has not been any book written on this topic before and the findings reported upon in the present volume are based on more than a dozen detailed studies on the learning of a wide range of sociolinguistic variants pertaining to the different components of language (phonology, lexicon, morphology and morphosyntax). Furthermore, ours is the only research of which we are aware that investigates the effect of educational input on learners' sociolinguistic competence.

Before we provide more specific information about the goals and methodology of our research, we will situate the research on the learning of sociolinguistic competence by advanced second language learners in the broader fields of variationist sociolinguistics and second language acquisition (SLA) research. We will also provide a state-of-the-art review of studies that have focused specifically on the acquisition of sociolinguistic competence by advanced learners of French as a second language.

Sociolinguistic Variation in First Language Speech Communities

Language variation is observable in all components of every human language (syntax, morphology, lexicon and phonology). It involves an alternation between different elements of a given language whose meaning (or phonological status, if they are sounds) is identical. There are two types of language variation: linguistic and sociolinguistic. With linguistic variation, the alternation between elements is categorically constrained by the linguistic context in which they occur. With sociolinguistic variation, speakers can choose between elements in the same linguistic context and, hence, the alternation is probabilistic. Furthermore, the probability of one form being chosen over another is also affected in a probabilistic way by a range of extra-linguistic factors [e.g. the degree of (in)formality of the topic under discussion, the social status of the speaker and of the interlocutor, the setting in which communication takes place, etc.].

An example of linguistic variation is the grammatical notion of plurality in spoken English, which can be conveyed by various affixes whose use is constrained categorically by the linguistic context in which they occur: *finger* versus *fingers* [z]; *cheek* versus *cheeks* [s]; *bridge* versus *bridges* [ɘz]; *foot* versus *feet*; *ox* versus *oxen*, etc. By 'constrained categorically' we mean that in a given linguistic context L1 speakers of English will always use the same form to convey a notion. Thus, in the above example, with nouns that end in a voiceless consonant, L1 speakers will always use the plural affix [s], with nouns that end in a voiced occlusive consonant, they will always use the affix [z], etc. An example of linguistic variation in French is the alternation between full and contracted forms of the definite article. The full form occurs before all consonant initial nouns (e.g. *le livre* 'the book' and *la table* 'the table'), whereas the contracted form is found categorically before words beginning with a vowel (e.g. *l'avion* 'the plane' and *l'assiette* 'the plate'). In linguistics, the different forms that speakers alternate between are referred to as 'variants' and the notion they convey is referred to as the 'variable'.

An example of sociolinguistic variation is the *-ing* variable, which involves the alternation between two pronunciations of the final sound of English words ending in *-ing*, such as *morning*, *nothing* and *doing* (e.g. *good morning* [n] versus [ŋ] or *nothing* [n] versus [ŋ]). L1 speakers of English tend to use variant [n] more frequently when *-ing* occurs in verbal forms, as in *he's eatin'*, than in nouns, such as *morning* or *Kipling*, where it is less likely to occur (a probabilistic linguistic constraint), see Houston (1985). L1 speakers of English also use [n] more often when discussing an informal topic, telling a funny story, etc. or if they hail from the lower social strata (probabilistic extra-linguistic constraints), see Trudgill (1974) and Downes (1998). A similar example from French is the variable use or non-use of /l/, which is also influenced by linguistic and extra-linguistic constraints. L1 speakers of Canadian French delete /l/ much more frequently when it occurs in a subject pronoun (e.g. *i(l) faut* 'it is necessary') than in definite articles (e.g. *dans (l)a cave* 'in the basement'). Also, male speakers and speakers from the lower social strata tend to delete /l/ more often than female speakers and speakers from the upper social strata (across all linguistic contexts), see Sankoff and Cedergren (1976) and Poplack and Walker (1986). It should be noted that these probabilistic linguistic and extra-lingusitic constraints are shared across speakers in a given speech community and are a feature of their native language competence. Furthermore, to distinguish the variants that are involved in linguistic variation from those involved in sociolinguistic variation, the former can be referred to as 'linguistic variants' and the latter as 'sociolinguistic variants'. Likewise, the notions conveyed by linguistic variants are, as pointed out above, referred to as linguistic variables, while the notions expressed by sociolinguistic variations are referred to as sociolinguistic variables.

Sociolinguistic variants are of special interest to linguists and language educators because they can be used as markers of style or register, social status, group membership, etc. For instance, returning to the *-ing* variable, speakers of English may elect to use variant [n] along with other informal variants (e.g. informal content or grammatical words such as *pal* for *friend*, *juice* for *electricity*, *gonna* for *going to*, etc.) to reduce the psychological distance between themselves and their interlocutors, to impart a humoristic tone to their speech, etc., and, in contrast, they may choose to use [ŋ] and the other formal variants mentioned above to heighten the psychological distance, to show respect to their interlocutor, because they are delivering a formal speech, etc.

Given that the use of sociolinguistic variants is governed by a complex set of linguistic and extra-linguistic factors, sociolinguistic variation presents a special challenge to L2 learners and consequently it is, as a rule, introduced late, if at all, in L2 syllabi. Be that as it may, because sociolinguistic variation is commonplace and because it is a crucial property of all human languages, L2 learners must come to grips with it sooner or later in their learning of the target language. Therefore, it is important to conduct research on the learning of sociolinguistic variation by such learners, which could bring to light useful data for program assessment, curriculum and materials development and implementation. It is precisely this type of research that the present volume reports upon.

Variation in Second Language

Research on the learning of sociolinguistic variation by L2 learners is part of a large body of research investigating various dimensions of the communicative competence of L2 learners, a concept originally defined by Canale and Swain (1980) and refined and further developed by others (e.g. Bachman, 1987; Brown, 1987). Within this body of research, the study of the learning of sociolinguistic variation is usually recognized as belonging to the set of studies that investigates the sociolinguistic competence of L2 learners. Interestingly, research on the learning of sociolinguistic variation, as we have just defined it, by L2 learners has only recently developed. Prior to this, numerous studies investigated the variable nature of the interlanguage of L2 learners (e.g. Dickerson, 1974; Ellis, 1987; Gatbonton, 1978; Huebner, 1983, 1985; Tarone, 1988). They focused on L2 learners' alternation between native and non-native usages or between more than one non-native usage to express a given notion, and not on L2 learners' use of sociolinguistic variants. For instance, Gass and Selinker (2001, p. 254) provide examples of alternating forms of native and non-native interrogative sentences in the past tense documented in the speech of a young Japanese learner of English as a second language (e.g. *Do you saw these peppermint?*; *Did you see the ghost?*; *What do you do?*; *What did you do?*). Such alternations represent a transitional stage before the L2 learners use the native forms categorically.

In order to avoid confusion between sociolinguistic variation, as is observable in L1 speech, and variable interlanguage production, some SLA researchers have referred to the latter as 'variation along the vertical continuum' (see Andersen, 1981; Corder, 1981; Young, 1988) and to the former as 'variation along the horizontal continuum' (Corder, 1981; Young, 1988). In our own work, we refer to the first type of variation as Type 1 variation and the latter as Type 2 variation (Rehner, 2002, 2004), terminology that has been adopted by researchers such as Dewaele (2004a) and Bayley and Regan (2004).

Because Type 1 variation involves forms that are, for the most part, quite predictable and because such forms express the same notion, previous SLA research on variable interlanguage adopted some of the constructs of variationist sociolinguistics (e.g. the use of the term 'variant' to refer to both the native and non-native forms). One important contribution of this variable interlanguage research was to show that the L2 learners' alternations between native and non-native usages evolve through time. Thus non-native usages decrease in frequency and eventually disappear as learners progress in their learning of the target language, and they undergo qualitative changes (e.g. become more complex or closer to the target). This research also showed that the frequency of use of native and non-native usages is simultaneously influenced by linguistic factors and by some of the same extra-linguistic factors that have been found to have an impact on sociolinguistic variation in L1 speech varieties (e.g. differences based on the nature of the communicative tasks learners performed in their L2). Obviously factors that apply only to L2 learners were also found to be influential (e.g. input, time spent learning the target language, and transfer from the L1 of the learners to their L2). For an overview of such research, the reader is directed to, among others, Adamson (1988), Beebe (1988), Ellis (1999), and Tarone (1988, 1990).

Without denying the significance of research on Type 1 variation, it remains that this research has largely ignored Type 2 variation, that is to say the investigation of sociolinguistic variation by L2 learners. There are two main reasons for this. Firstly, this research is not necessarily focused on aspects of the target language where L1 speakers alternate between variants. Furthermore, when this research happens to examine such alternations (e.g. contracted versus non-contracted forms of English copula *to be* – *I'm* versus *I am*), it rarely investigates the learning of these alternations from within the perspective of variationist sociolinguistics. Thus, there was a gap in the field of SLA research that the new strand of studies on the learning of sociolinguistic variation by L2 learners has begun to fill. More specifically, this new strand of research focuses exclusively on sociolinguistic variables within the target language and investigates learners' mastery of such variables. What is of interest, though, is that in their investigation of the learning of sociolinguistic variation these new studies have documented non-native variants, in addition to native ones (e.g. the non-native use of a construction like **à ma maison* that alternates with two native variants, namely *chez moi* and *à la maison* – all three variants meaning 'to/at my house'). These non-native variants are not unlike the non-native forms investigated in research on Type 1 variation and their presence in the speech of L2 learners raises issues similar to those examined in that research (e.g. What are their sources?; What factors promote their fossilization or disappearance?). Thus it is clear that while this new strand of research brings with it significant innovations, it cannot ignore the findings of the research on variable interlanguage that has paved the way for it.

Research on the Learning of Sociolinguistic Variation by Second Language Learners

Methodology

Studies on the learning of sociolinguistic variation by L2 learners, like the research presented in this volume, have, for the most part, been conducted within the framework of 'variationist sociolinguistics'. This discipline was established by William Labov in the late 1960s and early 1970s. Labov (1966, 1972) conducted a series of seminal studies on the patterns of sociolinguistic variation observable in the varieties of English spoken in urban settings in the United States. Labov's work spurred further research on sociolinguistic variation in other varieties of English and in varieties of French, Spanish and Portuguese notably in the Americas but also in Europe during the 1970s and 1980s. Thanks to this research, we now possess a great wealth of detailed information on numerous aspects of sociolinguistic variation that can be found in the above-mentioned languages. Not only does this information document the specific variants used by L1 speakers of these languages, it also sheds light on how sociolinguistic variation is influenced by linguistic and extra-linguistic factors. Such information provides us with a better understanding of what it is that L2 learners would likely have encountered when interacting with L1 speakers, at least as far as languages like English, French, Spanish and Portuguese are concerned. That said, the use of corpus-based data on L1 sociolinguistic variation for the purpose of descriptive research does not entail that one should impose L1 sociolinguistic norms on L2 learners in a pedagogical context. In our view, this is a separate question that we will address in Chapters 5 and 6. The fact remains that one needs descriptive benchmarks when conducting research on the learning of sociolinguistic variation.

The main goal of these studies is to focus on specific sociolinguistic variables and to verify if L2 learners (1) use the same range of variants as do L1 speakers; (2) use these variants with similar levels of frequency as do L1 speakers; (3) adhere to the same kinds of linguistic and extra-linguistic constraints on sociolinguistic variation observable in L1 speech; and (4) use non-native variants (i.e. forms that are not used by L1 speakers of the target language). The second goal of these studies is to examine the effect of independent variables on these four dimensions of the learning of sociolinguistic variation. These independent variables involve factors such as (1) length of exposure to the target language; (2) opportunities to interact with L1 speakers; (3) influence of inter-systemic factors (e.g. influence of the learner's L1); (4) influence of intra-systemic factors (e.g. markedness of the variants); (5) influence of the learner's social characteristics (e.g. social standing, sex and age); and (6) influence of educational input, a variable that is particularly relevant when the L2 is learned in a classroom setting.

In attempting to reach the first of these two goals, research on the learning of sociolinguistic variation by L2 learners uses spoken language corpora. Such corpora are usually gathered among a socially stratified weighted sample of speakers designed to provide data on the patterns of variant choice associated with various speaker groups in a given speech community. Typically, such weighted speaker samples include roughly equal proportions of female versus male speakers, of speakers from different age groups and of speakers from the different socioeconomic strata. These weightings make it easier to assess the statistical significance of inter-group differences in the frequency of variant selection. The most common method to collect speech data from the speakers included in the sample is a semi-directed face-to-face taped interview. During such an interview the speaker is asked to answer and elaborate on a series of non-invasive and not overly challenging questions on a range of topics chosen to reflect various levels of (in)formality and of the speaker's personal involvement in the topics under discussion. For example, at the formal end of the topic continuum, a speaker may be asked questions about education and matters of language correctness; at the other end of the continuum the speaker may be asked to recall a frightening or humorous experience. At the end of the interview the speaker may be asked to read a short passage, a series of sentences and a list of words in isolation that all include variable sounds (i.e. sounds where speakers alternate between phonetic variants). The purpose of this sequence of reading tasks is to gradually heighten the speaker's consciousness of her/his speech and to produce speech of increasing formality. The data produced during the three reading tasks, along with the data produced during the interview while speaking on a variety of topics, provide some measurement of the extent to which speakers favor standard or non-standard variants at various points on the (in)formality style continuum.

The standard semi-directed interview is about one hour long, and thus speech corpora gathered with this technique usually contain enough occurrences (tokens) of the variants under study to carry out statistical analyses of sociolinguistic variation. Still, the sociolinguistic interview has, like other data gathering techniques, some limitations that can be mentioned here. It does not allow researchers to tap a wide range of speech styles and, in particular, it is not a very good tool to gather data on the less guarded (more casual) speech styles (e.g. the type of register a speaker might use at home with family members or with friends). Data on a broader range of registers can be gathered by using a technique where the speakers tape themselves while interacting with various speakers in different settings. This approach, however, has its own limitations as well. Although it allows the researcher to gather data on a wider range of speech styles, it usually leads to a reduction in the size of the speaker sample, since there are limits to how much speech data can be processed and analyzed in sociolinguistic research on variation. For instance, when the sociolinguists investigating sociolinguistic variation in Montreal French (Vincent et al., 1995) decided to gather a new corpus across several situations of communication, they ended up reducing their speaker sample size on a scale of 10 to 1 in comparison with a previous corpus they had gathered using the standard sociolinguistic interview method. Whether one should opt for one or the other of these two alternatives depends on the goals of the researcher and on the particular needs of the study. However, in order to ensure meaningful comparisons between L1 and L2 speech, it is important that the L1 and L2 data be gathered via the same or similar methods.

To reach its second goal, namely to examine the effect of independent variables on the learning of sociolinguistic variation, research on the learning of sociolinguistic variation by L2 learners gathers data on the independent variables that would be likely predictors of inter-individual differences in the learning of sociolinguistic variation. Such data are usually collected via questionnaires or during the taped interview. The independent variables provided by these data are then, as a rule, correlated with L2 learners' variable output by means of a multivariate factor analysis. The most commonly used tool to perform this kind of factor analysis in research on sociolinguistic variation has been Varbrul/GoldVarb (designed by Pintzuk, and Rand and Sankoff, respectively).

Previous research

To date, there has been considerably more research on the learning of sociolinguistic variation by advanced learners of French as a second language, referred to here for convenience as FL2 learners, than by learners of other second languages (including English). Furthermore, most of the studies that examine the sociolinguistic competence of FL2 learners focus on individuals who, although they learned French in a school setting, have spent a significant amount of time in a French-speaking environment during or after their schooling. In sharp contrast, our own research focuses on FL2 learners whose exposure to French has taken place primarily in a classroom setting and who have had limited contacts with native speakers of French (FL1 speakers), a situation that is typical of most FL2 programs in Canada (see Chapter 2).

Our review of previous research on the learning of sociolinguistic variation by L2 learners will start with studies that focus on FL2 learners and then move to studies that focus on L2 learners of languages other than French.

Learning of sociolinguistic variation by FL2 learners

Research on the learning of sociolinguistic variation by FL2 learners has focused on a range of sociolinguistic variants that differ in terms of their social and stylistic markedness (i.e. the degree to which variants conform to the rules of standard speech or not, whether they are associated with speakers from the upper or lower social classes and/or the formal and informal registers, and whether or not the use of variants is stigmatized). In our own research, we use a system of variant categorization that takes into account the degree of sociostylistic markedness of variants. One of the advantages of this system is that it makes it easier to compare findings across studies and to formulate generalizations.

Our typology of variants is based on a five-point distinction that can be placed on a continuum of sociostylistic markedness. These five points are defined below:

(1) Marked informal variants (often referred to as vernacular variants in sociolinguistic literature) do not conform to the rules of the standard language, are typical of informal speech, are inappropriate in formal settings, are associated with speakers from the lower social strata, usually with male speakers, and may be stigmatized. In the semi-formal situation of the Labovian semi-directed taped interview described above, such variants are usually less frequent than their standard counterparts, and if they are stigmatized, may be completely avoided by speakers from the upper social strata. Examples of marked informal variants documented in spoken Quebec French include the use of noun *char* to denote the concept of 'automobile', the pronunciation of object pronouns *toi* and *moi* as [twe] and [mwe] rather than [twa] or [mwa] and the use of *m'as* [ma] instead of *je vais* or *je vas* to express future time reference, for example *m'as partir ce soir* 'I'm gonna leave tonight'.

(2) Mildly marked informal variants, like marked informal variants, do not conform to the rules of the standard language and are typical of the informal register, but may also be used in formal situations. However, compared with marked informal variants, they demonstrate considerably less social or gender stratification, are not stigmatized and their frequency in the situation of the Labovian interview typically greatly surpasses that of their formal equivalents. Examples of mildly marked informal variants documented in spoken Quebec French include non-use of the particle *ne* in negative sentences, for example *je ne comprends pas* > *je comprends pas* 'I don't understand', and non-use of consonant /l/ in third person subject pronouns *il* and *ils* 'he/it'; 'they', for example *il* [i] *s'est trompé* 'he got it wrong'.

(3) Neutral variants conform to the rules of the standard language, but are not sociostylistically marked. Typically, the neutrality of such

variants is reflected in the fact that they stand as a default alternative to other marked standard or non-standard variants. Examples of neutral variants documented in spoken Quebec French include the use of the periphrastic future (i.e. auxiliary *aller* + infinitive, e.g. *il va neiger la semaine prochaine* 'it's going to snow next week') instead of the more formal and contextually constrained inflecture future, for example *il neigera la semaine prochaine* or the use of noun *auto* to refer to the above-mentioned notion of 'automobile' instead of marked informal *char* or formal *automobile* and *voiture*.

(4) Formal variants, like neutral variants, conform to the rules of the standard language. However, unlike neutral variants, they are typical of careful speech and/or written language, are associated with members of the upper social strata and usually with female speakers. As such, in the situation of the Labovian taped interview, their discursive frequency is lower than that of neutral or mildly marked informal variants. Examples of formal variants documented in spoken Quebec French include use of the verb *demeurer* 'reside' instead of its informal counterpart *rester*, the noun *automobile* (see above), or central vowel /ə/ in a word such as *cerise* [səRiz] as opposed to its non-use [sRiz].

(5) Hyper-formal variants, like formal variants, conform to the rules of the standard language and are typical of careful speech and/or written language. However, they are used almost exclusively by members of the upper social strata and are characterized by a low discursive frequency in the situation of the Labovian interview. Examples of hyper-formal variants documented in spoken Quebec French include the use versus non-use of negative particle *ne* in negative sentences (see above) and the use of construction *ne ... que* instead of its mildly marked informal counterpart *juste* 'only' to express the notion of restriction.

As pointed out above, the sizable body of studies on the learning of sociolinguistic variation by FL2 learners has focused primarily on individuals who have had considerable contacts with FL1 speakers. This research has brought to light a variety of findings that we synthesize below.

- FL2 learners, as a rule, use *marked informal* variants at levels far below that of FL1 speakers.

Dewaele and Regan (2001) found that Irish FL2 students used quite sparingly marked informal content words such as *sympa* 'swell', *mec* 'guy' and *moche* 'ugly', in spite of the fact that they had spent one year in France. According to Dewaele and Regan, the reason for this trend is that the use of marked informal variants involves a significant amount of sociopragmatic risk-taking. As such, learners will exercise caution in using such variants in their own spoken discourse, even though they may be aware of them. This interpretation echoes the findings of Kinginger's (2008) investigation of the acquisition of colloquial French lexical items by American students who took part in a study abroad in France. She found that after the study abroad, the students' understanding and self-reported ability to use appropriately a series of 25 colloquial French content words had improved considerably, except for the strongly marked words in the series (e.g. words like *con* 'jerk, dammed fool'), which they perceived as vulgar.[3]

It should also be noted that in their research on the learning of sociolinguistic variation by Anglophone FL2 learners in Montreal, Sankoff and her colleagues found that such learners make use of marked informal variants, for example subject doubling – *Jean il mange* 'John he is eating' (Blondeau & Nagy, 1998; Nagy *et al.*, 2003); informal discourse markers – *bon, ben, t'sais, comme* 'good', 'well', 'you know', 'like' (Sankoff *et al.*, 1997); and *rester* 'to reside', an informal lexical variant of formal counterparts *demeurer* and *habiter* (Sankoff, 1997). The findings of these studies further show that there is a positive effect of high levels of integration in the local Francophone community. That said, these authors do not always provide FL1 benchmark data to determine whether or not these learners use marked informal variants at levels comparable to those of FL1 speakers. The only study where FL1 benchmark data are used is Sankoff's (1997) study of verbs meaning 'reside'. This study shows that in comparison with FL1 speakers, FL2 learners use marked informal variant *rester* 27% of the time in comparison with 64% for FL1 speakers.

Having said this, previous research on the interlanguage of FL2 learners has documented usages that, at first sight, resemble informal variants (e.g. Kenemer, 1982; Mannesy & Wald, 1984). Such usages, however, are not the result of the learning of informal variants by FL2 learners since such learners have not had extensive contacts with FL1 speakers. Rather, they are forms that the learners produce 'spontaneously' in their L2 because certain standard variants that are part of the educational input of the learners are linguistically marked (i.e. infrequent, irregular, semantically opaque, etc.) and hence difficult to learn. An example of such forms is the use of *je vas* /va/ 'I go', modeled on *tu vas* /va/ 'you go', *il/elle va* /va/ 'he/she goes', *on va* /va/ 'we go', instead of the standard though irregular form *je vais*/ve/ 'I go'. Such forms, which are the results of regularization or overgeneralization, can be found in the speech of FL2 learners and, as pointed out by Kenemer, they are also well-known features of popular French. Such findings are not surprising since, whether they are recent innovations or long-standing usages, informal variants tend to be more regular, more semantically transparent, etc., than their standard counterparts (cf. Chaudenson *et al.*, 1986).

In addition to these exceptions, research has also found that linguistically marked standard variants can be, quite simply, a source of error in that the alternatives produced by FL2 learners are non-native usages. Examples of such non-native usages can be found in Dewaele (1998), who, for instance, lists non-native lexical usages calqued on English that his FL2 learners were using in place of French lexical variants they had not mastered (e.g. *table de tennis* 'table tennis' instead of native variants *tennis de table* or *ping pong*). Another example is found in research by Lealess (2005), who has documented usages of impersonal modal verb *falloir* ('must') with personal subject pronouns, for example *je faux partir, tu faux manger*, etc., in the speech of the Montreal Anglophone learners of French examined by Sankoff and her associates. These regularized forms, which are not in keeping with FL1 speech, underscore the exceptional status of modal *falloir* and the difficulty of the morphosyntactic rules that govern its usage. When *falloir* is used with an infinitive as in *il faut partir*, the subject of the action that must be performed is conveyed implicitly via the context and/or situation. Thus, depending on the situation, *il faut partir* could mean 'you must leave', 'we must leave' or even 'I must leave'. The use of a personal subject pronoun before *faut* by FL2 learners can therefore be viewed as a more transparent expression of the notion of necessity, since it specifies explicitly the agent of the action. Furthermore, it aligns the use of modal *falloir* with that of related modals such as *devoir, pouvoir*, etc., which are used with personal subject pronouns.

- FL2 learners tend to use *mildly marked informal* variants less frequently than FL1 speakers.

Dewaele (1992, 2004b), Regan (1996, 2004), Sax (2003), Regan *et al.* (2009) and Thomas (2002a) found that FL2 learners delete negative particle *ne* at rates below those of FL1 speakers, and Howard *et al.* (2006), Regan *et al.* (2009), Sax (2003) and Thomas (2000) found that FL2 learners delete /l/ less often than do FL1 speakers. That said, in contrast to the trend reported above for marked informal variants, FL2 learners' use of mildly marked informal variants greatly increases when such learners have significant contacts with FL1 speakers. Evidence of this effect is found in research by Dewaele (2004b), Regan (1996, 2005) and Regan *et al.* (2009) that shows that after a one-year stay abroad in France, FL2 learners' non-use of the negative particle *ne* was comparable with that of FL1 speakers in France. Such a correlation is also well documented in the research of Blondeau *et al.* (1995) that has focused on adult Anglophone FL2 learners who have learned French both in the school context and in the target-language community (Montreal) from the outset. For example, Blondeau *et al.* found that the FL2 learners in their study delete negator *ne* almost as often as do L1 speakers of Montreal French (89% versus 99.5%) and use an inclusive subject pronoun *on* ('we') in place of *nous* almost as often as do these latter speakers (97% versus 98%). Likewise, Trévise and Noyau (1984) found that among Spanish FL2 learners residing in Paris, those who deleted *ne* most had lived longest in Paris and had the highest level of contact with FL1 speakers. These results are not surprising given that such variants are, as we have pointed out, very frequent in spoken L1 French and are not stigmatized. Nonetheless, research on Montreal Anglophones' (Nagy et al., 1996) learning of phonological variation reveals that some mildly marked informal variants are only used at levels comparable to levels found for FL1 speakers by those few learners who have the very highest degrees of contacts with FL1 speakers (e.g. /l/ non-use and the assibilation of dental stops – [tˢy] for [ty] meaning 'you').

- FL2 learners' behavior in relation to *neutral* variants has not been the object of extensive investigation.

Only one such study reports on the use of a neutral variant by FL2 learners, namely that by Lealess (2005) who examined modal constructions that express the notion of obligation. Among such constructions, *il faut que* + verb in the subjunctive (e.g. *il faut que je/tu/il/etc. le fasse(s)* 'I/you/he/etc. must do it') is, according to the criteria used in our categorization of variants, sociostylistically neutral. Lealess found that the Montreal FL2 speakers examined by Blondeau and her colleagues used this variant less often than FL1 speakers of Canadian French. As we will see, this finding may reflect the morphosyntactic complexity of this variant, a factor that leads FL2 learners to favor its more simple counterparts (e.g. *falloir/devoir* + verb in the infinitive – *il faut/tu dois le faire* 'you must do it').

- FL2 learners tend to use *formal* and *hyper-formal* variants considerably more often than do FL1 speakers.

The prevalence of formal and hyper-formal variants in the speech of FL2 learners is a corollary of the preceding trends. This prevalence has been documented in studies by Dewaele (1992, 2004b), Regan (1996, 2004, 2005), Regan *et al.* (2009), Sax (2003) and Thomas (2002a). In these studies FL2 learners exhibit rates of *ne* use that are substantially higher than those of FL1 speakers. A similar result was found by Howard *et al.* (2006), Regan *et al.* (2009), Sax (2003) and Thomas (2000) in relation to /l/ use in subject pronouns. Not surprisingly, however, the use of formal and hyper-formal variants has been found to decrease dramatically when FL2 learners have had intensive contacts with FL1 speakers (e.g. the findings of Blondeau & Nagy (1998), Regan (1996) and Regan *et al.* (2009), in the preceding sections).

Unexpectedly, previous research has also revealed that when FL2 learning takes place primarily in a classroom setting, as is the case for French immersion programs, certain formal variants are used by the FL2 learners much less frequently than by FL1 speakers. For example, Harley and King (1989), Lyster (1994a), Lyster and Rebuffot (2002) and Swain and Lapkin

(1990) have found that French immersion students under-use (1) the formal address pronoun *vous* 'you'; (2) the formal generic subject pronoun *on* 'one';[4] (3) polite conditionals to attenuate requests; and (4) polite openings or closings in letters. These interesting exceptions reflect to a large extent the influence of the learners' educational input, which may offer them misleading or incomplete information regarding these formal versus hyper-formal variants (see the section 'Independent variables'), the linguistic markedness of the formal/hyper-formal variants themselves, the fact that some formal/hyper-formal variants may be at odds with the learners' L1s and/or the complexity of the sociopragmatic rules that govern their use.

In summary, the literature we have just outlined points to the fact that FL2 learners distinguish themselves from FL1 speakers in several important ways. FL2 learners use marked informal variants at levels well below those of FL1 speakers. In comparison with FL1 speakers, FL2 learners tend to under-use mildly marked informal variants (and conversely over-use the formal counterparts of mildly marked informal variants). However, we have also noted that FL2 learners who have had extensive contacts with FL1 speakers use certain marked and mildly marked informal variants (and their formal counterparts) on a par with FL1 speakers.

Linguistic and stylistic constraints on sociolinguistic variation

The learning of sociolinguistic variation involves more than using the same range of variants as do L1 speakers at similar rates of frequency in a given situation. It also involves the learning of the linguistic constraints on variation and the ability to shift between styles. Research on these two dimensions of the learning of sociolinguistic variation by FL2 learners in an educational setting can be summarized as follows:

- FL2 learners seem to observe many of the linguistic constraints of sociolinguistic variation found in FL1 speech.

The finding that FL2 learners observe the same linguistic constraints as do FL1 speakers has been documented in connection with (1) *ne* non-use (Goldfine, 1987; Regan, 1996, 2004, 2005; Regan *et al.*, 2009; Thomas, 2002a); (2) /l/ non-use (Howard *et al.*, 2006; Regan *et al.*, 2009; Sax, 2003); (3) subject doubling, for example *Jean il dort* 'John he is sleeping' versus *Jean dort* 'John is sleeping' (Blondeau & Nagy, 1998); (4) [r] versus [R]; (5) assibilation of dental stops, for example *tu* [t^{s}y] versus [ty] (Nagy *et al.*, 1996); and (6) inflected future versus periphrastic future versus present indicative (Dion & Blondeau, 2005; Regan *et al.*, 2009).[5] However, Thomas (2002a) arrived at a contrary finding in relation to *ne* non-use, namely that his FL2 learners had not learned one of the linguistic constraints of *ne* non-use, namely the one associated with the post-verbal negator, and Lealess (2005) found that the Anglophone Montreal learners mentioned above had only partially mastered the linguistic constraints of variant *il faut que*. It should be borne in mind, however, that the studies that found that FL2 learners learn the linguistic constraints observed by FL1 speakers all involve individuals who have had extensive contacts with FL1 speakers. It remains to be seen if similar results will obtain with FL2 learners who have not had such contacts.

- FL2 learners observe some of the stylistic constraints on sociolinguistic variation found in FL1 speech.

This finding was documented for *ne* non-use (Dewaele, 1992; Dewaele & Regan, 2002; Regan, 1995, 1996; Sax, 2003; Thomas, 2002a); /l/ non-use (Sax, 2003; Thomas, 2000); and schwa non-use, for example *sam[ə]di* versus *sam'di* 'Saturday' (Thomas, 2002b), the inflected future (Regan *et al.*, 2009) and *tu* versus *vous* (Kinginger, 2008).[6] It should be pointed out, however, that these studies have found that the extent to which learners have opportunities to interact with native FL1 speakers in a variety of situations has a significant impact on the learners' level of mastery of stylistic constraints. For example, in relation to *ne* non-use, Sax (2003) found that FL2 students who had stayed more than 16 weeks in France showed signs of having learned the style constraint, and the longer their stays in France had been the closer to the FL1 speaker norms they were. Students who had stayed less than 16 weeks in France, however, had not learned the style constraint under study. As for Regan (1995, 1996), she found that after a one-year stay in France her FL2 learners exhibited rates of *ne* non-use in both informal and formal registers that were much closer to the FL1 speaker norm than when they were interviewed prior to their stay. However, she also found that in the formal register they deleted *ne* more often than FL1 speakers. In other words, extended contacts with FL1 speakers in France had brought about an 'overgeneralization' of *ne* non-use in the FL2 learners' spoken French. Regan *et al.* (2009) found that among their Irish FL2 learners, those who had spent a year abroad had mastered the association between the inflected future and formal style. Finally, Kinginger (2008) found that after having taken part in a study abroad in France, many of the students she examined had made substantial progress in their mastery of *tu* versus *vous* in that they were able to consistently use these address pronouns in situationally appropriate ways and to mark (in)formality.

Unsurprisingly, several studies that focused on FL2 learners who have had limited opportunities to interact with FL1 speakers in a variety of situations have found that such learners do not reach FL1 norms in relation to the stylistic constraints of sociolinguistic variation. Thus, Swain and Lapkin (1990) found that French immersion students from an Early Immersion program used the informal address pronoun *tu* much more often than did FL1 speakers in formal situations of communication. Swain and Lapkin also found that when the French immersion students had to make a polite request in the formal register, they used significantly fewer conditionals than did same-aged FL1 speakers. According to these authors, this latter finding may also reflect the students' incomplete mastery of the tenses of the conditional mood whose synthetic morphology is at variance with the analytic conditional tenses of English. Lyster (1994a) found that French immersion students, before instructional intervention addressing these features, under-used polite conditionals, the formal address pronoun *vous* ('you') and polite closings in letters (e.g. *je vous remercie à l'avance* 'I thank you in advance'). A similar result is reported in Dewaele (2004c), who found that learners of European French only partially follow native speaker patterns with regard to *tu* usage. Such findings are also echoed in Dewaele's (2002) study of the use of first person plural subject pronouns *nous* and *on* by Dutch-speaking FL2 university students. These students had minimal contacts with native speakers of French and displayed rates of usage of *on* that did not vary between their written and spoken production.

That said, it is important to keep in mind that findings on the learning of stylistic constraints were arrived at using methodologies that varied from study to study. For instance, Regan (1996) compared the rates of *ne* non-use found in the first part of the interview (where the students had not yet warmed up to the task) with those found in the second part, Sax (2003) compared the rates of *ne* non-use found in speech produced during two role plays (an informal and a formal one), and in our own research we compared the rates of variant use found when the French immersion students talked about different formal/informal topics (e.g. religion, education, politics versus vacations and trips, jokes, hobbies). As for Swain and Lapkin (1990), they used a battery of tests and taped interviews, while Lyster (1994a) used a combination of tests and elicitation tasks. This heterogeneous methodological approach to the study of the learning of style constraints makes it difficult to compare findings across studies. It is hoped future research will display a greater level of methodological convergence across studies.

Influence of independent variables

In addition to the trends summarized above, research on the learning of sociolinguistic variation by FL2 learners has identified a number of factors that influence such learning. The results of this research can be summarized via the following points:

- As illustrated above, contacts with FL1 speakers bring about an increase in the frequency of use of marked and mildly marked informal variants by FL2 learners (and a decrease in the use of their formal and hyper-formal counterparts).
- Contacts with FL1 speakers are also conducive to the learning of gender constraints on variation.

Studies that have arrived at this conclusion include those of Blondeau and Nagy (1998) and Regan *et al.* (2009) for *ne* non-use, *on/nous*, the future variants and /l/ deletion. Blondeau and Nagy (1998) found that female Anglophone FL2 learners in Montreal used subject doubling less often than did their male counterparts. These two researchers hypothesized that this difference reflected the fact that their FL2 learners had internalized the effect of speaker gender on subject doubling as a result of frequent interactions with FL1 speakers. A similar association was found by Regan *et al.* (2009) in relation to *ne* non-use, *on/nous* and the future variants. However, in the case of /l/ deletion the reverse association was found, namely that females exhibited higher rates of /l/ deletion, a pattern matching that of FL1 speakers in France. One exception to these patterns is the study by Dewaele and Regan (2002), who found that sex had no effect on *ne* non-use in the speech of Dutch-speaking FL2 learners who had limited contacts with FL1 speakers.

- Correlations between social class background and sociolinguistic variation in FL2 speech have not been studied in previous research (see Chapter 4 for a discussion of the pattern associated with this variable).
- FL2 learners tend to favor variants that have a morphological and semantic equivalent in their L1.

This trend was found in relation to the use of *wh*-word + verb + subject interrogative sentences (e.g. *Où est-il?* 'Where is he?'; Dewaele, 1999); discourse marker *comme* 'like' (e.g. *j'étais comme fatigué* 'I was like tired'; Blondeau *et al.*, 1995, 2002; Rehner, 2004); restrictive *juste* and generic subject pronoun *tu* meaning 'one' (e.g. *tu ne sais pas ce qui peut arriver* 'you don't know what can happen'; Blondeau *et al.*, 1995, 2002); and verbs meaning 'reside' (e.g. *habiter, vivre, rester*, etc.; Sankoff, 1997). In fact, the effect of the learner's L1 is so strong that Blondeau *et al.* and Sankoff found that their learners used restrictive *juste*, discourse marker *comme*, and *vivre* meaning 'reside', all of which are variants with an English equivalent (i.e. *just, like, live*), more often than did local FL1 speakers. These patterns are particularly interesting because they underscore the fact that, as is the case for bilingual speakers in minority speech communities, advanced L2 learners show evidence of linguistic convergence by favoring target-language variants that have a counterpart in their other language.

Influence of educational input

In an effort to better understand the specific factors that could potentially influence the learning of sociolinguistic variation by L2 learners who have learned French primarily in an educational setting, several studies have examined three dimensions of the educational input of FL2 learners. These dimensions are (1) the frequency of use of specific variants in the

FL2 teaching materials; (2) the frequency of use of specific variants by FL2 teachers in the classroom; and (3) the presentation of information on sociolinguistic variation and the use of activities designed to develop the students' sociolinguistic competence in either the FL2 teaching materials or the FL2 teachers' classroom speech. The importance of these studies lies in the obvious fact that the FL2 learners in question learn the target language primarily in an educational context.

- FL2 textbooks tend to favor formal variants, under-use mildly marked informal variants and avoid marked informal variants.

These results have been arrived at by Auger (2002) and O'Connor Di Vito (1991). Auger's study examined the presence of informal Quebecois vocabulary in French immersion textbooks used in Quebec. Her results reveal that such texts contain a small number of examples of lexical variants that are not strongly stigmatized (e.g. *tannant* for *énervant* 'annoying'), while more stigmatized forms do not appear at all (e.g. *piasse* for *dollar* 'buck'). O'Connor Di Vito's research presents evidence that FL2 textbooks place undue emphasis on the use of morphosyntactic variants such as pre-verbal clitics *en* and *y* (e.g. *il en veut* 'he wants some', *il y va* 'he goes there') as opposed to post-verbal adverbial forms (e.g. *il veut de ça, il va là-bas*), in spite of the fact that the pre-verbal variants are not highly frequent in spoken French.

It should be pointed out, however, that the frequency of variant use in FL2 teaching materials has not been systematically measured by these authors. In Chapter 4, we provide a systematic, quantitative analysis of all the variants focused on in our research found in the materials used to teach French Language Arts in French immersion programs.

- When most FL2 textbooks and accompanying materials make use of marked or mildly marked informal variants, they usually provide no information regarding the sociostylistic status of these variants. These materials also tend to offer the students no opportunities to engage in activities designed to develop their receptive or productive skills in relation to the variants in question.

These findings have been arrived at in studies by Lyster and Rebuffot (2002) and O'Connor Di Vito (1991). Lyster and Rebuffot focused on the use of the address pronouns *tu* and *vous* 'you'. More specifically, they found that French Language Arts teaching materials present French immersion students with inconsistent uses of informal *tu* (and its formal counterpart *vous*) across the grades and in different communicative situations. They also found that, in the materials they examined, the sociostylistic mechanisms that underlie FL1 speakers' choice between these pronouns are not the object of explicit instruction. As for O'Connor Di Vito, she found, for instance, that in a set of FL2 materials, students were required to practice the use of negation with *ne* 'without explaining the distinction between written and spoken norms' (O'Connor Di Vito, 1991: 386) and, more specifically, without informing students that '*ne* is oftentimes reduced in formal speech and is virtually absent in the everyday conversations of educated native speakers of French' (O'Connor Di Vito, 1991: 386).

While the above research has shown that the pedagogical materials used in FL2 programs do not, in general, adequately inform students about sociolinguistic variation or offer them opportunities to develop their receptive and productive abilities in relation to sociolinguistic variation, some textbook authors (e.g. Valdman *et al.*, 2002) are notable exceptions. Further, Lyster (1994a, 1994b) has shown that materials that offer students such information and opportunities can have a positive effect on the sociolinguistic competence of FL2 learners. Specifically, Lyster carried out a pedagogical experiment where French immersion students were provided with opportunities to (1) heighten their awareness of sociolinguistic variation and (2) perform a series of functional analytic communicative tasks focused on sociolinguistic variation and on specific stylistic variants (e.g. address pronouns *tu* versus *vous* 'you' or formal and informal openings or closings of letters). Lyster found that the French immersion students in the experimental classes reached a level of mastery of sociolinguistic variation that was much higher than that of students in the control classes who used regular French Language Arts materials.

- Teachers' classroom discourse is not always in keeping with FL1 speech norms.

To our knowledge, only one study, namely that by Lyster and Rebuffot (2002), has examined the role of teachers' classroom discourse in the sociolinguistic competence of FL2 learners. These authors found that French immersion teachers make frequent use of the informal address pronoun *tu* 'you' and of the informal generic pronoun *tu* 'you' meaning 'one'. Lyster and Rebuffot also found that French immersion teachers did not correct students who addressed them with *tu*, a choice of variant that native speakers would consider sociostylistically inappropriate. Finally, French immersion teachers marginally used *tu* to address the whole class (approximately 3% of the time), an exceptional usage that is likely to further confuse the French immersion students. Indeed, pronoun *tu* is a singular pronoun that refers only to the interlocutor in all French varieties with which we are familiar. It should be pointed out, however, that in Lyster and Rebuffot's study, frequency of variant use by teachers in the classroom was assessed impressionistically. In Chapter 4, we provide detailed quantitative findings on the role of teacher discourse on the sociolinguistic competence of FL2 learners, a very much under-studied topic in SLA research.

The findings summarized above suggest that several dimensions of the educational input of FL2 learners may be crucial factors in the underdevelopment of sociolinguistic competence among such learners in that they may reinforce the negative effect of the paucity of interactions with FL1 speakers in educational settings. They also suggest that if FL2 materials were redesigned and focused on sociolinguistic variation, the sociolinguistic competence of FL2 learners would improve significantly.

Learning of sociolinguistic variation by L2 learners of languages other than French

As pointed out above, studies that focus on the acquisition of sociolinguistic variation by learners of languages other than French have not yet developed to the same extent as the FL2 studies discussed above. Still, these limited studies have arrived at findings that either echo those of FL2 studies or complement them. For instance, several studies have found that the intensity and duration of contact with L1 speakers has a positive effect on the acquisition of sociolinguistic variants as well as on several aspects of sociopragmatic competence. For instance, Bayley (1996) found that Chinese learners of English in the United States with extensive native speaker contacts approached target-language patterns of consonant cluster reduction in monomorphemic words. However, it is noteworthy that an increase in the overall rate of consonant cluster reduction by the more proficient speakers led to a decrease in the likelihood that regular past tense verbs would be marked for tense. That is, the partial acquisition of a native speaker pattern of variability led to a decrease in the use of an obligatory target-language form. Barron (2003) found that university-level Irish learners of German who had spent a year abroad had made significant progress in their acquisition of the speech acts of requests, offers and refusals of offers in that at the end of their stay they relied less on transfer of L1 ways of accomplishing these acts and came somewhat closer to approximating target-language norms. In a similar investigation, Matsumara (2001) examined the acquisition of advice-giving formulations by Japanese learners of English who were participating in an eight-month stay in Canada. The author found that learners at the end of the stay had made progress in their awareness of and their ability to produce these formulations according to native norms. Such results are in line with the numerous studies discussed above that have reported a positive effect of interaction with FL1 speakers on the acquisition of the sociolinguistic variants of French. On the other hand, several studies suggest that some aspects of sociolinguistic variation are not acquired despite the L2 being learned in a naturalistic setting. For instance, a number of studies point out that some aspects of the target language are so complex that even an extended stay in the target-language community is insufficient to bring L2 learners to the level where they can actually produce target-language variants. Thus, Hashimoto (1994) found that a stay in Japan is insufficient to bring about productive usage of various sociolinguistic markers of Japanese, although it does have a beneficial effect on the learner's sensitivity to such markers. This finding is in keeping with Dewaele (2004d) and Dewaele and Regan's (2001) study, which showed that, for advanced-level Irish university FL2 learners, a one-year stay in France is not enough to induce productive usage of marked informal lexical variants at levels comparable to FL1 norms. Finally, Wolfram *et al.* (2004) focused on the acquisition of the monophthongal variant of the diphthong /ai/ in the English spoken by Latino residents in the southern United States. They found only modest acquisition of the variant due to the strong demographic concentration of the local Latino population and resulting limited interactions with native speakers of the vernacular variety of southern US English. Wolfram *et al.* also point out that, as a result, these learners rely heavily on English as a Second Language (ESL) instruction, which does not favor the monophthongal variant, and hence further reduces their exposure to this vernacular variant.

Further, additional studies have examined the acquisition of stylistic and sex-based constraints of sociolinguistic variation by L2 speakers. These studies have found that L2 learners are successful in acquiring the sex constraints on variation; however, they are less successful in acquiring the associated stylistic constraints. For instance, Major (2004) found that Japanese and Spanish learners of English acquired the sex constraints on a range of phonological variables, while only the Spanish learners of English showed some measure of stylistic differentiation. Adamson and Regan (1991) found that female Cambodian learners of English in the United States had successfully acquired the formal variant *-ing* and the style constraint that governs its use. However, while the male learners exhibited a preference for the *-in'* variant, which they had correctly associated with male L1 speech, they had failed to master the style constraint. The finding that sex constraints are acquired before stylistic constraints may help explain why in the FL2 studies reviewed above learners are more successful in mastering the sex-based constraints on variation than they are in the style-based ones.

Several studies have considered L2 speakers' acquisition of politeness variants in a study abroad context and found that the link between such sojourns and mastery of this aspect of sociolinguistic competence is by no means straightforward. Using a role-play methodology, Marriott (1995) examines the mastery of Japanese honorifics using two groups of learners: those who have spent time abroad and those who have not. Her results reveal a great deal of individual variation. There is some evidence of exchange students having progressed with some of the variables under study, which suggests that contact with native speakers in a study abroad context is beneficial. However, the lack of significant difference between speaker groups suggests that stays of at least several years are necessary before noticeable improvement obtains.

The use of Japanese honorifics is also the object of study in Siegal's (1995) study of two female students having spent time in Japan. Her results reveal that students must grapple with conflicting norms (the desire to speak politely versus how they view themselves in the target culture) and, as such, they do not consistently use variants in a native-like manner. While this study does not provide a direct comparison with learners not having spent time in a study abroad context, its results are relevant in that they underscore the fact that time spent in the target-language community is not necessarily equivalent to being 'in' the target-language culture.

To conclude this section, we point out that the extant research on the acquisition of sociolinguistic variation by learners of languages other than French suggests that the time spent in the target-language community is indeed beneficial for improving one's sociolinguistic competence. However, this may be truer for the acquisition of linguistic variants than for the acquisition of sociopragmatic rules.

Chapter 2
Methodology

Research Goals

The students focused upon in our project are enrolled in an immersion program in a school district within the greater Toronto area. Our research project, centered on the learning of spoken French sociolinguistic variation, seeks to answer the following questions:

- Do the French immersion students under study use the same range of variants as do L1 speakers of Canadian French?
- Do the French immersion students use variants with the same discursive frequency as do L1 speakers of Canadian French?
- Is the French immersion students' use of variants correlated with the same linguistic and stylistic constraints observable in L1 spoken Canadian French?
- What influence do the following independent variables have on the French immersion students' learning of sociolinguistic variation: (1) opportunities to interact with FL1 speakers; (2) the learners' L1(s); (3) intra-systemic factors (e.g. markedness of the variants); and (4) the learners' social characteristics (e.g. social standing)?
- To what extent is sociolinguistic variation reflected in the speech of French immersion teachers in the classroom and in the French Language Arts materials used in French immersion programs?
- Do these materials provide students with opportunities to reflect on and practice sociolinguistic variation?

To answer the first three questions, we take as a starting point several sociolinguistic variables that have been attested by the numerous sociolinguistic studies on the speech of Francophones in Quebec. These studies were chosen because they are based on corpora that, like our French immersion corpus, were collected via semi-formal, semi-directed taped interviews (see Appendix A for the French immersion students' interview schedule). This allows us to compare the French immersion students with L1 speakers of Canadian French in the same communicative situation.

Our comparison of the French immersion students with speakers of Quebec French is also motivated by the fact that it is primarily with these speakers that our French immersion students have had extra-curricular interactions in French (i.e. they stayed with Francophone families in Quebec, or went on trips to Quebec). In our research we assess the extent to which these contacts have enabled them to learn some features of marked informal French. An additional motivation for choosing Quebec French as a benchmark is the existence of economic, cultural and academic ties between Ontario and Quebec. This means that when they reach adulthood, Ontario French immersion students will likely continue to have contacts with Francophones from Quebec. Finally, the Ontario Ministry of Education's (2000) guidelines for the teaching of French in high school immersion programs stress the fact that students should develop familiarity with varieties of Canadian French.[7]

To assess the correlations between independent variables and French immersion students' use of sociolinguistic variants, we appeal to data on the students' sociological characteristics (namely sex and social class background), their patterns of language use at home and the extent of their contacts with FL1 speakers (see the questionnaire in Appendix B). These data were examined as independent variables in a multivariate factor analysis in order to assess possible correlations between the students' use of variants.

In order to examine the presence of sociolinguistic variants in the French immersion students' educational input, we analyze Allen *et al.*'s (1987) corpus of spoken French produced by a sample of seven French immersion teachers from the greater Toronto and Ottawa areas who were taped while teaching French immersion students,[8] and two series of textbooks and accompanying exercise books, one used in the school district where we gathered our French immersion student corpus and the other used in another Toronto area school district.[9] It is essential to stress the importance of having recourse to these two educational corpora since, as we will see, the immersion students under study have learned French primarily within French immersion settings. The importance lies in the extent to which variants in these sources of educational input are used in ways that approximate or differ from the L1 spoken French norms and, secondly, in the degree to which such similarities or differences are reflected in the students' own patterns of variant use.

Finally, it should also be pointed out that our research project provides data useful for French immersion educators interested in determining whether the sociolinguistic competence of French immersion students meets the expectations set forth by the Ministry of Education. Regarding these expectations, the Ontario Ministry of Education's (2000) guidelines for the teaching of French as a second language in the final two years of French immersion programs state, among other things, that students should have the following productive abilities: incorporate colloquialisms and idiomatic expressions into their speech; debate formally and informally issues arising from their reading of literary and other works; and express clearly and confidently their personal point of view in informal discussions (see Appendix C for further details). It is interesting that the concern expressed in these guidelines is reflected in the perception of French immersion students in relation to various aspects of their sociolinguistic competence. More specifically, 67% of Grade 12 French immersion students from a Calgary school district said that they are concerned about matching the style of their speech to their interlocutor (Hart *et al.*, 1989). While only 58% of these same students said that they would like to speak French the way Francophone professionals do, nearly 75% said that they would like to speak French the way same-aged FL1 speakers do. This finding is in line with that of Tarone and Swain (1995) who report that some of the immersion students lamented the fact that informal registers were not taught in immersion classrooms: 'So I'd like to be able to sit in a classroom and have someone teach me how to say, "Well, come on guys, let's go get some burgers" and stuff like that' (Tarone & Swain, 1995: 172). It is also echoed by Auger (2002) who points to the fact that graduates from French immersion programs in Montreal are frustrated at not being able to use their FL2 in real-life situations, despite their many years of classroom learning. Further, she suggests that the type of French that these immersion students are being taught is an impediment to their integration into the local Francophone community (see also Swain & Lapkin, 2005). The importance for immersion students to develop an adequate control of the informal register has also been underscored by Lyster (2007) who, drawing on research by Genesee (1987), observes that French immersion students perceive greater social distance between themselves and FL1 speakers as they progress through their program. This leads him to remark that:

> As the need to use the vernacular becomes increasingly important to pre-adolescents and adolescents for communicating among themselves, they use their first language to do so since they are familiar with its vernacular variants. The second language remains the language of academic discourse and not for social interaction among peers. (Lyster, 2007: 16)

An additional reason for investigating the acquisition of sociolinguistic competence by French immersion students is found in an experimental study carried out by Segalowitz (1976). This author found that there were social and psychological costs associated with the use of too formal a register by L2 speakers (Montreal FL2 learners in Segalowitz's study) when they interacted with L1 speakers of the target language (Montreal

FL1 speakers). These latter speakers perceived the L2 learners as too distant and uncooperative, etc. Segalowitz's findings were arrived at by using a collaborative task involving FL2 learners who interacted with FL1 speakers. One can surmise that if the FL2 speakers had a better command of the informal register, they would have interacted more smoothly and been judged more favorably by the FL1 speakers.

Further on this topic Segalowitz remarked that:

> Very often the second language speaker does not possess the full sociolinguistic competence permitting him or her to choose a particular speech style appropriate to the situation. [...]. The second language learner may have some ability to recognize and interpret some of the speech style characteristics of the interlocutor's speech but probably not at the same sophisticated level as for native language speech. This means then that the functional bilingual is largely unable to send and receive the non cognitive social and affective messages normally conveyed in every conversation. This may have the consequence of making second language communication very difficult and awkward in a social sense; the functional bilingual is cut off from one channel of social contact inherent in conversation. If the awkwardness that is caused by this is great enough, it may discourage the speaker from attempting cross-linguistic communication again. (Segalowitz, 1977: 184, 185)

Segalowitz's remarks are quite pertinent, since they suggest that while fully functional in their L2, French immersion students may not have the kind of sociolinguistic repertoire that would enable them to have smooth and natural interactions with FL1 speakers. Our book seeks to verify this hypothesis and will discuss the appropriate curriculum goals and pedagogical strategies that could improve French immersion students' mastery of sociostylistic variation.

In sum, we believe that the acquisition of sociolinguistic competence should be an essential part of French immersion students' linguistic and cultural learning experience because (1) it is deemed important by government agencies such as the Ontario Ministry of Education; (2) it is desired by the students themselves; and (3) there is evidence that FL1 speakers would react favorably to FL2 learners who could display some measure of linguistic accommodation toward them.

Characteristics of the French Immersion Student Population under Study

In order to draw a sample of French immersion students for our investigation of the learning of spoken French sociolinguistic variation, Mougeon and Nadasdi carried out a questionnaire survey in 1996 among the entire population ($N = 322$) of French immersion students in the school district under study in the greater Toronto area. These students were enrolled in three high schools that offer a type of French immersion program designated as 'Extended French'. In the school district where the survey was carried out, Extended French is characterized by 50% French-medium instruction in Grades 5–8, followed by 20% in high school. It should be pointed out that Extended French is one of several programmatic options available for French immersion in Ontario. One notable difference that sets Extended French apart from, for example, early total French immersion programs is that it provides students with a delayed start and does not involve 100% French-medium instruction in the initial stage. Thus, the Extended French option does not provide students with as high a level of classroom exposure to French as does early total French immersion.

It should also be made clear that the French immersion programs in these three high schools are housed in regular English language schools where the vast majority of the administrative, teaching and maintenance staff, and also students, are not French speaking. In other words, the classrooms where these students take their French-medium courses and the resource rooms attached to the French immersion programs are about the only settings in which these students have the chance to use or be exposed to French. This situation is not unusual in Ontario where most school boards offering French immersion education do so via French immersion programs rather than via designated French immersion schools, also known as single-track French immersion programs, where a French ambiance is created by the presence of French-speaking teachers, support staff, administrators and other sources of exposure to spoken and written French.

Let us now turn to the results of our student survey.[10] The data in Table 2.1 provide basic sociological information about the 322 French immersion students. As can be seen, female students outnumber male students by a ratio of 2:1. Such an imbalance in the ratio of females to males may be a characteristic feature of French immersion programs in Canada; however, we do not know of any study that has documented this. Table 2.1 also shows that the majority of the 322 students were born either in the greater Toronto area or elsewhere in Ontario (70%), 7% are from Quebec and, interestingly, nearly 20% were born outside of Canada. This percentage of foreign-born French immersion students is in line with the percentage reported by Hart *et al.* (1991) for foreign-born French immersion students in the Toronto area. It is also possible to make a comparison here with Bienvenue's (1983) study of French immersion programs in Winnipeg and with Hart *et al.*'s (1994) study of French immersion programs in a Northern Ontario City. Bienvenue found that 13% of the parents of students enrolled in these programs were born outside of Canada. As for Hart *et al.* the figure was less than 20%.

Table 2.1 Immersion students' sex, place of birth and grade

Factor	N	%
Sex		
Male	108	34
Female	211	66
Total[a]	319	100
Place of birth		
Greater Toronto Area (GTA)	193	60
Ontario (outside GTA)	32	10
Quebec	21	7
Canada (outside Ontario/Quebec)	13	4
Poland	17	5
Other	45	14
Total[a]	321	100
Grade		
9	93	29
10	93	29
11	77	24
12	56	17
13	3	1
Total[a]	322	100

[a]Factor totals of less than 322 indicate that some students did not provide the information necessary for categorization.

Finally, Table 2.1 shows that the proportion of students in Grades 9 and 10 is identical and that it decreases after that. The startlingly low proportion of students in Grade 13 likely reflects, in part, the fact that this is a level of schooling designed for those students who intend to continue on to university.[11] The drop between Grades 10 and 11 and Grades 11 and 12, however, may reflect a process of attrition similar to that documented in a report by the North York Board of Education (1986) on French as a second language program.[12]

Table 2.2 provides data on the social class background of students and their parents. Social class was measured as a function of parents' jobs as described by the students. We assigned rankings to both the mother's and

Methodology

Table 2.2 Immersion students' social class background: mother, father and combined

Factor	N	%
Social class: mother		
Upper-middle	44	19
Middle	141	62
Working	42	19
Total	227	100
Social class: father		
Upper-middle	85	34
Middle	120	47
Working	49	19
Total	254	100
Social class: combined		
Upper-middle	107	37
Middle	146	51
Working	33	12
Total	286	100

father's jobs, based on Blishen's *Socioeconomic Index for Occupations in Canada* (Blishen et al., 1987), with some adaptations for the new occupations that were not included in that index. Upper-middle class was defined as having a Blishen score greater than 60, middle class as having a Blishen score between 40 and 60 and working class as having a Blishen score less than 40. To determine the students' social class background, we combined the data for the mother and father (where two unequal rankings were assigned for the parents within one family, the higher of the two was taken to be the student's social class background). Note, also, that we were able to establish social class for only about two thirds of the student population and their parents because students' descriptions of their parents' jobs were at times vague, ambiguous or simply missing.

The combined measure of social class background reported in Table 2.2 shows that over half of the students are from the middle class (51%) and that 37% are from the upper-middle class. Although these proportions indicate that the students are predominantly from middle and upper-middle-class backgrounds, it is interesting that in other studies of French immersion students in the Toronto area, the proportion of students who are from the upper-middle class is considerably higher, approximately 65% (Hart & Lapkin, 1998). Hart and Lapkin contrast this figure of 65% in the French immersion programs with the figure of less than 20% in the regular English language programs in the same school district. Findings such as those of Hart and Lapkin have led some researchers to level charges of elitism at French immersion programs (e.g. Olson & Burns, 1983). However, Hart *et al.* point out that late partial immersion programs are 'more successful than early immersion in attracting and holding students with lower SES backgrounds' (Hart *et al.*, 1991: 8). This would seem to be supported by our own data.

It should be noted, however, that two authors have documented the absence of significant differences between the social class of parents with children in French immersion programs and those with children in the regular English stream (Bienvenue, 1986; Dicks, 2001). One possible explanation for Dicks' finding is that his study was focused on French immersion programs in New Brunswick that, in comparison with other French immersion programs in Canada, Quebec excepted, attract a much higher proportion of students and hence are more representative of the general student population.

Information on the number and range of languages spoken by the parents of the 322 students under study and by the students themselves is displayed in Tables 2.3–2.6. Table 2.3 shows that the vast majority of the parents speak more than one language fluently (61%) and that approximately 10% of the parents are fluent in three or more languages. Approximately 97% of the parents are fluent in English, 19% in a Romance language other than French and 36% in a non-Romance language other than English. Interestingly, approximately 20% of the parents are fluent in French. In a study of the social characteristics of French immersion students in Winnipeg, Manitoba, Bienvenue (1983) found that 35% of the students' parents were fluent in more than one language. This may be indicative of an increase in the multicultural makeup of Canada over the last 20 years.

As for which languages the parents use within the home, Table 2.4 shows that over 40% of the parents use a language other than English or French in this setting. This figure is higher than that reported by Hart *et al.* (1991), who point out that just over a third of the French immersion students in their Toronto data come from homes where a language other than English or French is spoken. It is also higher than the proportion of 12–30% reported by Hart *et al.* (1994) for French immersion programs in a Northern Ontario city. Table 2.4 also shows that approximately 15% of the parents speak a Romance language other than French at home and 27% of the parents speak a non-Romance language other than English in this setting. Table 2.4 also shows that approximately 10% of the parents of the students in the present study speak French at home. This percentage is

Table 2.3 Languages spoken fluently by immersion students' parents

Factor	N	%
Number of languages spoken fluently: mother		
1	126	39
2	168	52
3	22	7
4	5	2
Total	321	100
Number of languages spoken fluently: father		
1	125	39
2	149	47
3	35	11
4	9	3
Total	318	100
Languages spoken fluently: mother		
English	311/322	97
English only	116/322	36
French	71/322	22
Romance (other than French)	54/322	17
Non-Romance (other than English)	104/322	36
Languages spoken fluently: father		
English	308/322	96
English only	116/322	36
French	57/322	18
Romance (other than French)	64/322	20
Non-Romance (other than English)	117/322	36

higher than the 5% reported by Hart *et al.* (1991) for the parents of the late partial immersion students in their study of Toronto French immersion programs, but lower than the 21% reported for the parents of early French immersion students in Toronto and the 28% for Northern Ontario. The differences between the data concerning the languages parents speak fluently and the languages parents speak at home are very informative.

Table 2.4 Languages spoken at home by immersion students' parents

Factor	N	%
Number of languages at home: mother		
1	190	59
2	124	39
3	7	2
Total	321	100
Number of languages at home: father		
1	196	61
2	113	36
3	9	3
Total	318	100
Languages spoken at home: mother		
English	284/322	88
English only	155/322	48
French	42/322	13
Romance (other than French)	44/322	14
Non-Romance (other than English)	88/322	27
Languages spoken at home: father		
English	287/322	89
English only	165/322	51
French	24/322	7
Romance (other than French)	49/322	15
Non-Romance (other than English)	88/322	27

We have seen that while 61% of the parents speak more than one language fluently, only 40% speak more than one language at home. Looking at specific languages, we find that this difference between languages of fluency and languages used at home is most marked for French. This does not necessarily indicate that more Francophone parents abandon this language at home. Rather, it likely reflects the fact that, although French is not their mother tongue, many of these parents speak French fluently as a result of having learned it at school or in other settings. It should be

Table 2.5 Languages spoken at home by the immersion students

Factor	N	%
Language spoken at home: English		
Always	203	63
Often	76	24
Half the time	27	8
Rarely	12	4
Never	4	1
Total	322	100
Language spoken at home: French		
Always	5	2
Often	17	5
Half the time	18	5
Rarely	169	53
Never	112	35
Total	321	100
Language spoken at home: Romance		
Always	5	2
Often	14	4
Half the time	9	3
Rarely	20	6
Never	274	85
Total	322	100
Language spoken at home: other		
Always	7	2
Often	21	7
Half the time	21	7
Rarely	34	10
Never	239	74
Total	322	100

Table 2.6 Languages spoken outside of the home by the immersion students

Factor	N	%
Language outside home: English		
Always	217	67
Often	95	30
Half the time	4	1
Rarely	6	2
Never	0	0
Total	322	100
Language outside home: French[a]		
Always	2	1
Often	26	8
Half the time	41	13
Rarely	197	62
Never	51	16
Total	317	100
Language outside home: Romance		
Always	3	1
Often	8	2
Half the time	5	2
Rarely	22	7
Never	284	88
Total	322	100
Language outside home: other		
Always	0	0
Often	7	2
Half the time	8	2
Rarely	42	13
Never	265	83
Total	322	100

[a]It is not possible to determine what percentage of the use of French outside the home was within the school setting and how much was within the community.

borne in mind here that in some Canadian provinces, including Ontario, French is a required subject in school, while in others it is recommended. In those provinces where French is a recommended subject, it is the second language subject most often chosen. Also of interest is the fact that the number of parents speaking only English at home is higher than the number of parents speaking only English fluently. This difference suggests that some multilingual parents are choosing to use only English at home. Two factors come to mind to explain this shift to English. Firstly, the various languages other than English, including French, are minority languages in the greater Toronto area. Secondly, the French immersion students in this study receive about 60% of their instruction in English. The greater utilitarian value attributed to English and attested by these two factors, among others, would seem to encourage parents to shift to English at home, even if it is not their first language.

Table 2.5 displays the frequency of use of various languages at home by the French immersion students. It is clear from these data that these students overwhelmingly favor English at home, since 95% of the respondents report using this language at home 50% of the time or more. Interestingly, 12% of the students report using French 50% of the time or more at home, 9% do likewise for a Romance language other than French and 16% for 'other' languages.

A comparison of the languages used at home by the students and their parents (Tables 2.4 and 2.5) reveals the following patterns. English is used at home by 99% of the students, but by only 89% of the parents. In contrast, 15% of the students and 15% of the parents speak a Romance language, and 26% of the students and 27% of the parents speak 'other' languages. This contrast reflects the fact that the students have opportunities to be exposed to English outside the home, including the school, whereas their exposure to the minority language is primarily restricted to the home setting. As for French, 65% of the students report using this language at home, while this is the case for only 10% of the parents. It should be made clear, however, that most of the students who report using French at home use this language only rarely in this setting. The rare use of French at home by French immersion students may involve primarily communication with siblings or fellow students also enrolled in French immersion. If one omits the students reporting rare use of French at home, the discrepancy between the proportions of parents and students who report using French at home is considerably reduced, with 12% of the students who report using French half of the time or more and 10% of the parents who report using French at home.

As Table 2.6 shows, outside the home considerably fewer students report using minority languages than within the home. For example, while 16% of the students report using 'other' languages at home at least 50% of the time, only 4% report doing so outside the home. This difference underscores the normative pressure that minority students likely feel to use the majority language outside the home in the greater Toronto area. The only apparent exception to this trend is the use of French, where more students report using this language outside the home at least 50% of the time (22% of the students) than they do within the home (12%). This surprising result is probably, in part, an artifact of the wording of the question that did not specify whether this out-of-the-home use included or excluded the school. Finally, as might be expected, the proportion of students who report using the majority language of English outside the home at least 50% of the time is higher than the proportion of students reporting similar frequency of use of this language at home (98% versus 95%, respectively).

Tables 2.7–2.13 provide more detailed information on the students' use of and exposure to French that will allow us to gain a better sense of how much exposure to this language the students receive in and outside the French immersion programs. Table 2.7 provides information on the students' use of French in a variety of settings. For instance, it provides data on their use of French with family members. It is interesting that this information confirms the statistics reported above on the students' use of French at home. Recall that 12% of the students reported using French at home 50% of the time or more. Here we can see that 14% of the students usually use French with their family members when they have the chance. When the students are outside the home and interact with their friends, 11% report usually using French when they have the chance. Interestingly, 23% of the students report usually using French in stores and restaurants when the opportunity presents itself. This surprisingly high figure echoes a finding in the North York Board of Education (1986) report that points out that in their survey questionnaire several students felt the need to add additional comments indicating that they occasionally used French in restaurants within the greater Toronto area.[13] In contrast, Table 2.7 shows that only 3% of the students report usually using French on the street with strangers. This difference reflects the fact that the students reside in overwhelmingly English-speaking communities where they are unlikely to meet Francophone strangers on the street, but that they are more likely to take the opportunity to speak French with bilingual waitstaff in the greater Toronto area's many French restaurants.

Table 2.8 focuses on the students' use of French in the school setting. This table underscores the fact that French is the language used primarily in class with teachers, since 84% of the students report usually using French in this situation when they have the chance. However, the students overwhelmingly use English when they communicate among themselves in the classroom (71% rarely or never use French) or outside of the classroom (90% rarely or never use French). Having said this, it is interesting to note that the proportion of students reporting nil or marginal use of French outside the classroom is nearly 20% greater than within this

Methodology

Table 2.7 Use of French by the immersion students within and outside the home

	Never have the chance to use French		Sometimes have the chance, rarely use French		Often have chance, rarely use French		Sometimes have chance, usually use French		Often have chance, usually use French		Total*	
	N	%	N	%	N	%	N	%	N	%	N	%
With family members	235	73	34	11	5	2	42	13	3	1	319	100
Out of school with friends	204	64	65	20	15	5	30	9	5	2	319	100
In stores and restaurants	145	46	92	29	7	2	71	22	4	1	319	100
With strangers on the street	288	89	12	4	15	4	6	2	1	1	322	100

*A total of less than 322 signifies that one or more of the students did not indicate their French use in the situation.

Table 2.8 Use of French by the immersion students in the school setting

	Never have the chance to use French		Sometimes have the chance, rarely use French		Often have chance, rarely use French		Sometime have chance, usually use French		Often have chance, usually use French		Total*	
	N	%	N	%	N	%	N	%	N	%	N	%
Out of class with friends	171	54	90	29	24	7	27	9	4	1	316	100
In class with friends	47	15	95	30	84	26	56	18	33	11	315	100
In class with teacher	2	1	20	6	27	9	76	24	192	60	317	100

*A total of less than 322 signifies that one or more of the students did not indicate their French use in the situation.

Table 2.9 Languages of media use by the immersion students

Factor	N	%
Language use: television		
Always French	0	0
Often French, sometimes English	1	1
Half French, half English	5	2
Often English, sometimes French	100	31
Always English	204	63
Another language	11	3
Total	321	100
Language use: radio		
Always French	0	0
Often French, sometimes English	1	1
Half French, half English	3	1
Often English, sometimes French	26	8
Always English	278	87
Another language	11	3
Total	319	100
Language use: music		
Always French	0	0
Often French, sometimes English	1	1
Half French, half English	3	1
Often English, sometimes French	64	20
Always English	234	73
Another language	18	5
Total	320	100
Language use: magazines		
Always French	0	0
Often French, sometimes English	0	0
Half French, half English	17	5

(Continued)

Table 2.9 *Continued*

Factor	N	%
Often English, sometimes French	65	20
Always English	229	72
Another language	9	3
Total	320	100
Language use: books		
Always French	0	0
Often French, sometimes English	8	2
Half French, half English	79	25
Often English, sometimes French	146	46
Always English	83	26
Another language	4	1
Total	320	100

Table 2.10 Time spent in Francophone environments by the immersion students

Factor	N	%
No time	213	66
1–3 days	22	7
4–14 days	49	15
15–50 days	16	5
51–100 days	6	2
101–365 days	4	1
More than 365 days	12	4
Total	322	100

setting, a finding that likely reflects the presence of an authority figure, represented by the French immersion teacher, within the classroom. Hart et al. (1989), in their study of French immersion programs in Calgary, have also reported low levels of use of French outside the classroom in the school setting. For instance, only 20% of the students report using French at least some of the time between classes.

Table 2.11 Time spent in Francophone environments by immersion students as a function of place

Factor	N	%
Time in Quebec		
No time	99	31
1–3 days	35	11
4–14 days	108	34
15–50 days	35	11
51–100 days	11	3
101–365 days	7	2
More than 365 days	26	8
Total	*321*	*100*
Time in Ottawa		
No time	291	90
1–3 days	20	6
4–14 days	9	2
15–50 days	1	1
51–100 days	1	1
101–365 days	0	0
More than 365 days	0	0
Total	*322*	*100*
Time in other Canadian locations		
No time	302	92
1–3 days	2	1
4–14 days	5	2
15–50 days	5	2
51–100 days	1	1
101–365 days	0	0
More than 365 days	7	2
Total	*322*	*100*

(*Continued*)

Table 2.11 Continued

Factor	N	%
Time in France		
No time	279	85
1–3 days	8	2
4–14 days	22	7
15–50 days	5	2
51–100 days	2	1
101–365 days	5	2
More than 365 days	1	1
Total	322	100
Time in other non-Canadian locations		
No time	314	96
1–3 days	0	1
4–14 days	2	1
15–50 days	2	1
51–100 days	2	1
101–365 days	0	0
More than 365 days	2	1
Total	322	100

Table 2.12 Time spent with a Francophone family by the immersion students

Factor	N	%
No time	218	71
1–3 days	9	3
4–14 days	38	12
15–50 days	9	3
51–100 days	11	3.5
101–365 days	1	0.5
More than 365 days	21	7
Total	307	100

Table 2.13 Time spent with a Francophone family by immersion students as a function of place

Factor	N	%
Time in Quebec		
No time	261	85
1–3 days	6	2
4–14 days	28	8
15–50 days	5	2
51–100 days	4	2
101–365 days	0	0
More than 365 days	3	1
Total	307	100
Time in Ontario		
No time	296	96.5
1–3 days	2	0.5
4–14 days	4	1
15–50 days	1	0.5
51–100 days	3	1
101–365 days	0	0
More than 365 days	1	0.5
Total	307	100
Time in other Canadian locations		
No time	288	94
1–3 days	1	0.5
4–14 days	1	0.5
15–50 days	0	0
51–100 days	0	0
101–365 days	0	0
More than 365 days	17	5
Total	307	100

(*Continued*)

Table 2.13 *Continued*

Factor	N	%
Time in France		
No time	297	96
1–3 days	0	0
4–14 days	5	2
15–50 days	1	0.5
51–100 days	3	1
101–365 days	1	0.5
More than 365 days	0	0
Total	307	100
Time in other non-Canadian locations		
No time	304	99
1–3 days	0	0
4–14 days	0	0
15–50 days	2	0.5
51–100 days	1	0.5
101–365 days	0	0
More than 365 days	0	0
Total	307	100

Data on the students' media consumption also reveal limited use of French. As Table 2.9 shows, 34% of the students report watching French television at least some of the time, 10% report listening to French radio at least some of the time, 22% report likewise for French music and 5% report such use of French magazines. These results are in line with the findings of several studies. For instance, the North York Board of Education (1986) reported that French immersion students never or hardly ever watched French television or French movies or read French newspapers or French magazines. Similar findings on French immersion students' use of the French language media have been reported by Genesee (1990) for French immersion students in Montreal, and for French immersion students in Ottawa by Parkin *et al.* (1987) as well as by Wesche *et al.* (1986). In relation to the reading of books in French, our survey revealed a high proportion of students (73%) who read French books at least some of the time. This may reflect, in part, the fact that a certain proportion of the French books the students read are for school purposes. Unfortunately, the question as phrased in the survey did not ask the students to make this distinction.

Table 2.10 reveals that two thirds of the students have spent no time in a Francophone environment and that for those students who have stayed in such an environment, most have stayed between four and 14 days. This finding stands in sharp contrast to those reported in several studies where only a small proportion of French immersion students have never stayed in a Francophone environment. For instance, only 13% of the Toronto area French immersion students in Hart et al.'s (1989) study report never having spent a week in a Francophone environment. Furthermore, among their students who have spent time in a Francophone environment, the highest proportion of students falls into the category 5–8 weeks.

One possible explanation for the difference in stays in a Francophone environment between the French immersion students in our data and those in the Hart et al.'s data is that, as we have pointed out, the former students include a much smaller proportion of upper-middle-class individuals. It is possible that the lower socioeconomic status of the students in our research would make it more difficult to afford frequent and/or long stays away from home.

Table 2.11 provides information on where and for how long the stays in a Francophone environment by the students have taken place. As can be seen, these stays have taken place primarily in Quebec and, to a much lesser extent, in France. This echoes a finding reported by Hart et al. (1994) that the stays in a Francophone environment by the French immersion students in their research have been almost invariably in Quebec. Concerning Quebec, it is interesting that one third of the students in our research have spent between four and 14 days in this location. That 8% of the students report having spent more than a year in Quebec mirrors the fact that 7% of the students were actually born in Quebec. This location is also the only one where a substantial percentage of the students have spent between 15 and 50 days. These findings reflect the geographical proximity of Quebec in relation to Ontario and hence the long-standing tradition of class trips to Quebec.

In terms of time spent staying with a Francophone family, Table 2.12 reveals that the proportion of students who have never had such an experience is even higher than the figure for time spent in a Francophone environment (71% versus 66%, respectively). Once again, most students having stayed with a Francophone family spent between four and 14 days. Table 2.13 further reveals that it is almost exclusively in Quebec that these stays have occurred. It is also interesting that the proportion of students who have spent more than a year with a Francophone family in Quebec is only 1%, a sharp contrast to the 8% of students who report having spent more than a year in Quebec. Since 7% of the students were born in Quebec, the fact that only 1% of the students have stayed with a Francophone family in Quebec suggests that many of these Quebec-born students may have been raised in non-French-speaking families. In fact, over half of the Quebec-born students report speaking no French at home. Furthermore, the clear majority of students who do speak French at home were actually born in the greater Toronto area. This may be an indication that Francophones from Quebec who come to the greater Toronto area do not necessarily have a strong inclination to enroll their children in French immersion programs.

Table 2.14 provides attitudinal data on how the students feel toward the value of French in Canada, the value of learning French and the value of French-Canadian culture. These data are the result of combining several items from the survey questionnaire. The value of French in Canada represents the students' reactions to the following statements: 'I think it is important to learn French because you need it more and more for most things you do in Canada'; 'I think it is important to learn French because it is an official language of Canada'; and 'I think it is important to learn French because if we don't, the French language in Ontario might disappear'. The value of learning French represents the students' reactions to the following statements: 'I want to learn as much French as possible'; 'Learning French is a waste of time'; 'I really enjoy learning French'; 'When I leave school, I will give up the study of French entirely because I'm not interested in it'; and 'If it were entirely up to me whether or not to take French, I would drop it'. Finally, the value of the French-Canadian culture represents the students' reactions to the following statements: 'The French-Canadian culture is an important part of our Canadian heritage' and 'If Canada were to lose the French culture, it would certainly be a great loss'.

As Table 2.14 shows, a great majority of the students hold positive or fairly positive attitudes toward the French-Canadian culture (a mean of 0.83 out of a maximum of 1.0). This result is in keeping with that of Van der Keilen (1995) who reported a mean that is equivalent to 0.78 out of a maximum of 1.0. She found this mean, which differed significantly from that for students in non-immersion programs, among Grades 5–8 French immersion students from Sudbury, Ontario, in relation to attitudes toward French Canadians. The finding that concerns the high school French immersion students in the present study is interesting because the majority of studies have looked at the attitudes of French immersion students at the elementary level. These latter studies (e.g. Genesee *et al.*, 1977; Lambert & Tucker, 1972) have found that French immersion students initially have positive attitudes toward French Canadians or French-Canadian culture, but that these positive attitudes decrease gradually over the first few years of their programs to become indistinguishable from those of their non-immersion peers. In contrast, among the students in the present study, not only is there a very high overall positive attitude toward the French-Canadian culture, but also an increase in the mean value

Table 2.14 Values associated by the immersion students with the importance of the French language within the Canadian context, the learning of French and the French-Canadian culture

Factor	N	%
Value attributed to French-Canadian culture		
Negative	1	1
Fairly negative	6	2
Neutral	41	13
Fairly positive	69	21
Positive	199	63
Total	316	100
Overall mean and standard deviation	Mean 0.83, S.D. 0.18	
Value attributed to learning French		
Negative	1	1
Fairly negative	4	2
Neutral	32	10
Fairly positive	76	24
Positive	199	63
Total	312	100
Overall mean and standard deviation	Mean 0.83, S.D. 0.15	
Value attributed to French in Canadian context		
Negative	27	8
Fairly negative	80	25
Neutral	54	17
Fairly positive	72	23
Positive	85	27
Total	318	100
Overall mean and standard deviation	Mean 0.58, S.D. 0.27	

attributed as one progresses through the high school grades (Grade 9, 0.81; Grade 10, 0.82; Grade 11, 0.84; Grade 12, 0.86; and Grade 13, 0.90). It would be interesting to conduct further research to see if such an increase reflects student attrition and self-selection from Grade 10 onward (see above) or whether it is a reflection of longitudinal changes in student attitudes.

As for the value attributed to learning French, Table 2.14 shows also that the great majority of the students hold a positive or fairly positive attitude (a mean of 0.83 out of a maximum of 1.0). Again, this result is in line with that of Van der Keilen (1995) who reported a mean that is equivalent to 0.86 out of a maximum of 1.0 for the value attributed to learning French by the Grades 5–8 French immersion students she examined.

However, Table 2.14 shows a mean of only 0.58 out of a maximum of 1.0 attributed to the value of learning French because of its special value and status in the Canadian context. This difference may represent an interesting split between a utilitarian motivation toward learning French and a more general and undifferentiated motivation to learn this language, which may include cultural and intellectual enrichment.

Speaker Sample

Our research on the learning of spoken French sociolinguistic variation by French immersion students is based on a sample of 41 Grade 9 and 12 French immersion students selected from the 322 French immersion students whose questionnaire survey answers were examined above.[14] Two sampling criteria were used to select the subset of 41 students. The students were drawn in equal proportions from three levels of French-language competence (high, mid and low) as judged by their teachers and came from homes where French was not used as a means of communication. Students raised in Francophone homes were excluded in order to focus on the spoken French competence of students for whom French is a second or third language and who constitute the majority of students in those schools where the data were collected.[15]

Each of the 41 students took part in a face-to-face, individual, semi-directed interview conducted by the same native Francophone, followed a set of non-challenging, non-invasive questions about the students' daily activities. The interview design was inspired by that employed in Mougeon and Beniak's (1991) sociolinguistic research on the spoken French of Franco-Ontarian adolescents, which in turn reflected that used by previous sociolinguistic research on L1 French in Quebec (e.g. Sankoff and Cedergren's research on Montreal spoken French) and follows the principles of the Labovian sociolinguistic interview described in the previous chapter.

Frequency counts of the questionnaires for the 41 student sub-sample are presented in Tables 2.15 and 2.16.

Table 2.15 Chief characteristics of the 41 student sample

Grade	Sex	Social class[a]	French-medium schooling (%)	Exposure to TV and radio in French	Time in the Francophone environment	Length of stay with Francophone family	Languages spoken at home
9 ($n = 21$)	Female ($n = 13$)	Middle ($n = 10$)	0–25 ($n = 2$)	Never ($n = 16$)	<1 day ($n = 8$)	0 h ($n = 15$)	English ($n = 10$)
			26–37 ($n = 14$)		1–6 days ($n = 6$)	1–13 days ($n = 5$)	Romance ($n = 4$)
	Male ($n = 8$)	Upper working ($n = 9$)	38–100 ($n = 5$)	Occasional ($n = 5$)	1–3 weeks ($n = 6$)	>2 weeks ($n = 1$)	Other ($n = 7$)
					>3 weeks ($n = 1$)		
12 ($n = 20$)	Female ($n = 17$)	Middle ($n = 14$)	0–25 ($n = 6$)	Never ($n = 9$)	<1 day ($n = 4$)	0 h ($n = 12$)	English ($n = 10$)
					1–6 days ($n = 3$)	1–13 days ($n = 1$)	Romance ($n = 4$)
			26–37 ($n = 13$)	Occasional ($n = 11$)	1–3 weeks ($n = 9$)	>2 weeks ($n = 7$)	Other ($n = 6$)
	Male ($n = 3$)	Upper working ($n = 6$)			>3 weeks ($n = 4$)		
Total = 41	Female = 30	Middle = 24	0–25 = 8	Never = 25	<1 day = 12	0 h = 27	English = 20
			26–37 = 27		1–6 days = 9	1–13 days = 6	Romance = 8
	Male = 11	Upper working = 15	38–100 = 6	Occasional = 16	1–3 weeks = 15	>2 weeks = 8	Other = 13
					>3 weeks = 5		

Table 2.16 41 students' curricular and extra-curricular patterns of French language use

Media usage	Always English	Often English	Half English, half French	Often French	Always French
Television	26	15	0	0	0
Radio	39	2	0	0	0
Music	31	10	0	0	0
Books	10	21	9	1	0
Magazines	29	10	2	0	0
Usage of French	Never have the chance to use French	Sometimes have the chance, rarely use French	Often have chance, rarely use French	Sometime have chance, usually use French	Often have chance, usually use French
In class with teachers[a]	0	2	3	7	27
In class with friends[a]	4	13	10	8	4
At school with friends[a]	23	12	3	2	0
Outside school with friends	28	9	1	3	0
At home with family members	29	8	2	2	0
In stores and restaurants	22	12	0	7	0
On the street with strangers	32	4	0	5	0

[a] One or more of the students did not indicate their French usage in these situations.

As can be seen in Table 2.15, there are roughly equal numbers of Grades 9 and 12 students, proportionally more females than males, and more students from middle class than from upper-working class backgrounds. Sixty-six percent of the students have received 26–37% of their schooling in French. Many of those students with higher values than this have attended an exclusively French-medium school at some point. While 61% of the students report never watching French television or listening to French radio, it is interesting to note that proportionally more Grade 12 students report occasional use of these French media than do the Grade 9s. A similar situation obtains with the students' stays in a Francophone environment and with a Francophone family. There are proportionally more Grade 12 than Grade 9 students who have spent time in a Francophone environment or with a Francophone family. Furthermore, the average length of stay both in a Francophone environment or with a Francophone family, for those students who have had these types of experiences, is a relatively modest 16 days and the majority of these stays are in Canada, particularly in Quebec.[16] Finally, Table 2.15 shows that 51% of the students come from homes where a language other than English is spoken. More specifically, among those students speaking a non-French/English language at home, 38% speak a Romance language (Italian or Spanish) and 62% speak a non-Romance language (e.g. Chinese, Croatian, German, Korean, Polish, Tagalog and Vietnamese).

Table 2.16 provides data on the use of French by the 41 immersion students inside and outside of the school setting. It shows that beyond the confines of the classroom, these students lack or do not seek opportunities to use French. Specifically, in relation to the media they clearly favor English television, radio, music and magazines, demonstrating 76% use exclusively in English. The only activity that shows any marked deviation from this pattern is reading books, with 24% of the students undertaking this activity as often, or more often, in French than in English, though likely for school purposes.

Table 2.16 also shows the students' limited interpersonal uses of French both on and off the school premises. Only 'in class with teachers' indicates that most students often have and take advantage of the occasion to use French. In contrast, 'in class with friends' and 'at school with friends' indicate respectively that 69% and 95% of the students rarely or never use French in these situations, whether they report having the chance to do so or not. Outside the school with their friends and family, in stores, restaurants and on the street, the great majority of the students rarely or never use French, primarily because they do not have many opportunities to do so.

Corpora Used as Comparative Norms

Recall that the present research takes a comparative approach in its description of the French immersion students' sociolinguistic competence.

To this end, we use findings from studies based on Quebec native speaker corpora. For sociolinguistic variables where studies of Quebec spoken French have not been carried out, we also use findings from studies on corpora of Ontario spoken French. This decision is based on the close genetic ties between Ontario and Quebec French (i.e. Ontario French may be rightly looked upon as a variety of Quebec French, transplanted into Ontario due to at least a century and a half of migration from Quebec). Finally, we also analyze a corpus of French immersion teachers' in-class speech and written materials used for French Language Arts in French immersion programs.

The Quebec corpora

The majority of sociolinguistic variation studies of Quebec French are based on Sankoff and Cedergren's corpus of Montreal French (see Sankoff *et al.*, 1976 for a description of the corpus). This corpus was gathered in 1971 and comes from semi-directed taped interviews following Labovian methodology. The speakers from this corpus are 120 native Francophones from Montreal and the corpus is stratified according to sex (60 men and 60 women), age (16–85) and socioeconomic status. A second Montreal corpus was gathered in 1984 by Thibault and Vincent (1990). This corpus is composed of 60 speakers from the 1971 Sankoff and Cedergren corpus coupled with 12 new speakers (aged 15–25). The goal of these two corpora was to generate natural conversations focusing in particular on life in Montreal. The major themes of the 1971 interviews were religion and politics, as well as life events such as marriage, birth of children, etc. Another important topic was the question of language in Quebec. Most of these topics were again discussed in the 1984 interviews.

The Ontario corpora

The spoken FL1 data we use from speakers residing in Ontario are from two different corpora, that of Poplack and of Mougeon and Beniak. Poplack's (cf. Poplack, 1989) corpus of spoken French was collected in 1982 from 120 native Francophones in the twin cities of Ottawa and Hull.[17] Once again, a Labovian methodology was followed and the corpus is stratified according to social factors. There are 60 men and 60 women from five neighborhoods (three in Ottawa and two in Hull) from a full range of socioeconomic backgrounds and age groups.

Mougeon and Beniak's (1991) corpus was gathered in 1978 in four Ontario communities: Hawkesbury, Cornwall, North Bay and Pembroke. The 117 speakers in this corpus are Grades 9 and 12 adolescents enrolled in French language high schools. The semi-directed interviews of this corpus follow a Labovian methodology and center on various topics. As with other Canadian French corpora, speakers in this corpus represent both sexes and a range of socioeconomic status. While all the adolescent speakers in this corpus are of French-Canadian extraction, they use French in and outside the French language school to varying degrees. Some make almost categorical use of French in all domains (unrestricted speakers), while others use it very infrequently (restricted speakers). Still others use it at an intermediate level (semi-restricted speakers). This reflects the fact that in spite of recent measures taken to provide institutional support for the maintenance of French in Ontario, Franco-Ontarians are still undergoing assimilation into Ontario's Anglophone majority. It should be pointed out that when we use the Mougeon and Beniak corpus for the FL1 comparative norm, we use only the data produced by the unrestricted speakers of French (i.e. those speakers who come closest to FL1 Quebeckers).

That said, the restricted speakers are also of special interest for our research since their sociolinguistic profile shares some similarities with that of the French immersion students. In both cases, their use of French is restricted primarily to an educational setting (i.e. the classroom). Still, one must bear in mind that, unlike the French immersion students, these restricted speakers have been entirely schooled in French. Moreover, in the French language schools where they are enrolled, the restricted speakers are exposed to the marked informal spoken French of peers who come from homes where French is maintained. In Chapter 5, we will carry out a comparison of the speech of the French immersion students with that of Mougeon and Beniak's restricted speakers. This comparison will highlight similarities and differences in the way both groups of students use sociolinguistic variants and the importance of factors such as the amount of French language instruction and peer group exposure to marked informal French for the learning of sociolinguistic variation.

The French immersion teacher corpus

The corpus of French immersion teachers' in-class speech that we use for comparative purposes was gathered by Allen *et al.* (1987). The speech in this corpus was produced by a sample of seven French immersion teachers from the greater Toronto and Ottawa areas who were taped while teaching Grades 3 and 6 French immersion students. It should be pointed out that these teachers are not the actual instructors of the French immersion students under study here, and that no sociolinguistic background data on the teachers were gathered. However, one should also bear in mind that our systematic use of this teacher corpus to shed light on the spoken French competence of French immersion students is a methodological innovation. While we hope to gather a corpus of teachers' speech and accompanying sociolinguistic background data in the school district where the French immersion student corpus was gathered, the Allen *et al.* corpus of classroom speech gives a sense of the type of educational input that the French immersion students are likely to have had. In fact, as we will see in Chapter 4, there is often a striking degree of convergence between the patterns of sociolinguistic variation found in the speech of these teachers and the French immersion students.

The corpus of French Language Arts materials

Our corpus of French Language Arts materials consists of two series of textbooks and accompanying exercise books that are commonly used in French immersion programs in the greater Toronto area. We have examined in their entirety two series of materials, one called *Portes ouvertes sur notre pays* that included series 1A and B (Roy Nicolet & Jean-Côté, 1994) and 3A and B (Le Dorze & Morin, 1994), which is used in the school district where we gathered our student corpus, and the other called *Capsules* (Deslauriers & Gagnon, 1995, 1997), which is used in the Toronto District School Board, in spite of the fact that it was initially designed for FL1 students. This reflects the fact that it is not uncommon for immersion programs to rely on materials that were designed for FL1 students, given that immersion programs are not considered a sufficiently lucrative market for publishers to tailor materials specifically to their needs. In addition, in relation to the *Capsules* series, there is a positive perception of its content on the part of French immersion educators.

Research Hypotheses

Variants used by the French immersion students

On the basis of previous research (see Chapter 1) and also taking into account the important fact that the French immersion students under study have had only limited contacts with FL1 speakers outside the school context, and consequently received the vast majority of their exposure to French in a classroom setting, our research seeks to verify the following general hypotheses concerning the frequency of variant use by the French immersion students in our research and the type of variants they will use:

(1) The French immersion students will make only marginal use of marked informal variants.

(2) The French immersion students will use mildly marked informal variants less often than would FL1 speakers.

(3) The French immersion students will use forms that look like marked or mildly marked informal variants, but which are, in fact, symptomatic of their incomplete mastery of difficult standard variants.

(4) The French immersion students will use non-native forms that are not used by FL1 speakers and which also reflect their incomplete mastery of difficult standard variants.

(5) The French immersion students will over-use certain formal and hyper-formal variants.
(6) The French immersion students will use some neutral variants, but not others, depending on their systemic properties (e.g. the presence of a semantically and morphophonetically similar form in English, the structural complexity of the variant, etc.).[18]

Linguistic and stylistic constraints

Previous research on the learning of the linguistic constraints of sociolinguistic variation by FL2 learners found that FL2 learners observed the same linguistic constraints on variation as did FL1 speakers. However, it should be borne in mind that this research involves learners who have had considerable contacts with FL1 speakers, which is not the case of the immersion students in our sample. Consequently, these French immersion students might lack the kind of higher-level linguistic proficiency necessary to master the more subtle and complex dimensions of the linguistic constraints of sociolinguistic variation. As such, we hypothesize that the French immersion students will likely not display native-like mastery of the linguistic constraints of sociolinguistic variation in our own research.

Most of the studies that have investigated the learning of the stylistic constraints of sociolinguistic variation by FL2 learners have focused on French immersion students. They have found that by and large these FL2 learners have an inadequate mastery of this dimension of sociolinguistic variation. We expect to arrive at the same results in our own research.

Independent variables

In our research we examine correlations between French immersion students' sociolinguistic competence and four independent variables, namely (1) sex; (2) social class; (3) contacts with FL1 speakers; and (4) students' L1.

The reader will recall that, aside from our research, only one study (Blondeau & Nagy, 1998) has documented the correlation between sex and the learning of sociolinguistic variation by FL2 learners. Since this study has focused on FL2 learners in a naturalistic environment, we are curious to discover whether this parameter correlates with the learning of sociolinguistic variation by French immersion students in an educational context and notably if female students display a preference for the formal variants that are part of their repertoire. This hypothesis is premised on results from L1 sociolinguistic studies that have found that female speakers make greater use of standard variants than do male speakers, and we expect that the French immersion students will carry this pattern over from their L1 to their L2.

While no previous research has yet examined correlations between social class on variation in FL2, sociolinguistic research of L1 speakers has shown that middle class speakers use standard variants more often than lower-middle or working class speakers. We are therefore interested to find out if, as in the case of the sex variable, French immersion speakers who hail from the middle class will display a preference for standard variants.

As is evident in our review of research on the sociolinguistic competence of FL2 learners, many studies have found a positive effect of intensity of contacts with FL1 speakers and frequency of use of marked or mildly marked informal variants. We also expect to find such an effect in our research. However, given that the French immersion students have not had extensive contacts with FL1 speakers, and that some of the French immersion students had had no contacts at all with FL1 speakers, we hypothesize that the effect of this variable will be relatively modest.

As for the effect of the French immersion students' L1 on their sociolinguistic competence, given the findings of previous research, we expect to find such an influence. Specifically, we hypothesize that variants that have a morphologically and or semantically similar counterpart in the students' L1 will be used with greater frequency. The reader will recall that about half of the French immersion students who speak a language other than English at home, speak a Romance language (Spanish and Italian). We therefore entertain two hypotheses. Firstly, we hypothesize that variants with English equivalents will be used more often by students for whom English is their only L1 and secondly, that variants with Italian or Spanish equivalents will be used more often by students who speak such Romance languages at home in comparison with other students.[19]

Variation in the educational input of French immersion students

As pointed out in Chapter 1, neither French immersion teachers' classroom speech nor FL2 teaching materials accurately reflect the norms of L1 spoken French. This observation allows us to formulate several hypotheses regarding the presence of sociolinguistic variants in French immersion students' educational input.

As concerns teachers' classroom speech, we expect to find that teachers will (1) make frequent use of hyper-formal and formal variants; (2) make only modest use of mildly marked informal variants; and (3) avoid marked informal variants.[20]

As for the French Language Arts materials used by the French immersion students, we expect they will strongly favor hyper-formal, formal, variants. Conversely, we expect that these same materials will make sparse use, if any, of marked informal variants. However, it is possible that in the texts that are meant to represent oral French, we will find occurrences of mildly marked informal variants, although we are uncertain as to the extent to which this will be the case.

Lyster's (1994a) finding that pedagogical materials centered on specific sociolinguistic variables significantly improved the sociolinguistic competence of French immersion students is one of the reasons we decided to examine the treatment of sociolinguistic variation in the French Language Arts materials used in French immersion programs. Aware of the fact that the materials that we examine are based on the communicative approach, we do not expect to find many activities involving explicit analysis or practice of linguistic forms. In contrast to traditional views of language learning, which focus primarily on formal linguistic accuracy, communicative approaches to language teaching and learning have always emphasized the use of language in 'authentic' and unrehearsed contexts and focus on dimensions of the language in addition to the grammatical, such as the sociolinguistic, sociocultural, strategic and discursive (cf. Canale, 1983; Canale & Swain, 1980; Celce-Murcia *et al.*, 1995; Savignon, 1983, 1997). Still, assuming that the materials include certain mildly marked informal variants, we are curious to determine if these variants are the object of special emphasis, either in the form of information about their sociostylistic status or in the form of activities meant to develop the students' receptive or productive abilities to use such variants.

Data Analysis

As mentioned, the main goal of our research is to determine the range and frequency of the variants used by the 41 French immersion students, the influence exerted on variant use by certain linguistic and stylistic constraints, as well as other independent variables. The computerized concordance program MonoConc Pro (Barlow, 1998) has been employed to identify within the corpus instances (tokens) of the variants under study, along with their context of occurrence. GoldVarbII (Rand & Sankoff, 1990), a logistic regression factor analysis program, has been used to obtain frequency counts and factor effect weightings that allow us to identify which of the linguistic and stylistic constraints and which of the other independent variables under study are significantly correlated with variant choice. This program does a stepwise regression analysis yielding an ordered selection of the factors that are associated with variant choice by the immersion students. The factor effects vary between 0 and 1, with values greater than 0.5 indicating that a sociolinguistic variant is favored and values less than 0.5 indicating that it is disfavored. GoldVarbII also gives two more general measures: the overall 'goodness of fit' (log likelihood), and the probability of the application of the rule irrespective of the contribution of the factors (input probability) – see Appendix D for examples of the GoldVarb outputs for the sociolinguistic variables focused upon in this volume and Young and Bayley's (1996) overview of the use of GoldVarb in second language variationist research.

As pointed above, we also analyzed the data in the Allen *et al.* immersion teacher classroom speech corpus and in our sample of French Language Arts materials used in immersion programs, to determine the range and frequency of all the variants focused on in our research. In the sample of materials, we also assess the extent to which the authors' frequency of use of variants in dialogues and similar types of discourse was different from their frequency of use of the same variants in the parts of the materials that illustrated various forms of written texts (see further down). In the teacher classroom speech corpus, our analysis is limited to a calculation of the frequency of each of the variants under study.

Chapter 3
Variation in L1 Spoken French

Introduction

The goal of this chapter is to review the results of previous variationist research on L1 varieties of Quebec and Ontario French that focused on the same 15 sociolinguistic variables examined in our research. This review is the first such synthesis of the findings of research on sociolinguistic variation in spoken L1 Quebec and Ontario French. The 15 variables examined belong to a range of language components including grammatical, lexical and phonological variables. In our review of this literature, we will provide information on the frequencies with which FL1 speakers use the different variants under study in an interview situation. Frequency will be expressed via relative percentages (e.g. variant a = 20%, variant b = 80%). We will also provide information on the linguistic, social and situational constraints that condition their use.

Unfortunately, as pointed out in Chapter 2, the vast majority of sociolinguistic studies on variation in Quebec and Ontario spoken French have been based on corpora that are now more than 20 years old (i.e. 1971, 1984 for Montreal French; 1978 for Ontario adolescent French and 1982 for Ottawa–Hull French). As such, they do not necessarily represent the varieties spoken at the time we gathered our own immersion corpus (1996). Still, these are the only studies in existence that use similar data-gathering techniques as our own, namely, the Labovian semi-directed interview. Further, since the students in our sample who have had interactions with FL1 speakers have been primarily exposed to French in Quebec, we had to use the findings of studies focused on variation in Quebec spoken French or in a variety of Canadian closely related to Quebec French, namely Ontario French.[21] Thus such studies, and the corpora they are based on, provide the most suitable L1 benchmarks of sociolinguistic variation that immersion students might be expected to approximate during a semi-directed interview.

Grammatical Variation

Nine grammatical variables will be examined: (1) the first person plural subject pronouns *on* and *nous*; (2) use versus non-use of the negative particle *ne*; (3) alternation between the auxiliaries *avoir* and *être*; (4) future verb forms in all persons; (5) first person singular periphrastic future; (6) locutions of restriction; (7) third person plural verb forms; (8) expressions of consequence; and (9) location at/motion to one's dwelling.

Use of *on* versus *nous* as first person plural subject pronouns

In many varieties of contemporary spoken French, the notion of first person plural can be expressed via either of two subject pronouns: *on* and *nous*, meaning 'we'. This alternation dates back to at least the 17th century. In her study of subject pronoun use in Montreal French, Laberge's (1977) documented these two pronouns, as well as two secondary doubled variants (i.e. *nous-autres on* and *nous on*) as illustrated by examples (1)–(4), taken from the 1971 Montreal spoken French corpus.

(1) *on allait à l'école moi pis lui*
    'we used to go to school me and him'
(2) *c'est évident que **nous** n'avons pas l'accent*
    'it's clear that we don't have the accent'
(3) ***nous-autres on** reste dans la même merde qu'eux-autres*
    'Us, we're stuck in the same shit as they are'
(4) *Il trouve qu'il est très bien formé, aussi bien que **nous on** l'était*
    'He finds that he is very well educated, as well as us we were'

Laberge's research of this variable in the 1971 Montreal French corpus shows widespread use of *on* (98%), with or without preceding stressed pronouns *nous* or *nous-autres* [as in examples (1)–(4)].[22] In contrast, the frequency of the variant *nous* is quite marginal (2%). Laberge's study does not provide information on the frequency of the variants *nous-autres on* and *nous on*; therefore we had to use the Mougeon and Beniak corpus of Ontario French to gain a sense of how frequent these two variants are in relation to *on*. In the Mougeon and Beniak corpus we found 4% of *nous-autres on*, 1% of *nous on* and 95% of *on*. Thus it is reasonable to assume that in Montreal spoken French *nous-autres on* and *nous on* are secondary variants as well and that *on* is a highly frequent default alternative. In a subsequent study, based on a corpus of spoken French collected in Quebec City, Deshaies (1991) arrived at results similar to those of Laberge (1997), namely that *nous* is virtually non-existent in the speech of her informants.

Studies of contemporary spoken French from France have also documented the variable use of *on* and *nous* (see notably Coveney, 2000;

Fonseca-Greber & Waugh, 2002) and found that the variant *on* is also highly frequent in this variety of French. Coveney's (2000) study is based on a corpus collected in 1982 and Fonseca and Greber's on a corpus collected in the mid-to-late 1990s. In Coveney's corpus *on* was used in 96% of occurrences and in Fonseca and Greber's corpus *on*'s frequency is nearly categorical (99%).

Interestingly, in European French, the predominance of *on* over *nous* is the result of a relatively recent sociolinguistic change, which was rooted in the speech of the working class and which spread to the speech of all social groups during the 20th century, in spite of the negative reactions of grammarians, who have prescribed the use of the standard variant *nous* (see King *et al.*, 2009).

Linguistic constraints

Laberge's (1977) study did not examine the role of linguistic factors in the use of *on* and *nous*. However, a non-variationist study by Boutet (1986) of the use of *on* in spoken French in France has considered linguistic factors relevant for the alternation between *on* and *nous*. Boutet categorizes the uses of *on* and *nous* into three groups according to the semantic specificity and restriction of the referent: (1) when the referents are specific groups of individuals whose size is restricted (e.g. *moi et ma soeur* 'me and my sister'); (2) are specific but not restricted (e.g. *les élèves de mon école* 'the students at my school'); and (3) are neither specific nor restricted (e.g. *les gens* 'people'). Each of these contexts is illustrated through examples (5)–(10), taken from the Mougeon and Beniak corpus of adolescent spoken Ontario French.[23]

Context 1

(5) *puis dans ma famille* **nous** *sommes six – cinq garçons une fille*
  'and in my family we are six – five boys one girl'
(6) *pis* **on** *a un chalet entre Lancaster pis Lewiston*
  'and we have a cottage between Lancaster and Lewiston'

Context 2

(7) **nous** *avons une école ici ... 'xxx'*
  'we have a school here ...' ''name deleted''
(8) *pis* **on** *a deux écoles bilingues pis* **on** *a 'xxx' ça c'est anglais*
  'and we have two bilingual schools and we have 'name deleted' that one is English'

Context 3

(9) *quand* **nous** *sommes avec des personnes et si on va pour un 'job interview'*
  'when we are with people and if we go for a job interview'
(10) *dans l'avenir ben* **on** *aura pas d'gaz d'après qu'est-ce qu'eux-autres i' dit*
  'in the future well we will have no gasoline according to what they say'

One of the merits of Boutet's classification is that it is based on semantic factors that have been found to influence the evolution of the *on* versus *nous* alternation during the history of French. Thus, in their investigation of the trajectory of *on* and *nous* from the 17th to the 20th century in European French, King *et al.* (2009) found that *nous* was used much more often when the referents are restricted and specific, and conversely, that *on* was clearly the preferred option when the referents are unrestricted. Further, they found that this linguistic constraint remained stable from the 17th century up to the point when *on* started to win the competition with *nous*. In other words, at that point of time *on* started to encroach into contexts where pronominal reference is restricted and specific.

Extra-linguistic constraints

As concerns the social distribution of first person plural subject pronouns, it should be pointed out that the occurrences of *nous* that do exist in Quebec French are found primarily in the speech of those older than 50. In addition, it is particularly women and upper-middle-class speakers who make use of *nous* (see Deshaies, 1991; Laberge, 1977). This suggests that in Montreal French *nous* is a prestige variant and may be disappearing from the spoken language. The prestige status of *nous* is further confirmed by the fact that it is used with greatest frequency in the most formal part of the interview (see Deshaies, 1991; Laberge, 1977). In contrast, the variant *on* is used by all speakers in the Montreal and Quebec City corpora and its frequency varies little across the different social groups. As for the main secondary variant, *nous-autres on*, Laberge and Deshaie's studies do not provide information on its social and stylistic correlates. However, Blondeau's (2001) study revealed that in the Montreal 1971 and 1984 corpora, the compound forms of the plural personal pronouns (*nous-autres, vous-autres* 'you' and *eux-autres* 'them') are used more often than their simple counterparts *nous, vous* and *eux* by speakers from the lower social strata than by speakers from the upper social strata, by males than by females and when discussing informal topics than when discussing formal ones. These findings suggest that the variant *nous-autres on* may also be associated with working class speakers, male speakers and informal topics.

In sum, in relation to the continuum of sociostylistic markedness, which we have outlined in Chapter 1, in Quebec spoken French, *nous* can be placed at the hyper-formal end of the continuum, *on* has the features of a mildly marked variant and *nous-autres on* can be looked upon as a marked informal variant.

Use versus non-use of the negative particle *ne*

As has been attested in several dialects of the Romance languages (e.g. Brazilian Portuguese, Provençal, and Romansh), modern French expresses the notion of negation via a pre-verbal and a post-verbal negator (e.g. *ne* + verb + *jamais* 'never', *pas* 'not', *personne* 'nobody', *plus* 'no longer' or *rien* 'nothing'). However, in modern casual spoken French, a strong tendency to drop the pre-verbal negative particle *ne* has been documented. Examples (11) and (12), taken from Sankoff and Vincent's (1977) study of this variable in L1 Montreal French, illustrate this tendency and its formal equivalent use of *ne* use.

(11) *notre parler Ø est pas tellement différent*
 'our speech is not very different'
(12) *ma mère **ne** parle pas un mot anglais*
 'My mother does not speak a word of English'

Sankoff and Vincent found that *ne* is deleted 99.5% of the time in spoken Montreal French. Furthermore, *ne* is present in the speech of only 15 of the 60 speakers they studied. Similar results for this variable have been arrived at by Poplack and St-Amand (2007) who found *ne* to be present in only 0.2% of occurrences in their Ottawa–Hull corpus, while Sandy (1997) found 1.5% *ne* usage in Mougeon and Beniak's corpus of Ontario French. In addition, research on this variable in the French spoken in France (cf. Ashby, 1981, 2001; Coveney, 1996, among others) has documented *ne* non-use although their overall rates of non-use are not as high as for the studies of Canadian French. In a corpus collected in Tours in 1976 and in a second corpus collected in the same city in 1995, Ashby found overall rates of *ne* non-use of respectively 63% and 80%. As for Coveney, he found an overall rate of *ne* non-use of 82% in his Picardy corpus collected in 1982. More recently, Armstrong (2001) found that in a corpus of adolescent spoken French collected in Northern France in 1990, *ne* deletion had reached the near categorical levels documented in the studies of Canadian French.

Linguistic constraints

Sankoff and Vincent (1977) examined the effect of the type of post-verbal negator on the frequency of *ne* use versus non-use. However, they were not able to establish a clear pattern due to the overwhelming non-use of *ne* in their corpus. Ashby's (1981) study also examined the effect of this linguistic constraint. He found that *ne* non-use is highest with *pas* (67%) and lowest with *personne* (25%).

The various contexts taken into consideration are found in examples (13)–(20), taken from the Mougeon and Beniak corpus of adolescent spoken Ontario French.

Jamais

(13) *je **n'**ai jamais ben ben eu la chance d'en lire*
 'I never really really had the chance to read some'
(14) *ils Ø parlent jamais sur la rue*
 'they never talk on the street'

Pas

(15) *il **n'**a pas de contrôle*
 'he has no control'
(16) *il Ø parle pas l'anglais du tout*
 'he does not speak English at all'

Personne

 no examples of *ne* use with *personne* were found in the corpus

(17) *personne Ø le comprenait dans la classe*
 'no one in the class understood him'

Plus

(18) *on lui a dit qu'il **n**'était plus professeur de français*
 'they told him that he was no longer a French teacher'
(19) *t'sais je Ø m'souviens plus quel moyen qu'on a été*
 'you know I don't remember any more how we went'

Rien

 no examples of *ne* use with *rien* were found in the corpus

(20) *ça Ø sert à rien parce que la plupart du temps ...*
 'it's pointless because most of the time ...'

Extra-linguistic constraints

The speakers of Montreal French who did make occasional use of *ne* were slightly older, occupied the higher rungs of the linguistic marketplace (those for whom Standard French was of high importance in the work domain), and had slightly higher levels of education, thus lending support to the claim that *ne* use is a prestige variant (cf. Sankoff & Vincent, 1980). Note, however, that no difference along sex lines was reported. Sankoff and Vincent also pointed out that style is relevant for this sociolinguistic variable – those occurrences of *ne* usage documented in their research were mostly found when speakers discussed formal topics such as religion and education. Similar results have been documented by Poplack and St-Amand (2007) for Ottawa–Hull French, who found similar associations for both style and social class. In contrast, Sandy's (1997) study of Ontario French found that neither social class nor (in)formality of topic had a significant effect on variant choice. In relation to topic, it should be pointed out that, unlike the studies of Sankoff and Vincent or Poplack and St-Amand, Sandy's finding is based on a systematic assessment of the frequency of both variants (i.e. *ne* usage and *ne* deletion) across a range of formal and informal topics.

In sum, in relation to our continuum of sociolinguistic markedness, the findings of research on *ne* usage vs *ne* deletion in Quebec and Ontario

French point to the fact that *ne* usage is a hyper-formal variant and that its counterpart, *ne* deletion, is a mildly marked informal variant.

Etre versus *avoir* as past auxiliaries

One noteworthy difficulty of French is that in the compound past tenses two auxiliaries are used, *être* 'to be' and *avoir* 'to have'. According to the rules of Standard French, auxiliary *être* is required with: (1) verbs that are used with a reflexive object pronoun (e.g. *se nourrir* 'to feed oneself' and *se coucher* 'to go to bed'); and (2) a small subset of verbs of motion and state (e.g. *entrer* 'to enter', *venir* 'to come', *sortir* 'to leave', *rester* 'to stay' and *demeurer* 'to remain'), when these verbs are used intransitively (*je suis sorti hier* 'I went out yesterday'). However, when these verbs of motion and state are transitive, they take auxiliary *avoir* (*j'ai sorti le chien hier* 'I took the dog out yesterday'). As for auxiliary *avoir*, it is required with all other verbs.

In many contemporary varieties of spoken French, FL1 speakers do not consistently observe the above rules and variably replace irregular auxiliary *être* with the more regular auxiliary *avoir*. As far as Quebec French is concerned, Sankoff and Thibault (1980) show that *avoir* is widely used as an auxiliary with the verbs that must, according to Standard French, be conjugated with auxiliary *être*. Auxiliary *avoir* occurs in 34% of the examples they examined. Note also that in modern vernacular European French use of auxiliary *avoir* with *être* verbs is widespread (see Gadet, 1992) and that such use has existed in casual spoken French for at least several centuries (see Willis, 2000).

Examples (21) and (22), where the motion verb *rentrer* 'to go in' is used in the compound past (i.e. *passé composé*) with either *être* or *avoir*, are taken from the Sankoff and Cedergren corpus.

(21) *je suis plus jamais rentré dans les pavillons*
'I never went back into the buildings'
(22) *Ils m'ont donné une place pour que je rentre dans l'hôpital puis j'ai pas rentré*
'They gave me a spot so that I could get into the hospital, but I didn't go'

Linguistic constraints

By far the most important linguistic factor conditioning this sociolinguistic variable is the relative frequency of the verb. Thus, with *aller*, the most frequent of all the *être* verbs, Sankoff and Thibault (1980) found a rate of auxiliary *avoir* use as low as 0.7%, whereas with verbs of lesser frequency the rate of auxiliary *avoir* use was as high as 90% (*passer* 'to go/come'). They also found that verbs with a transitive counterpart were more favorable to the use of auxiliary *avoir* than were those that did not have such a counterpart. The most in-depth study of the linguistic factors conditioning the auxiliary alternation is Willis' (2000) study of Ottawa–Hull French. She found that auxiliary *avoir* was favored by the following factors: (1) all the verbs whose past participle has the ability to be used as an adjective (e.g. *maintenant il est parti à Kingston* 'he is away in Kingston now' – the reasoning here is that with such verbs there will be a greater tendency to use auxiliary *avoir* in the compound past to avoid the possibility of an adjectival interpretation); (2) presence of a locative complement (the reasoning here is that grammarians in the 1800s recommended that auxiliary *avoir* be used with verbs followed by a locative complement, while auxiliary *être* was to be used with verbs followed by an infinitival complement); (3) verbs that cannot be used reflexively; (4) non-adjacency between the auxiliary and the past participle (the reasoning here is that the presence of intervening material may be a distracting factor in auxiliary choice and that the greater the distance between the auxiliary and the verb, the greater the likelihood that unmarked auxiliary *avoir* will be used); and (5) ability of the verb to be used transitively (the reasoning here is that since the transitive counterparts of the verbs of motion are normally used with auxiliary *avoir*, the association between the verbs of motion and auxiliary *avoir* may carry over to the intransitive uses of these verbs).

These contexts are illustrated by examples (23)–(32), taken from the Mougeon and Beniak adolescent corpus of spoken Ontario French.

Verbs whose past participles can be used adjectivally

(23) *il pouvait pas bouger pis on **a** parti hein*
       'he could not move and we left eh'
(24) *pis on **est** parti avant que la joute a fini*
       'then we left before the game was over'

Presence of a locative complement

(25) *j'**ai** allé à l'école 'xxx' avant*
       'I went to "name deleted" school before'
(26) *avec mes parents on **est** allé en Floride*
       'with my parents we went to Florida'

Verbs that cannot be used reflexively

(27) *puis après il **a** venu la chercher*
       'then after he came to get her'
(28) *c'était Grease qui **est** venu ça c'était pas pire*
       'then Grease came and it wasn't bad'

Non-adjacency between the auxiliary and the past participle

(29) *oui ça m'**a** déjà arrivé*
       'yes that's happened to me before'

(30) *oui ça m'est déjà arrivé*
'yes that's happened to me before'

Ability of the verb to be used transitively, as well as intransitively

(31) *ils **ont** sorti les trans-ams des affaires*
'they took out trans-ams and things'
(32) *pis le gars il **est** sorti ... il était pas mal gros*
'then the guy went out ... he was pretty fat'

Extra-linguistic constraints

A number of social factors have been shown to correlate with the auxiliary *avoir* versus *être* variable. For example, Sankoff and Thibault (1980) found that speakers with higher socioeconomic status used more auxiliary *être* than did those speakers with lower status and women used more auxiliary *être* than did men. They also noted that speakers with high linguistic marketplace indices used more auxiliary *être* than did those speakers with lower indices. Similar results were reported by Willis (2000) who found a strong correlation with education (the higher the education, the more likely one is to use auxiliary *être*)[24] and age (older speakers showed a preference for auxiliary *être*).

In sum, in Quebec and Ontario spoken French, the auxiliary *avoir* versus *être* variable represents an alternation involving a marked informal variant, namely *avoir* and a formal counterpart namely *être*, which is conditioned by several linguistic and extra-linguisnic factors.

Use of inflected future versus periphrastic future versus futurate present

Since at least the 15th century, spoken French has used two variants to express the notion of futurity: (1) the inflected future, a tense that is formed by adding a suffix to the verb stem (e.g. *il mangera* 'he will eat'); and (2) the periphrastic future, a tense formed with semi-auxiliary *aller* 'to go' followed by an infinitive (e.g. *il va manger* 'he's going to eat'). Deshaies and Laforge (1981) found these two forms of the future tense in their study of Quebec City spoken French and Emirkanian and Sankoff (1985) did likewise in their study of Montreal French. However, a more recent study based on the Ottawa–Hull spoken French corpus (Poplack & Turpin, 1999) has underscored the fact that the future can be expressed with yet another variant, namely the present indicative (i.e. the 'futurate present'). Each of these variants is presented in examples (33)–(35), taken from Poplack and Turpin (1999).

Periphrastic future

(33) *... quand tu **vas** te marier*
'... when you get married'

Inflected future

(34) *on se **mariera** pas*
'we will not get married'

Futurate present

(35) *ma petite nièce elle se **marie** là le 21 août*
'my little niece is getting married on August 21'

Poplack and Turpin (1999) found the following frequency rates: (1) inflected future 20%; (2) periphrastic future 73%; and (3) futurate present 7%. These results show that the preferred variant for indicating future verb reference is clearly the periphrastic future. This same general tendency has been found in the spoken French of France (cf. notably Bonami, 2002; Jeanjean, 1988; Le Goffic & Lab, 2001; Söll, 1969). However, among these studies those that examined speech corpora have found frequency rates for the periphrastic future which are not as high as in the studies of Canadian French. For instance, Jeanjean found that, in her corpus, the periphrastic and inflected future were used at almost equal levels of frequency.

Linguistic constraints

Poplack and Turpin (1999) point out that in most of the contexts which, according to traditional grammatical descriptions of Standard French, should not be associated with use of the periphrastic future (e.g. hypothetical events and temporally distant events), speakers use periphrastic verb forms far more often than the inflected future. The authors summarize this trend in saying that far from being reserved for the expression of some marked future eventuality, the periphrastic future functions as the basic default future marker in Canadian French. Thus, these authors found numerous examples of the periphrastic future when the verb refers to either a distal event (e.g. *dire que dans quatre cents ans d'ici il va avoir encore des Asselin* 'to think that four hundred years from now there will still be Asselins') or a proximal one (e.g. *ce soir on va te ramener* 'tonight we will bring you back'). The only contexts where a strong association with the inflected future is observable are (1) negative sentences; (2) formulaic utterances (e.g. quotes from the Bible and predictions); and (3) verbs used in the polite second person plural (i.e. with address pronoun *vous* 'you').[25] As concerns the futurate present, Poplack and Turpin point out that it is found principally in sentences that have a time-specific adverb (e.g. *demain* 'tomorrow' and *ce soir* 'this evening') since the present indicative does not explicitly mark futurity and hence is more likely to occur when this information can be recovered from an adverb.

Linguistic contexts favoring either the inflected future or the futurate present are exemplified below with examples (36)–(39) from the Poplack corpus.

Negative sentences (favorable to the inflected future)

(36) *Mais tu paieras plus de taxes*
'But you won't pay taxes anymore'

Formulaic utterances (favorable to the inflected future)

(37) *Le Bon-Dieu a dit, 'Tu ne **tueras** point'*
'the Good Lord' has said 'Thou shalt not kill'

Polite second person plural (favorable to the inflected future)

(38) *Il dit, 'Monsieur Rémillard, on est douze, vous **passerez** pas'*
'He says, 'Mr. Rémillard, there are twelve of us, you won't get by'

Time-specific adverb (favorable to the futurate present)

(39) *J'y **vas** ce soir-là*
'I'm going there tonight'

Extra-linguistic constraints

Surprisingly, when Poplack and Turpin (1999) examined correlations between the periphrastic and present forms, on the one hand, and speakers' occupation and education, on the other, no significant results were obtained. Given that these two variants lack a marked or mildly marked informal counterpart, they can be classified as neutral (see Chapter 1). A lack of correlation with speakers' occupation and education was also found for the inflected future. However, it should be noted that studies of 'written' Quebec French (cf. Lesage & Gagnon, 1992) reveal that the inflected future is by far the most frequent variant in that register. This, coupled with an association of this variant in spoken French with formulaic utterances and address pronoun *vous*, suggests that there is an association between the inflected future and formal usage. The only social factor found to correlate with this sociolinguistic variable is age. The finding that the inflected future is used significantly less by younger speakers, coupled with the low frequency of the inflected future and its narrow contextual distribution, led Poplack and Turpin to suggest that this tense is undergoing a sharp decline in informal speech. This pattern of change is reminiscent of what happened to the simple past in relation to the compound past.

In sum, in relation to the continuum of sociolinguistic markedness, research on the expression of the future in Quebec and Ontario spoken French has revealed that both the periphrastic future and the futurate present are neutral variants and that the inflected future is a formal variant. Further, such research has found only one linguistic factor influencing variant choice, namely negative sentences, which are strongly associated with the inflected future.

Use of *je vais* versus *je vas* versus *m'as* as auxiliaries of the periphrastic future

As we have seen, in Canadian French the future variable involves three variants. However, when one focuses on verb forms used in the first person singular, there are, in fact, several variants within the periphrastic future, namely *je vais*, *je vas* and *m'as*. It is worth pointing out that alternation between *je vais* and *je vas* dates back to the 16th century and that, in fact, in the early part of that century, *je vas* was considered a feature of educated speech. It was only later in that century that grammarians prescribed the use of *je vais* and that *je vas* became progressively associated with vernacular spoken French. While *je vas* has a long history of robust usage on both sides of the Atlantic Ocean in vernacular varieties of French, it has now become virtually extinct in urban European French (Martineau & Mougeon, 2005). In contrast, *je vas* is still quite frequent in many varieties of contemporary Canadian spoken French.

As for *m'as*, it is used mostly in Quebec French (Deshaies *et al.*, 1981) and in the varieties of French spoken in the Canadian provinces west of Quebec (Hallion, 2000; Mougeon *et al.*, 2008).[26]

Note also that in comparison with *je vas*, *je vais* is irregular, since it is phonologically distinct from other singular persons (*je vais* /vɛ/ versus *tu vas* /va/, *il va* /va/ and *elle va* /va/). Variant *m'as* is an interesting and exceptional instance of a conjugated verb whose subject pronoun (*je* 'I') has undergone deletion. This variant has never been attested in standard or literary written French. Its attestation in several French-based Creoles and in dialects of French spoken in Picardy suggests that it was probably used in informal spoken French during the French colonial period (1608–1750), see Mougeon (1996) and Mougeon and Beniak (1991) for further information on the history of *m'as* and the other two variants.

The alternation among the first person singular periphrastic future variants was not examined separately in Poplack and Turpin (1999). However, Mougeon and Beniak (1991) have carried out an analysis of this alternation in their corpus of spoken French by Franco-Ontarian adolescents. Uses of the first person singular periphrastic future variants, taken from Mougeon and Beniak's (1991) study, are illustrated in examples (40)–(42).

(40) O.K. *je vais t'aider*
    'OK I'm going to help you'
(41) *ben je vas y aller à l'université*
    'well I'm going to go to university'
(42) *m'as le retourner*
    'I'm going to bring it back'

Mougeon and Beniak (1991) documented the following frequencies for each of these variants in the speech of the unrestricted Franco-Ontarian adolescents: (1) *vais* 6%; (2) *vas* 64%; and (3) *m'as* 30%.

Linguistic constraints

Mougeon and Beniak (1991) did not examine linguistic constraints for this sociolinguistic variable. This owes to the fact that since the variants in question are part of the same general form, namely the periphrastic future, and all occur in the same person, it is not obvious which elements in the linguistic environment would condition this sociolinguistic variable.

Extra-linguistic constraints

There is a clear pattern of social stratification for this sociolinguistic variable. *Je vais* is the preferred form of middle class and female speakers and *m'as* is associated with male and working class speakers. In contrast, *je vas* shows no discernable pattern of social stratification and it clearly outranks *je vais* and *m'as* in terms of frequency.

In relation to our scale of sociostylistic markedness, *je vais* and *m'as* occupy, respectively, the formal and marked informal ends of the continuum. *Je vas*, however, can be categorized as a mildly marked variant, reflecting the fact that, while it does not conform to the rules of standard French, it is devoid of social connotations in a semi-directed taped interview situation.

Use of *seulement* versus *ne ... que* versus *juste* versus *rien que* to express restriction

In several varieties of spoken French, the notion of adverbial restriction has been found to be expressed via four alternatives: *juste, ne ... que, rien que* and *seulement*, all meaning 'only'. These variants have been found in Montreal French, as shown by examples (43)–(46), taken from Thibault and Daveluy (1989).

(43) *le joual pour moi c'est **rien qu'**une question de mots*
 'slang for me it's only a question of words'
(44) *il y a une voisine qui a **juste** un enfant*
 'there's a neighbor who only has one child'
(45) *mais le hockey on prenait **seulement** les éliminatoires*
 'but hockey we would only watch the play-offs'
(46) *il **n'y a qu'**une source de dissension*
 'there's only one source of dissent'

It should be noted that Montreal French has two variants of *seulement* – *seulement* and *seulement que*. These forms were considered occurrences of the same variant, since as Massicotte (1986) observed, the alternation between them is not influenced by linguistic or social factors.

According to Massicotte, the frequency of the variants in Montreal French is as follows: (1) *juste* 52%; (2) *rien que* 31%; and (3) *seulement (que)* 17%. As for the variant *ne ... que*, given that it is extremely rare in the Montreal corpus, it was excluded from quantitative analysis. The difference in variant frequencies found in both corpora suggests that *juste* has undergone an increase, *seulement* a decrease and *rien que* has remained relatively stable. Concerning the French of France, to our knowledge the variable has not been the object of any corpus-based sociolinguistic study. However, the existence of all four variants is attested in several reference works on European Standard French (e.g. Grevisse, 1988; Le Petit Larousse, 1993).

Linguistic constraints

According to Thibault and Daveluy (1989), each of the variants appears in three different linguistic contexts: (1) before a verb; (2) before circumstantial complements; and (3) before noun phrases. These contexts are illustrated in examples (47)–(55). They are drawn from the Sankoff and Cedergren corpus of Montreal spoken French.

Verb

(47) *j'ai juste été écorniflé dans les magasins*
 'I was only being spied on in the stores'
(48) *c'est pas seulement que d'aller à la messe*
 'it is not only to go to mass'
(49) *c'est rien que faire du cannage*
 'it's only canning'

Circumstantial complement

(50) *Je vais y aller juste pour le fun*
 'I am going to go there only for fun'
(51) *On ouvrait nos cadeaux seulement à Noël*
 'we would open our presents only on Christmas'
(52) *Toute la nuit je pense rien qu'à ça*
 'all night I think only of that'

Noun phrase

(53) *Il y a une voisine qui a juste un enfant*
 'there is a neighbor who has only one child'
(54) *Elle revenait seulement le soir*
 'she came back only in the evening'
(55) *Le joual pour moi c'est rien qu'une question de mots*
 'slang for me is only a question of words'

Thibault and Daveluy's (1989) analysis of the effect of linguistic context on variant choice reveals that *juste* is associated with verbs, *rien que* with noun phrases, while *seulement (que)* occurs mostly with circumstantial complements and noun phrases. However, as pointed out by Mougeon and Rehner's (1997) study of this sociolinguistic variable in Ontario French, there is another possible context for adverbial restriction in French, namely before adjectives, as in examples (56)–(58).

Adjective

(56) *il est **juste** intéressé dans le hockey*
'he is only interested in hockey'
(57) *la personne qui travaille là est **seulement** français*[27]
'the person who works there is only French'
(58) *mais je dis que c'est **rien que** normal c'est la vie*
'but I say that it's only normal that's life'

The results from Mougeon and Rehner reveal that *seulement* is the most frequent variant before adjectives.

Extra-linguistic constraints

Massicotte (1986) and Thibault and Daveluy (1989) established the following facts concerning the influence of social factors: (1) *ne ... que* is, as we have pointed out, highly infrequent in spoken discourse and used only by highly educated speakers (even among these speakers the variant remains rare); (2) *rien que* is associated with speakers from working class backgrounds;[28] (3) *juste* is particularly frequent with younger speakers, who use it 73% of the time and infrequent with older speakers, who use it only 22% of the time; (4) *juste* is not associated with clear frequency differences reflecting social class stratification; and (5) *seulement* is used more often by speakers who are on the top half of the social ladder than by those who are on the bottom half.

The absence of clear findings regarding the effect of social class on *juste* may be a reflection of the fact that *juste* has only recently entered spoken Montreal French (as indicated by the infrequency of this variant in the speech of the older speakers and its rise in the 1984 corpus). Thus it is possible that *juste* may not be considered part of standard French by all speakers. Such a perception may be reinforced by the fact that variant *juste* is morphophonetically similar and semantically identical with English restrictive adverb *just*. Thus some speakers may believe that the rise of *juste* in spoken Montreal French may reflect the influence of English.[29]

In sum, in relation to their sociostylistic markedness in spoken Canadian French, the four variants discussed above can be categorized as follows: (1) *ne ... que* (hyper-formal); (2) *seulement* (formal); (3) *juste* (mildly marked variant); and (4) *rien que* (marked informal).

Use of plural versus singular verb forms in the third person plural

While a great many French verbs are homophonous in the third person singular and plural (e.g. *mon frère parle* /paRl/ *italien* 'my brother speaks Italian', *mes parents parlent* /paRl/ *italien* 'my parents speak Italian'), a small number of irregular verbs explicitly mark person in the third person by means of a morphological alternation. This can take the form of complete suppletion, as in the case of *être*, for example *il est* versus *ils sont* 'he is versus they are', denasalization (e.g. *il vient* /vjẽ/ versus *ils viennent* /vjɛn/ 'he comes versus they come'), change in final vowel quality (e.g. *il va* /va/ versus *ils vont* /võ/ 'he goes versus they go'), the adding of a final consonant, (e.g. *il dit* /di/ versus *il disent* /diz/ 'he says versus they say') or a combination of these last two processes (e.g. *il sait* /se/ versus *ils savent* /sav/ 'he knows versus they know'). It can be pointed out that these morphological alternations are quite diverse and not entirely predictable. As such they constitute a major difficulty in the learning of the French verb system.

In several varieties of contemporary spoken French, including popular European French (cf. Gadet, 1992), a trend to use a singular verb form instead of the distinctive third person plural one has been attested. While this trend has not been documented in spoken Quebec French, a study by Mougeon and Beniak (1991) has attested its existence in Ontario French in 2% of third person plural contexts, as shown by examples (59) and (60), taken from their study.

'Singular' form[30]

(59) *il y a beaucoup de choses qui se **produit*** /prodyi/ (for *se produisent*/prodyiz/)
      'there are many things that happen'

'Plural' form

(60) *quand qu'ils **disent*** /diz/ *que c'est fini*
      'when they say that it's over'

Linguistic constraints

Mougeon and Beniak's (1995) analysis of the influence of linguistic constraints on this sociolinguistic variable revealed that the 'singular' forms are used only after *qui* 'who' and *ils* 'they'. This is likely due to the fact that in informal Canadian French *ils* and *qui* are morphophonetically singular (i.e. without plural markers) and, as such, cause speakers to interpret the subject as singular and to therefore use a singular verb form. Indeed, pronoun *ils* is pronounced /i/ or /j/, and is homophonous with the singular pronoun *il* (*ils mangent* versus *il mange* [imãž] 'they versus he eat', *ils arrivent* versus *il arrive* [jaRiv] 'they versus he arrive') and pronoun *qui* is always pronounced /ki/ regardless of whether the antecedent is plural or singular.

Each of these contexts is illustrated in examples (61)–(64), taken from the Mougeon and Beniak corpus.

Ils

(61) *ils parlent, comme ils **peut** parler très vite*
'they speak, like they can speak really fast'
(62) *ils comprennent le français mais ils **peuvent** pas le parler*
'they understand French but they can't speak it'

Qui

(63) *il y a des personnes qui **peut** le parler plus ou moins*
'there are people who can speak it more or less'
(64) *les personnes âgées qui **peuvent** pas parler l'anglais*
'the elderly people who cannot speak English'

Extra-linguistic constraints

Social class and sex were considered in Mougeon and Beniak's (1995) analysis of this sociolinguistic variable. However, neither of these factors was shown to exercise a significant effect on the variable. These findings suggest that this sociolinguistic variable is not sociostylistically salient. Furthermore, given that the 'singular' variant is so infrequent, it is reasonable to look upon the plural variant as neutral. As for the 'singular' variant, its social class value has yet to be clearly determined. It is, however, very infrequent and since it is clearly not part of Standard French, we have classified it as a marked informal variant.

Use of *donc* versus *alors* versus *(ça) fait que* to express consequence

In varieties of contemporary spoken French, the relationship of cause and effect between two clauses is expressed via several variants that all mean 'so': conjunctions *alors* and *donc*, locutions *(ça) fait que, si bien que*, etc. All of the above-mentioned variants have been attested in European French (e.g. Grevisse, 1988; Le Nouveau Petit Robert, 1996).[31] In Montreal French, consequence is expressed most often via *(ça) fait que* and *alors*, while *donc* is a much less frequent option (see Dessureault-Dober, 1974).[32] These three variants are exemplified in examples (65)–(67), taken from the Sankoff and Cedergren corpus.

(65) *il est dans un niveau beaucoup moins avancé que moi **ça fait que** je le vois plus*
'he's at a much less advanced level than me so I don't see him anymore'
(66) *il est avocat **donc** il a fait son classique*
'he's a lawyer so he went to a collège classique'
(67) *il y en a qui ont un vocabulaire très limité **alors** ils sacrent*
'there are some who have a very limited vocabulary so they swear'

As pointed out by Dessureault-Dober (1974), these three variants can also function as discourse markers fulfilling two functions, namely the introduction of a topic or idea at the beginning of a conversational turn and an indication that the speaker has finished a conversational turn. These discursive uses will not be discussed here and are not included in our analysis of the French immersion corpus.

The frequencies of *(ça) fait que, alors* and *donc* documented by Dessureault-Dober are as follows: (1) *(ça) fait que* 55%; (2) *alors* 43%; and (3) *donc* 2%. There are thus two principal variants, *(ça) fait que* and *alors*, and one marginal one, *donc*.

This sociolinguistic variable has also been the object of a corpus-based study of Ontario French. For this variety of French, all three variants exist, as well as a fourth form, namely the English conjunction *so*, whose use is by no means marginal (cf. Mougeon & Beniak, 1991). Although no quantitative analysis of this sociolinguistic variable has been undertaken for the French of France, reference works, as we have pointed out, attest the use of *alors, donc, (ça) fait que* and several other variants.

Linguistic constraints

Dessureault-Dober (1974) considered a number of linguistic constraints (e.g. verb tense, type of syntactic structure, etc.). However, none of these appeared to have an effect on variant choice.

Extra-linguistic constraints

According to Dessureault-Dober (1974), working class speakers use only *(ça) fait que*. Within the professional class, the following distribution is reported: (1) *alors* 73%; (2) *(ça) fait que* 23%; and (3) *donc* 4%. These results reveal that *alors* is clearly the preferred variant among the professional class while *donc* is a marginal variant mostly among the professional class. Mougeon and Beniak (1991) and Mougeon *et al.* (2009) arrived at similar results in relation to the influence of speaker social class in their corpora of Ontario French: *donc* and *alors* are correlated with speakers from the higher social strata and *(ça) fait que* is the preferred variant of speakers from the lower social strata. Dessureault-Dober (1974) also examined the effect of topic (in)formality on variant choice. She found that speakers used (1) *(ça) fait que* more often when discussing informal topics than when discussing formal ones and (2) *alors* and *donc* more often when discussing formal topics than when discussing informal ones.

In sum, in relation to our scale of sociostylistic markedness, the three variants can be categorized as follows: *donc* (hyper-formal); *alors* (formal); and *(ça) fait que* (marked informal).

Use of *chez* versus *à la maison* versus *su'*, etc. to express 'movement to' or 'location at' one's home

Unlike most varieties of Romance languages, French expresses movement to or location at one's home via a specialized preposition, namely *chez*. However, French also uses a prepositional locution that more transparently expresses this notion, namely *à la maison* 'at home/home'. This prepositional locution is more transparent than *chez* because the words it includes correspond directly to the different components of the meaning of *chez* (i.e. *à* = 'at/to', *la* = 'the' and *maison* = 'home').

While there is no corpus-based study of this interesting sociolinguistic variable for Quebec French or for European French, it is safe to assert that both *chez* and *à la maison* are instantiated in these two varieties of French. Mougeon *et al.* (1981) and Mougeon and Beniak (1991) have studied this sociolinguistic variable extensively in their corpora of French spoken by Franco-Ontarian adolescents.[33] In the speech of the unrestricted speakers, these authors have documented not only the two forms mentioned above, but also several other variants. Further, they have distinguished three contexts in which the entire set of variants can be used. The first context is when *chez* is followed by a pronoun and when the speaker or the grammatical subject resides in the home in question. The second context is also when *chez* is followed by a pronoun, but when the speaker or grammatical subject does not reside in the home in question. The final context is when *chez* is followed by a full noun phrase.

Examples (68)–(77), taken from the Mougeon and Beniak corpus, illustrate the entire set of variants in each of the three contexts.

Context 1 (*chez, à la maison, dans la maison, à* + possessive adjective + *maison*)

(68) ils_1 *étaient pas* **chez** eux_1[34]
    'they were not at home'
(69) $elle_1$ *travaille* **à la maison**$_1$
    'she works at home'
(70) *des personnes$_1$ parlent français comme* **dans la maison**$_1$
    'people speak French like at home'
(71) il_1 *est arrivé à* **sa maison**$_1$
    'he arrived home'

Context 2 (*chez, à* + posessive adjective + *maison*)

(72) *tout le monde$_1$ vient* **chez** *nous$_2$*
    'everyone comes to our house'
(73) *quand j$_1$'vas à* **leur maison**$_2$
    'when I go to their house'

Context 3 *(chez, su', à la maison de* + noun, *à)*

(74) j₁'étais *chez* mon cousin₂
'I was at my cousin's'
(75) moi j₁'restais *su'* ma cousine₂
'I was staying at my cousin's'
(76) on₁ se recontre *à la maison de* son ... mon ami₂
'we get together at his ... my friend's house'
(77) j₁'ai été *à* mon grand-père₂
'I went to my grandfather's'

As pointed out by Mougeon *et al.* (1981) and Mougeon and Beniak (1991), the above variants can be regrouped into four categories: (1) opaque variants, that is those whose meaning is not reflected in their form (i.e. prepositions *chez* and *su'*); (2) semi-transparent variants, that is those whose meaning is partially reflected in their form (i.e. *à la maison, dans la maison*); (3) transparent variants, that is those whose meaning is fully reflected in their form (i.e. *à* + possessive adjective + *maison, à la maison de* + noun); and (4) generic locative preposition *à* (which usually means 'at', 'to' or 'in'). Concerning *dans la maison*, it should be made clear that this prepositional phrase was counted as a variant of *chez* only when it had a generic locative meaning, that is when the preposition could be translated as 'at' or 'to' (as opposed to 'inside'). Finally, it should be borne in mind that as far as Standard French is concerned, Context 1 allows only *chez* and *à la maison*, and Contexts 2 and 3 allow only *chez*. The use of *su'* in Context 3 is a longstanding feature of marked informal Canadian French.

Mougeon *et al.* (1981) found the following frequencies for the above-mentioned variants in Contexts 1 and 3 (the frequency of occurrence of variants in Context 2 was too low to calculate reliable statistics):

- Context 1 – *chez* 67%, *à la maison* 28%, *dans la maison* 4% and *à* + possessive adjective + *maison* 2%.
- Context 3 – *chez* 66%, *su'* 28%, *à* 5% and *à la maison de* 1%.

As can be seen, the statistics found for Context 1 are not too different from the norm of Standard French, since the combined frequency of the non-standard variants (*dans la maison* and *à* + possessive adjective + *maison*) is quite low –6%. It is also interesting that among the two standard variants, *chez* clearly outranks *à la maison* as the most frequent option. As for Context 3, we see that it is also associated with two main variants, namely the standard variant *chez* (which occurs two thirds of the time) and the marked informal variant *su'* (whose frequency is not marginal – close to 30%). The other two non-standard variants (*à* + noun and *à la maison de* + noun) are used infrequently – combined frequency of 6%.

Linguistic constraints

Mougeon and Beniak (1991) examined a linguistic constraint that is associated with the choice of *chez/à la maison* in Context 1, namely whether the speaker or grammatical subject is moving to or is at the home in question. They found that utterances involving movement to the home in question are favorable to the use of *chez*.

Extra-linguistic constraints

In Context 1, the opposition between *chez* and *à la maison* is not associated with sex or social class differences and thus represents an interesting sociolinguistic variable that, like that of the future discussed above, is devoid of social connotations; hence it is another example of what we have referred to as neutral variants. The alternation, however, is associated with the degree of contact with English and restriction in the use of French, as indicated by a much higher frequency of use of *chez* in the speech of the adolescents from the strong Francophone majority community of Hawkesbury, which stands in contrast with significantly lower frequencies in localities where French is a minority language (see Chapter 5).

In Context 3, *su'* is strongly associated with working class background and with unrestricted use of French. Given that *su'* is a marked informal variant, it is not surprising to find a correlation with working class background. As for its association with lack of restriction in the use of French, it reflects the fact that the unrestricted adolescent speakers of Ontario French are those who use French outside the school context and especially at home, where the marked informal variety is handed down. In contrast, the restricted speakers speak French primarily in the school context and hence are less likely to be exposed to variants such as *su'*.[35]

Finally, while the remaining variants found in Contexts 1 and 3 are marginal in the speech of the unrestricted Franco-Ontarian adolescents, they are used with non-negligible frequency by the restricted Franco-Ontarian adolescents (see Chapter 5). This difference may be taken as an indication that high levels of restriction in the use of French and/or concomitant high levels of contact with English can bring about a phenomenon of convergence toward variants that are more transparent or more regular and also similar to English locutions (e.g. 'at/to one's home' and 'at/to someone's'). While these marginal variants are non-standard, their sociostylistic status is unclear. Mougeon and Beniak (1991) did not examine the effect of speaker social class and sex on these remaining variants and they have not been reported in general works on Canadian French. Consequently, we have opted to categorize them as neutral, by default.

Lexical Variation

Lexical variation has received less attention than grammatical variation in research concerning L1 French in Canada. To our knowledge, only four such studies exist. Sankoff *et al.* (1978) examined words used to indicate (1) 'remunerated work' and (2) words used to indicate 'one's place of residence'.[36] Martel (1984), using a corpus of spoken French from Sherbrooke,[37] Quebec and Nadasdi *et al.* (2004), using the Mougeon and Beniak corpus of spoken Ontario French, examined variants used to express the notion of 'automobile'.

Travail versus *emploi* versus *job* versus *ouvrage*

Let us begin by examining the ways one refers to 'remunerated work' in L1 Montreal French. As Sankoff *et al.* (1978) point out, seven lexical items express this notion. Examples (78)–(84) are taken from the Sankoff and Cedergren corpus.

(78) *il y a des gens qui ont du **travail** depuis quarante ans*
 'there are people who have had jobs for forty years'
(79) *je vais avoir un autre **emploi** mais que je revienne*
 'I'm going to have another job as soon as I get back'
(80) *ils m'ont offert la **job** de chef de police*
 'they offered me the job of chief of police'
(81) *je peux toujours me trouver un **ouvrage** dans mon métier*
 'I can always find myself a job in my field'
(82) *c'était pour les administrateurs de conserver leur **poste***
 'it was for the administrators to keep their jobs'
(83) *mon père avait une bonne **situation***
 'my father had a good job'
(84) *des gens [...] qui perdaient leur **position***
 'people [...] who lost their job'

However, it should be noted that the final two variants are marginal in Sankoff *et al.*'s (1978) data and were excluded from further analysis. The frequencies of the remaining variants are as follows: (1) *travail* 35%; (2) *job* 29%; (3) *ouvrage* 14%; (4) *emploi* 14%; and (5) *poste* 8%. These frequencies indicate that there are two main variants, namely *travail* and *job*, and two secondary ones, namely *ouvrage* and *poste*. Note, finally, that as far as European French is concerned, although we are unaware of any corpus-based study of this sociolinguistic variable, six of the above-mentioned variants (i.e. all but *ouvrage*) are also used in European Standard French (e.g. Le Nouveau Petit Robert, 1996).[38]

Linguistic constraints
Sankoff *et al.* (1978) did not examine linguistic constraints in their study.

Extra-linguistic constraints
Sankoff *et al.*'s (1978) analysis of the effect of extra-linguistic factors on variant choice, focusing on the main variants: *emploi, travail, job* and

ouvrage, revealed that *ouvrage* and *job* are most frequent in the speech of working class speakers. In contrast, *emploi* is most frequent in the French of speakers from the professional class. As for *travail*, no clear pattern of social stratification emerged. Thus in relation to our scale of sociostylistic markedness the four variants can be categorized as follows: (1) *ouvrage* and *job* (marked informal variants); (2) *emploi* (formal variant); and (3) *travail* (neutral variant).

Use of habiter versus vivre versus rester versus demeurer

In their analysis of verbs that express residence in a given place, Sankoff *et al.* (1978) identified four variants in L1 Montreal French. These variants are exemplified in examples (85)–(88), taken from the Sankoff and Cedergren corpus.

(85)   on **restait** à Rosemont avant
       'we lived in Rosemont before'
(86)   si on **demeure** en dehors de la ville ...
       'if one lives outside the city ...'
(87)   ... peut avoir ses responsabilités aussi, tout en **habitant** avec la fille
       '... could assume his responsibilities, as well, even while living with the girl'
(88)   mon père a **vécu** à Sarnia
       'my father lived in Sarnia'

According to Sankoff *et al.* (1978), the frequencies of these forms in Montreal French are as follows: (1) *rester* 64%; (2) *demeurer* 20%; (3) *vivre* 10%; and (4) *habiter* 6%. These frequencies reveal that the most frequent verb used to express residence in a given place is *rester*. *Demeurer* can be characterized as a secondary variant, while *vivre* and *habiter* can be considered marginal in Montreal French. As for European French, we are, once again, unaware of any corpus-based study that has examined this variable in that variety of French. However, the same variants used in Montreal French are found in European Standard French, with the exception of *rester* (Le Nouveau Petit Robert, 1996).

Linguistic constraints
In Sankoff *et al.*'s (1978) study no linguistic constraints were examined for this sociolinguistic variable.

Extra-Linguistic Constraints

Sankoff *et al.* (1978) point out that while the majority of the speakers of L1 Montreal French use *rester*, only a small number of individuals use *habiter* and are, for the most part, highly educated women belonging to the professional class. As for *demeurer*, these authors describe it as 'a stylistic resource... particularly as a "high-style" form for those who usually use *rester*' (Sankoff *et al.*, 1978: 28). While *rester* is used by members of all social classes, the heavy users of this variant, that is those who use it more than 50% of the time, are concentrated in the working class. Finally, the authors do not report on the sociostylistic status of *vivre*. This may be taken as an indication that this variant is neutral in the sense that we have given to this term.

In sum, in relation to our scale of sociostylistic markedness the four variants mentioned above can be categorized as follows: *habiter* (hyperformal); *demeurer* (formal); *vivre* (neutral); and *rester* (marked informal).

Use of *automobile* versus *voiture* versus *auto* versus *char*

Nouns used to indicate an automobile in L1 Canadian French have been studied by Martel (1984) in Sherbrooke (in the Eastern Townships of Quebec) and by Nadasdi *et al.* (2004) for adolescent Ontario French. Examples (89)–(92) are taken from the Mougeon and Beniak corpus.

(89) *j'étais en-dessous du **char***
'I was underneath the car'
(90) *c'est à peu près une demi-heure de **voiture** d'ici*
'it's about a half hour by car from here'
(91) *une **auto** pouvait te durer au moins 10 ans*
'a car could last you at least 10 years'
(92) *peutêtre j'm'acheterais une **automobile***
'maybe I'll buy myself a car'

It should be noted that a further variant, *machine*, was documented in Martel (1984), although no examples of this variant were found in the Mougeon and Beniak corpus.

According to Martel (1984), the frequencies of these forms in Sherbrooke French are as follows: (1) *auto* 42%; (2) *char* 23%; (3) *machine* 19%; (4) *automobile* 14%; and (5) *voiture* 2%. These frequencies reveal that the most frequent word used to refer to an automobile is *auto*. *Char*, *machine* and *automobile* can be characterized as secondary variants, while *voiture* can be considered marginal in Sherbrooke French.[39] As far as European French is concerned, we are unaware of any corpus-based study that has examined this variable. However, in European Standard French the same variants found in Canadian French are used, with the exception of *char* and *machine* (Le Nouveau Petit Robert, 1996). Interestingly, in its entry on variant *auto* this dictionary points to the fact that *voiture* is used more frequently than *auto*. In other words, *voiture* is the primary variant in European French, contrary to Quebec and Ontario French, where it is considerably less frequent than *auto*.

Linguistic Constraints

In Martel's (1984) study, no linguistic constraints were examined for this variable. However, Nadasdi *et al.* (2004) identified two linguistic factors influencing variant choice, namely interviewer priming and preceding element. Lexical priming by the interviewer is illustrated in example (93a), taken from the Mougeon and Beniak corpus.

Lexical Priming
Interviewer:

(93a)   *ah l'école garde l'**auto**?*
         'ah the school keeps the car?'

Response:

(93b)   *oui elle garde l'**auto***
         'yes it keeps the car'

Nadasdi *et al.* (2004) found that when the interviewer asked a question containing one of the variants, this variant was used categorically in the response [see example (93b)].

Concerning preceding element, three contexts were examined: (1) preceded by a preposition; (2) preceded by an adjective; and (3) preceded by a determiner. These three contexts are presented below. Note, however, that the effect of context was examined only in relation to *auto* and *char*. The other two variants, namely *automobile* and *voiture* were not frequent enough to lend themselves to this type of analysis. Examples (94)–(99) are taken from the Mougeon and Beniak corpus.

Preposition

(94)   *comment je me rends là? en **auto***
        'how do I go there? by car'
(95)   *non en en **char***
        'no by by car'

Adjective

(96)   *bien j'aimerais avoir une belle **auto**[40]*
        'well I would like to have a nice car'
(97)   *il était le plus beau **char** au monde*
        'it was the most beautiful car in the world'

Determiner

(98)   *il y a un **auto** stationné là-bas*
        'there is a car parked over there'

(99) *il avait un **char***
       'he had a car'

Consideration of this group of factors led to the conclusion that, unlike *char*, *auto* is favored in contexts where there is a preceding preposition, primarily in the collocation *en auto*.

Extra-linguistic constraints

Martel (1984) made several observations concerning the effect of social factors on variant choice. He found for example that *char*, which he describes as a marked informal variant, is favored by working class speakers and is used only marginally by those in the professional class. On the other hand, *auto* is used by speakers from all social groups, and is particularly frequent with speakers under 30 years of age. The form *automobile* is found, in particular, in the speech of middle-aged speakers.[41] As for the variant *machine*, it is associated with older speakers and is marginal in the speech of both younger speakers and those of the professional class (hence the absence of this variant in the Mougeon and Beniak corpus of Franco-Ontarian adolescent speech). Finally, Martel describes *voiture* as a prestige variant found almost exclusively in the speech of the professional class.

In sum, in relation to our scale of sociostylistic markedness, the five variants that refer to a car in Quebec French can be categorized as follows: *auto* (neutral); *char* (marked informal); *machine* (marked informal and used almost exclusively by older speakers); *automobile* (formal); and *voiture* (hyper-formal).

Phonetic Variation

In this section we consider two phonological variables in L1 Canadian French, namely the variable non-use of the mid vowel [ə], known as schwa, that occurs in open unaccented syllables (e.g. *demain* 'tomorrow' /dəmẽ/ versus /dmẽ/) and the variable non-use of the consonant /l/ in a variety of function words (e.g. *il comprend vite* 'he understands quickly' /il/ versus /i/).

Use versus non-use of schwa

The variable presence of schwa in French has been the object of a number of historical and synchronic studies of spoken French. The onset of schwa non-use is thought to date as far back as the 15th century. As pointed out by Uritescu *et al.* (2004), very little is known about the sociolinguistic distribution of schwa in Quebec French, since this sociolinguistic variable has not been the object of any systematic corpus-based study in that variety of French.[42] The only study of this kind for Canadian French is that conducted by Uritescu *et al.* (2002) with 51 Franco-Ontarian adolescent speakers from the Mougeon and Beniak corpus. Examples (100) and (101) of variable schwa non-use are taken from the Mougeon and Beniak corpus.

(100) *j' m'en souviens plus*
'I don't remember any more'
(101) *je m'en souviens plus*
'I don't remember any more'

In this study, the overall rate of schwa non-use in the speech of the unrestricted Franco-Ontarian adolescents is 62–68% in the taped interview and a much lower rate of 22% in the reading passages. The variable has also been studied quantitatively in the French of France (see notably Hansen, 1994; Walter, 1977, 1990) where the deleted variant has also been shown to be frequent.

Linguistic constraints

Mougeon *et al.* (2002) studied 12 phonetic contexts that in previous studies were found to be either favorable or unfavorable to schwa non-use. These contexts are exemplified below with brackets around the schwa to indicate that this phoneme is either present or deleted. Examples (102)–(113) are taken from the Mougeon and Beniak corpus.

A. Word initial syllable following a pause or a vowel

(102) *ça va v(e)nir*
'it will come'

B. Monosyllable at the beginning of a rhythm group, not followed by: a foreign word, a word beginning by an aspirated [h] and a syllable containing another schwa

(103) *j(e) sais pas*
'I don't know'

C. Sequence of monosyllables not following a consonant or another schwa

(104) *j(e) m(e) baignais beaucoup*
'I used to go swimming a lot'

D. Group medial monosyllable following a vowel

(105) *beaucoup d(e) monde*
'a lot of people'

E. Word medial following a single consonant

(106) *je gagne un peu d'argent maint(e)nant*
'I'm making a little money now'

F. Word initial syllable following a word ending in a consonant or a monosyllable containing a schwa, or followed by another schwa

(107) *il essaie de v(e)nir*
       'he is trying to come'

G. Monosyllable at the beginning of a rhythm group, preceding a foreign word, a word beginning with an aspirated [h] or with a syllable containing another schwa

(108) *l(e) hockey*
       'hockey'

H. Sequences of monosyllables following a consonant or another schwa

(109) *hier j(e) m(e) suis levé tard*
       'yesterday I got up late'

I. Group medial monosyllables following a consonant

(110) *je pense qu(e) c'est difficile*
       'I think it is difficult'

J. Word medial following more than one consonant

(111) *exact(e)ment*
       'exactly'

K. Phrase final *que* preceded by a consonant

(112) *qu'est-ce qu(e) tu fais?*
       'what are you doing?'

L. Forms such as *quelque* pronounced [kek]

(113) *j'ai lu quelqu(e)s [kek] livres*
       'I read some books'

Contexts A–E have been consistently found to be favorable to schwa non-use in previous research based on European French, while Contexts F–K were not usually examined in that research because they were hypothesized to be quite unfavorable to schwa non-use. As for Context L, it was also not included in these previous works, even though it is quite favorable to schwa non-use, as Mougeon *et al.* (2002) have found. The results of their examination of the effect of linguistic context on schwa use versus non-use are presented in Table 3.1.

As Table 3.1 shows, although the contexts, which have previously been found to be favorable to schwa non-use in European French, are also favorable to this phenomenon in Ontario French, two contexts

Table 3.1 Effect of linguistic context on schwa use and non-use[a]

Linguistic context	Schwa use (N)	Schwa non-use (%)	Schwa use (N)	Schwa non-use (%)
L.	348	97	9	3
E.	1226	95	70	5
J.	**783**	**81**	**180**	**19**
C.	397	77	121	23
D.	2992	67	1437	33
H.	**98**	**60**	**64**	**40**
B.	2373	59	1614	41
A.	712	51	679	49
F.	315	42	444	58
I.	521	22	1839	78
K.	115	20	472	80
G.	43	19	187	81
Total	9923	58	7116	42

[a]Note that these figures are for the speakers across all three levels of French language use restriction (i.e. unrestricted, semi-restricted and restricted).

hypothesized to be unfavorable in European French are, on the contrary, favorable in Ontario French. These two contexts, J and H, are presented in bold in Table 3.1. The remaining contexts hypothesized to be unfavorable to schwa non-use in European French are also unfavorable in Ontario French. Finally, concerning Context L, its favorable effect on schwa non-use reflects, to a large degree, the fact that it includes *quelque*, a determiner that is often realized as [kek] in Canadian French.

Extra-linguistic constraints

Mougeon *et al.* (2002) found that the factors of sex and social class had little or no effect on schwa non-use. This suggests that this variable has only weak social marking in Ontario French, a finding that is also reflected in the weak effect of topic (in)formality during the taped interview (formal topics 65% versus informal topics 73%). However, when a sharper contrast between formal and informal speech was made (the interview versus the reading passages), a strong pattern of style shifting was documented. Schwa was deleted more often in the taped interview (65%) than in the reading passages (17%).[43] Because of this, schwa use can be classified as a formal variant and schwa non-use as a mildly marked informal variant.

Use versus non-use of /l/

Another longstanding feature of the pronunciation of French is the variable non-use of /l/ in several linguistic environments. This development is thought to have started as early as the Middle Ages in words like *pulce* which became *puce* 'flea'. This phenomenon later spread to word final position with the onset of final consonant deletion and was once considered to be a feature of educated speech, for instance in pronouns like *il* and *elle*, pronounced /i/ and /e/. It was not until centuries later that /l/ was reintroduced under the influence of orthography.

Contrary to schwa, the variable non-use of /l/ in articles and subject and object pronouns has been the object of a number of sociolinguistic studies of Quebec French (cf. Poplack & Walker, 1986; Sankoff & Cedergren, 1976). Examples (114) and (115) of variable /l/ non-use are taken from Poplack and Walker's (1986) study of Ottawa–Hull French.

(114) *i' tombait des gros morceaux*
 'big pieces were falling'
(115) *il va travailler en bicyclette*
 'he goes to work on bike'

Sankoff and Cedergren (1976) found very high frequencies of this phenomenon, particularly with personal pronouns. For example, in the case of the impersonal subject pronoun *il*, the /l/ is deleted in 97.8% of occurrences. Studies of the French spoken in France have also documented this same phenomenon (cf. Ashby, 1984, where /l/ non-use in impersonal *il* also occurs frequently (76%) before a consonant in the 1976 Tours corpus and Armstrong, 1996, who found almost categorical rates of /l/ deletion in *il* in a corpus of adolescent spoken French collected in Lorraine).

Linguistic constraints

This sociolinguistic variable is influenced by a number of linguistic factors, notably the category of word in which /l/ appears and the phonological segment following /l/. According to Sankoff and Cedergren (1976), the rates of non-use by word category are as follows:[44] (1) *il* (impersonal subject pronoun 'it') 97.8%; (2) *ils* 'they' 92%; (3) *il* (personal pronoun 'he') 89%; (4) *elle* 'she' 63.2%; (5) *les* (object pronoun 'them') 46.8%; (6) *la* (object pronoun 'her') 27.7%; (7) *la* (singular article 'the') 29.3%; and (8) *les* (plural article 'the') 18.7%. Poplack and Walker (1986) arrived at very similar results in their analysis of /l/ deletion in the Ottawa–Hull corpus.[45] It is interesting that subject pronouns are overwhelmingly favorable to /l/ non-use, while the same cannot be said for object pronouns and definite articles. As for the influence of the following segment, Sankoff and Cedergren (1976) and Poplack and Walker (1986) found that the probability of /l/ deletion in *il* is much higher when the following segment is a consonant than when it is a vowel.

Examples (116)–(123), taken from the Mougeon and Beniak corpus of Ontario French, illustrate the various lexical contexts in which /l/ can undergo deletion.

Il (impersonal subject pronoun 'it')

(116) *i(l) me semble qu'il vient de France*
'it seems to me that he is from France'

Ils ('they')

(117) *les docteurs i(l)s trouvent toutes sortes de maladies*
'doctors they find all sorts of diseases'

Il (personal pronoun 'he')

(118) *elle a dit 'oui' puis i(l) m'a donné un dollar*
'she said 'yes' then he gave me a dollar'

Elle ('she')

(119) *c'est une fille puis e(ll)e est heu aveugle*
'it's a girl and she is um blind'

Les (object pronoun 'them')

(120) *je (l)es connais plus que les autres*
'I know them better than the others'

La (object pronoun 'her')

(121) *il s'en va pis il (l)a laisse avec l'autre homme*
'he goes and he leaves her with the other man'

La (singular article 'the')

(122) *en neuvième année ben là j'ai eu de (l)a misère t'sais*
'in ninth grade well like I had trouble you know'

Les (plural article 'the')

(123) *la femme qui choisissait (l)es élèves*
'the woman who would choose the students'

Extra-linguistic constraints

The studies that have examined /l/ non-use in Quebec French suggest that this variable is stratified according to social class, sex and the speaker's place in the linguistic marketplace. However, there is a clear difference in

Variation in L1 Spoken French

Table 3.2 Sociostylistic status of variants in L1 Canadian French

	Sociostylistic status of variants				
Linguistic variables	Marked informal	Mildly marked informal	Neutral	Formal	Hyper-formal
Negative particle		*ne* non-use			*ne* use
Restrictives	*rien que*	*juste*		*seulement*	*ne … que*
Consequence	*(ça) fait que*			*alors*	*donc*
First person future	*m'as*	*je vas*		*je vais*	
Future			Periphrastic, present	Inflected	
First person plural pronouns	*nous-autres on*	*on*			*nous*
Third person plurals	Singular verbs		Plural verbs		
Auxiliaries	*avoir*			*être*	
chez 1			*chez, à la maison*, other		
chez 3	*su'*		*chez*, other		
'Work'	*job, ouvrage*		*travail*	*employ*	*poste*
'Living'	*rester*		*vivre*	*demeurer*	*habiter*
'Car'	*char, machine*		*auto*	*automobile*	*voiture*
schwa use/non-use		schwa non-use		schwa use	
/l/ use versus /l/ non-use in subject pronouns		/l/ non-use			/l/ use

the extent to which these patterns obtain when one considers the subject personal pronouns versus the object pronouns and the definite articles. Specifically, /l/ non-use in subject pronouns is much less sharply stratified according to social class and sex than in the object pronouns and the definite articles. For instance, Sankoff and Cedergren (1976) found that the difference between the working and professional class speakers in relation to /l/ non-use in impersonal pronoun *il* is 99% versus 89%, whereas this difference in article *la* is 44% versus 11%. The /l/ non-use in subject pronouns, inasmuch as it is highly frequent and only weakly associated with social stratification, is a clear example of the type of mildly marked informal variant we have discussed in Chapter 1.

No study of Quebec French has examined the variable non-use of /l/ according to style. However, such an analysis was conducted in Tennant's (1995) study of the variety of French spoken in North Bay, Ontario (using the Mougeon and Beniak corpus). His results showed that, while frequent in the interview, /l/ non-use is rare in the reading passages. This is particularly clear in the case of subject pronouns: while /l/ is deleted 94% of the time in the interview, it is deleted in only 7% of the time in the reading passages.

In sum, in terms of sociostylistic markedness, the use of /l/ in pronoun *ils* is a hyper-formal variant and /l/ non-use in the same context is a mildly marked one.

Conclusion

The overview of the findings of studies on sociolinguistic variation in Canadian French provided in the preceding sections shows that our research on the learning of sociolinguistic variation by French Immersion students has investigated 15 variables that belong to the different components of language (e.g. lexicon and phonology) and that span the sociostylistic continuum discussed in Chapter 1. Table 3.2 provides summarized information on where the variants fit on such a continuum.

In the next chapter, we will first consider the extent to which (1) this wide range of variants is found in the immersion students' educational input and, ultimately, in their speech; (2) the students have mastered the linguistic and extra-linguistic constraints that influence variant choice by FL1 speakers; and (3) independent variables, such as contacts with FL1 speakers, have an effect on the learning of variants by the immersion students.

Chapter 4
Students' Learning of Variation

Frequency and Treatment of Variants in the French Immersion Students' Educational Input

Given that the immersion students have learned French primarily in a school context, it is important to obtain detailed information on the use of sociolinguistic variants in their educational input. We will therefore start the present chapter with a review of the results of our investigation of the frequency and treatment of variants in the French immersion students' educational input. Two principal sources of classroom input have been considered: (1) the French Language Arts materials used in immersion programs, including those where we gathered the immersion student corpus; and (2) the speech of French immersion teachers in a classroom setting (see Chapter 2).

Frequency of variant use in the teacher corpus

The reader will recall that our general expectations were that the French immersion teachers in the Allen *et al.* (1987) corpus would (1) avoid marked informal variants, (2) make only modest use of mildly marked informal variants and (3) favor formal and hyper-formal variants.

The data on the frequency of informal marked variant used by the French immersion teachers displayed in Table 4.1 reveal that our first expectation has been confirmed. However, the data in this table also show that FL1 speakers make frequent use of the majority of these marked informal variants in the context of a taped interview. Nonetheless, the French immersion teachers essentially avoid marked informal variants. This is evidenced by the nil rates found for *m'as, nous-autres on, su', job, ouvrage, char, machine, rester* and 'singular' verbs and by the very low frequency of *rien que* (0.1%), *(ça) fait que* (1%) and auxiliary *avoir* (5%). These frequencies can be explained by several factors. Firstly, the teachers are likely aware that these are non-standard variants and hence that they are in appropriate in a classroom context. Secondly, they may not use these

Table 4.1 Marked informal variants in the French immersion teachers' classroom speech and in L1 Canadian French

Marked informal variants	Immersion teachers (%)	L1 Canadian French (%)
rien que	0.1	31
(ça) fait que	1	55
m'as	0	30
nous-autres on	0	4
Auxiliary avoir	5	34
su'	0	28
job	–[a]	29
ouvrage	–[a]	14
char	0	23
machine	0	19
rester	0	64
Singular verbs	0	2

[a]The – symbol has been used when a variable (and, thus, its associated variants) was never used.

variants often themselves in casual speech. Finally, as will be seen further down, these variants are absent in the French Language Arts materials and such absence may reinforce the French immersion teachers' perception that they are inappropriate in the classroom context.

The frequency of mildly marked informal variants in the teachers' speech is illustrated in Table 4.2. As can be seen in Table 4.2, our expectations have been largely met. The teachers make at best modest use of three of the four mildly marked informal variants under study, namely *ne* non-use (29%), *juste* (15%) and *je vas* (1%). These low rates stand in sharp contrast to the much higher ones found in the taped speech of FL1 Quebeckers.

The factors that account for these findings are similar to those we have invoked in relation to the rarity of marked informal variants. The teachers likely feel that in the formal context of the classroom they should not use mildly marked informal variants frequently, even though they may use these forms frequently in their casual speech. Another explanation may lie once again in the rarity or absence of these forms in the French Language Arts materials (see further down), a factor that may reinforce the teachers' tendency to use them infrequently in the classroom. While the teachers' infrequent use of mildly marked informal

Table 4.2 Mildly marked informal variants in the French immersion teachers' classroom speech and in L1 Canadian French[a]

Variants	Immersion teachers (%)	L1 Canadian French (%)
ne non-use	29	99.5
juste	15	52
je vas	1	64
on	83	94

[a]We were not able to analyze the immersion teacher corpus for phonetic variation, since we did not have access to the tapes from which the transcripts came. Therefore, the table provides no information on schwa and /l/ non-use.

variants is understandable in terms of their perceived non-standard status of such variants and assumed inappropriateness in a classroom setting, the net result is that French immersion students are under-exposed to variants that are very frequent in FL1 speech (even in the context of a semi-formal taped interview). What we have said here does not apply for *on*, where the immersion teachers come very close to L1 Quebec French. One explanation for this pattern lies in the fact that the French Language Arts teaching materials, as we will see, do make substantial use of pronoun *on*, especially in dialogues – a fact that the teachers may have become aware of. Another explanation may be that the teachers are accommodating to the students by using a pronoun associated with unmarked singular verb forms that are easier for the students. This second explanation is in line with the results of the study of *tu/vous* by Lyster and Rebuffot (2002) who found that contrary to the general trend, immersion teachers over-expose students to the informal pronoun *tu* perhaps also in an attempt to accommodate to their students by using a pronoun associated with unmarked singular forms that are easier to learn.

The use of formal and hyper-formal features in the teachers' speech, compared to that of FL1 speakers, is illustrated in Tables 4.3 and 4.4. Here again, the expected pattern obtains since the teachers make frequent or very frequent use of the formal and hyper-formal variants (a corollary of the two trends we have just discussed).[46] Specifically, teachers use the formal variants *seulement, alors, je vais*, auxiliary *être* and *chez* 3 at frequency rates that contrast markedly with the lower rates displayed by the FL1 speakers. As for hyper-formal variants, the fact that the teachers use these variants more frequently than do FL1 speakers is especially apparent for *ne, donc, nous, habiter* and *voiture*.

The high frequency of these forms in the French immersion teachers' speech can be attributed to the following factors. Firstly, these forms are typical of Standard (written) French and hence are considered to be appropriate

Table 4.3 Percentage of formal variants in the French immersion teachers' classroom speech and in L1 Canadian French

Variants	Immersion teachers (%)	L1 Canadian French (%)
seulement	79	17
alors	76	43
Inflected future	18	20
je vais	99	6
Auxiliary être	95	66
emploi	–	14
demeurer	0	20
schwa use	n/a	32
automobile	0	14

Table 4.4 Percentage of hyper-formal variants in the French immersion teachers' classroom speech and in L1 Canadian French

Variants	Immersion teachers (%)	L1 Canadian French (%)
ne usage	71	0.5
ne … que	5	1
donc	23	2
nous	17	2
poste	–	8
habiter	80	6
voiture	67	2
/l/ use (in subject pronouns)	n/a	7

in the classroom context. Secondly, as we will see next, these variants are prevalent in the French Language Arts materials. They are also prescribed in French reference works. Note, however, that the teachers do not make frequent use of *ne … que* (5%) or the inflected future (18%), which are also prescribed variants. The reader will recall that *ne … que* is a highly formal variant that is marginal in the speech of FL1 speakers. They use this variant in only 0.6% of occurrences. This might explain why the French immersion teachers use this form only sparingly even though it is highly favored by the authors of French Language Arts teaching materials (see below). As for the inflected future, the unexpectedly low frequency of this variant may reflect the teachers' perception that it is too complex for the French immersion students (and that the alternative, the periphrastic future, also conforms to the rules of Standard French). This same explanation also applies to the teachers' lower than expected use of the hyper-formal variant *ne ... que*, a complex variant that alternates with a simpler formal counterpart, namely *seulement*.[47] Finally, the unexpected absence of the formal variant *automobile* in the teachers' classroom speech may be attributed to the availability of another formal and simpler variant, namely, *voiture*.

In sum, while the general trend on the part of the French immersion teachers to strongly favor formal and hyper-formal variants can be explained by the academic situation in which they find themselves and the treatment of these variants in the teaching materials they use, French immersion students end up being over-exposed to variants that are for the most part marginally used by FL1 speakers in the context of a semi-directed taped interview.

Finally, with respect to the neutral variants (see Table 4.5), we see that the immersion teachers' frequency of use is essentially in keeping with that of FL1 speakers for the periphrastic future, futurate present and plural verbs. This finding underscores the neutrality of these variants. However, a different pattern obtains in the case of *chez 1* and *à la maison*, where the immersion teachers use the latter variant substantially more often than do the FL1 speakers. One explanation is that in an educational context,

Table 4.5 Percentage of neutral variants in the French immersion teachers' classroom speech and in L1 Canadian French

Variants	Immersion teachers (%)	L1 Canadian French (%)
Periphrastic future	79	73
Futurate present	3	7
Plural verbs	100	98
chez 1	32	67
à la maison	56	28
Other	12	5
chez 3	100	66
Other	0	6
travail	–	35
vivre	0	10
auto	33	42

teachers typically use *à la maison* in front of the class when discussing work that should be completed at home. Indeed, we will see that in the teaching materials, *à la maison* is used very frequently in students' pedagogical activities. In the case of *chez 3*, we can see that the immersion teachers use this variant categorically, while the FL1 speakers use it 58% of the time. This finding likely reflects the teachers' avoidance of or unfamiliarity with the marked informal variant *su'*. Finally, the absence of the variant *vivre* and of the variant *travail* in the immersion teachers' classroom discourse does not necessarily contradict our categorization of these two variants as neutral. Since in the classroom setting the teachers rarely expressed the notion of living and, as mentioned above, did not express the notion of remunerated work,[48] it is not possible to infer preferential variant choice on the part of the teachers.

In summary, our investigation of the frequency of variant use by the French immersion teachers in the Allen *et al.* corpus has revealed that, overall, the teachers avoid or make only infrequent use of marked or mildly marked informal variants, variants that in contrast are used frequently or quite frequently by FL1 speakers in the context of a semi-formal taped interview. Further, these same teachers make much greater use of formal and hyper-formal variants in comparison to FL1 speakers. We have seen that there are several factors that explain why this pattern obtains. Still, the chief consequence of this dual pattern is that French immersion students are under-exposed to a wide array of variants that are part and parcel of the normal speech of FL1 speakers and over-exposed to other variants that are not.

It can also be noted that our scrutiny of the teacher corpus yielded no examples where teachers made an effort to increase students' awareness of sociolinguistic variation. For example, none of the reactive strategies described by Lyster (2007) and Lyster and Rebuffot (2002) such as providing explicit feedback for students concerning the appropriateness of lexical choices were used. More generally, we also found no evidence that the teachers had employed activities to develop students' sociolinguistic competence.

Frequency of variant use in the corpus of French Language Arts materials

The reader will recall that our hypotheses regarding the French Language Arts materials used in French immersion programs are that they will (1) strongly favor hyper-formal, formal, variants and (2) conversely, will make sparse use, if any, of marked informal variants. However, we also consider the possibility that texts meant to represent oral French, will contain non-negligible occurrences of mildly marked informal variants.

As we pointed out in Chapter 2, the sample of teaching materials that we examined included textbooks and accompanying exercise books. Both sets of materials included texts that were meant to be a representation of everyday spoken French (e.g. a dialogue between two school children or a conversation among several members of a family at home) and texts meant to be read as written texts (e.g. instructions to the students regarding an assignment and background information for a project). In order to assess if the authors of the teaching materials had attempted to reflect the distinctive features of both registers by using marked or mildly marked informal variants more frequently in texts meant to represent oral French than in the regular texts, we calculated separate frequency rates of the different variants under study for these two types of texts.

Let us consider each category of variant in turn. The results concerning the distribution of marked informal variants in the teaching materials are presented in Table 4.6. As can be seen, the materials to which the students are exposed make no use whatsoever of marked informal features. This finding echoes that of Auger (2002) who notes that the more stigmatized variants of Quebecois French do not appear in French immersion teaching materials used in Montreal.

While we did not expect that such features would be frequent in the set of materials that we examined for our own research, it remains that even the high frequency marked informal forms such as *rester* and *ça fait que* are

Table 4.6 Marked informal variants in the French Language Arts teaching materials (compared to L1 Canadian French)

Variants	Text (%)	Dialogue (%)	L1 Canadian French (%)
rien que	0	0	31
(ça) fait que	0	0	55
m'as	0	0	30
nous-autres on	0	0	4
Auxiliary *avoir*	0	0	34
su'	0	0	28
job	–	0	29
ouvrage	–	0	14
char	0	0	23
machine	0	0	19
rester	0	–	64
Singular verbs	0	0	2

Table 4.7 Percentage of mildly marked informal variants in the French Language Arts teaching materials (compared to L1 Canadian French)

Variants	Text (%)	Dialogue (%)	L1 Canadian French (%)
ne non-use	0	1	99.5
juste	3	0	52
je vas	0	0	64
on	17	48	94
schwa non-use	0	0.1	68
/l/ non-use (in subject pronouns)	0	0	93

entirely absent. This is particularly disconcerting in the case of materials intended to represent spoken dialogues. The result is that students have been deprived of an opportunity to familiarize themselves with some of the distinctive features of informal Canadian French.

Table 4.7 reveals that mildly marked informal variants are almost as rare as the marked formal ones. The reader will recall that Auger (2002) found a small number of variants that are not strongly stigmatized in the teaching materials she examined. However, it is difficult to determine whether or not this goes against our own findings since she does not present data on the frequency of these variants in relation to their formal equivalents. Furthermore, she does not examine the same sociolinguistic variables that we have.

The only variant that occurs with some frequency in the materials we examined is *on* and interestingly it is associated with a clear difference in frequency between the written texts and the dialogues. While the rate of *on* in the dialogues is below that of FL1 speakers, it differs enough from the rate in the written texts to provide a clue to the students that this variant is likely to be used in oral French. Apart from variant *on*, essentially the same pattern observed in relation to the marked informal variants obtains for the remaining mildly marked informal variants, namely there is little or no difference between the frequency of variants found in the written texts compared to the dialogues and the frequencies are universally nil or marginal. This finding is surprising, given that we are dealing with variants that are part and parcel of the spoken French of FL1 speakers of Canadian French, and that even though they do not conform to the rules of Standard French are, for the most part, devoid of social connotations and are highly frequent. In the case of the two phonetic variants, namely schwa and /l/ non-use, it may be argued that the authors of the French Language Arts materials have felt reticent to alter French orthography, although the convention of marking such deletions with an apostrophe (e.g. *j' me brosse les dents* 'I brush my teeth') is found in literary works that aim at providing a 'flavor' of informal French. However, while there is a modest attempt to employ this convention in relation to schwa non-use in dialogues, it is unfortunate that it was not extended to /l/ non-use and, more generally, that it was not used more frequently. Interestingly, in the audio materials included in the series that we used for our analysis, there is a slightly better representation of these mildly marked informal phonetic variants, namely /l/ is deleted 2% of the time and schwa 8%. It should be noted, however, that these audio materials are unfortunately oralized versions of the written textbooks and not materials specially designed to bring about learning of the features of oral French.[49]

Concerning *ne* non-use, *juste* and *je vas*, there is no impediment to inserting these variants in the textbooks due to orthography and, hence, their quasi-total absence in the dialogues could easily be remedied. In contrast, the total absence of 'singular' verbs is understandable in view of its rarity in FL1 speech. Finally, it is interesting that, while there is very little difference in the frequency of *on* use and *ne* non-use in FL1 speech, their treatment in the French Language Arts materials is markedly different. One possible explanation for this difference may be that the authors feel that it is more acceptable to replace one pronoun with another than it is to delete an item, use a regularized verb form or use an adverb that may be perceived as the result of English influence. In support of the hypothesis that *on* may be viewed more favorably than the remaining mildly marked informal variants, we found in our examination of one of the student workbooks for the series *Pont vers le futur* (*Fiches d'activités 2*, McLaughlin & Niedre, 1998) an activity where the students were asked to use pronoun *on* as a synonym of *nous*. In contrast, in the *Capsules* series we examined (Deslauriers & Gagnon, 1995, 1997), *ne* non-use is discussed under the rubric *Ellipse fautive de NE* 'erroneous ellipsis of *ne*' and nowhere in any of the materials we analyzed are the students asked to practice *ne* non-use.

In summary, contrary to our perhaps optimistic prediction that the French Language Arts teaching materials would contain non-negligible occurrences of mildly marked informal variants, the materials we have examined are largely devoid of such variants. This is indeed regrettable since it is precisely these kinds of variants that one would expect authors to use at levels that more closely approximate the norms of FL1 speakers, in the materials meant to represent spoken French.

Let us turn now to results for formal variants in the French Language Arts teaching materials, presented in Table 4.8. The distribution of the formal variants is the opposite of what is found for the marked and mildly marked informal variants, that is, the formal variants are indeed frequent in the French Language Arts teaching materials and to a much greater

Table 4.8 Percentage of formal variants in the French Language Arts teaching materials (compared to L1 Canadian French)

Variants	Text	Dialogue	L1 Canadian French
seulement	11	0	17
alors	75	17	43
Inflected future	95	70	20
je vais	100	100	6
Auxiliary *être*	100	100	66
emploi	–	100	14
demeurer	4	–	20
schwa use	100	99.9	32
automobile	55	0	14

extent than what is found in FL1 speech. This result is reminiscent of O'Connor Di Vito's (1991) observation that sociostylistically marked, complex features of French were given significant emphasis in the FL2 materials she examined (although she fails to provide systematic quantitative support for the use of such forms in the teaching materials).

In our own analysis, we find that even in the case of dialogues, the formal variants abound. In fact, for three variants (i.e. *je vais*, auxiliary *être* and schwa) there is no, or almost no, difference in the distribution between the dialogues and texts. However, for four other variants (i.e. inflected future, *seulement*, *automobile* and *alors*), the frequency in the dialogues is lower than in the texts, a finding that goes in the right direction.

Turning to the hyper-formal variants, Table 4.9 reveals that they, too, are found extensively in the texts and dialogues.

The distribution of the hyper-formal variants reveals that the frequency for six of the eight variants, for which it is possible to compare frequency in the written texts with frequency in the dialogues, either hardly varies (i.e. *ne* use, *voiture*, *véhicule* and /l/ non-use), or varies in the opposite to expected direction (i.e. *ne ... que* and *donc*). This finding, coupled with the fact that seven of the hyper-formal variants are far too frequent in the context of dialogues, is unfortunate because it sends the wrong sociostylistic signals to students. This leads us to wonder if the authors of the materials have not become overly fond of hyper-formal variants and lost sight of the fact that they sound very stilted in spoken Canadian French. Further evidence of this penchant is found when one takes into account the syntactic distribution of the hyper-formal variant *donc* (see Table 4.10). In the materials *donc* is used overwhelmingly in intra-sentential position,

Table 4.9 Percentage of hyper-formal variants in the French Language Arts teaching materials (compared to L1 Canadian French)

Variants	Text	Dialogue	L1 Canadian French
ne usage	100	99	0.5
ne ... que	86	100	Very rare
donc	25	83	2
nous	83	52	1
poste	–	0	8
habiter	42	–	6
voiture	20	25	2
véhicule	6	0	Unattested
/l/ non-use (in subject pronouns)	100	100	2.2

that is after the verb within the sentence that expresses the consequence, as in example (124)

(124) *il se fait tard il faut **donc** partir*
'it is getting late it is therefore necessary that we go' (intra-sentential)

This intra-sentential use of *donc* is typical of elevated literary French and thus is even more formal than the simple use of *donc* between sentences, as in example (125)

(125) *il se fait tard **donc** il faut partir*
'it is getting late therefore we need to go' (inter-sentential)

To our knowledge, intra-sentential use of *donc* is unattested in corpora of spoken Canadian French. The fact that such use of *donc* is near categorical in the French Language Arts materials illustrates the extent to which textbook authors can become disconnected with the norms of L1 French.[50] In fairness to the textbook authors, it must be pointed out that for one of the hyper-formal variants (i.e. *nous*), we found a difference in frequency between the two types of texts that goes clearly in the expected direction and that does provide students with some degree of indication, albeit implicit, that these hyper-formal variants are definitely associated with written French.

Turning to the neutral variants, Table 4.11 shows that their frequency in the written texts and dialogues in FL1 speech displays a variety of different patterns. It is not surprising that both the written texts and the dialogues make categorical use of plural verb forms. This pattern is consonant with

Table 4.10 Frequency distribution of variants *alors*, *donc* and *(ça) fait que* in the pedagogical materials according to syntactic context

Position	Written texts							Dialogue					
	alors		*donc*		*(ça) fait que*			*alors*		*donc*		*(ça) fait que*	
	N	%	N	%	N	%		N	%	N	%	N	%
Inter-sentential	6	75	2	25	0	0		1	17	5	83	0	0
Intra-sentential	1	4	25	96	0	0		0	0	4	100	0	0

Table 4.11 Percentage of neutral variants in the French Language Arts teaching materials (compared to L1 Canadian French)

Variants	Text	Dialogue	L1 Canadian French
Periphrastic future	5	30	73
Futurate present	0	0	7
Plural verbs	100	100	98
chez 1	27	100	67
à la maison	73	0	28
Other	0	0	5
chez 3	100	100	66
Other	0	0	6
auto	19	75	42
vivre	54	–	10
travail	–	0	35

the very high frequency of these verb forms in FL1 speech. In a similar vein, the fact that there is no use of the futurate present in either the written texts or the dialogues is in keeping with the low frequency of this variant in FL1 speech. Concerning the periphrastic future, its low frequency in the written texts is, indeed, what one would expect given that written texts are strongly associated with the inflected future. However, the fact that the periphrastic future is used only 30% of the time in the dialogues is somewhat off-target in view of its much higher frequency in FL1 speech. Having said this, it is important to note that there are two instances where we find a marked difference in frequency between the two types of texts (the periphrastic future is six times more frequent in dialogues than in the written texts; *auto* is four times more frequent in the dialogues), which provides a useful signal to the students that these variants are likely to be used in oral French.

As for *chez* 1 and *à la maison*, the high frequency of the former variant in FL1 Canadian French is correctly reflected by its dominance over *à la maison* in the context of dialogues. In the written texts, it is not surprising to find both neutral variants *chez* 1 and *à la maison*. However, the fact that the frequency of *à la maison* so clearly outweighs *chez* 1 deserves an explanation. As was the case for the prevalence of *à la maison* in classroom teachers' speech, one possible explanation for this pattern is that in the instructions to students included in the French Language Arts materials, two types of work are often distinguished, namely work to be done 'at school' (*à l'école*) and work to be done 'at home' (*à la maison*). The fact that, with the former type of work, one can only use the preposition *à* may have led the authors to favor *à la maison*. A further explanation may be that *à la maison* allows the authors to avoid making a choice between *chez toi* and *chez vous* where *toi* refers to one student, while *vous* can refer either politely to one student or collectively to the whole class, because *à la maison* can mean either of the above. As for *chez* 3, its categorical presence in the teaching materials can be attributed to the fact that it competes with *su'*, a highly stigmatized marked informal variant and, as such, which may have been viewed as inappropriate by the authors of these materials.

The comparison of the frequency of variant use in both types of written texts has revealed that the French Language Arts materials used in French immersion programs are unsuccessful at providing learners with accurate information about the use of marked and mildly marked informal variants in spoken French. We say these because both kinds of informal variant are grossly under-represented in the dialogues. That said, it is interesting that with the three categories of standard variants (i.e. neutral, formal and hyper-formal), the authors do make an attempt to distinguish written and spoken registers by using such variants more frequently in the texts than in the dialogues. This suggests that if textbook authors were made aware of the actual frequency of marked and mildly marked informal variants in spoken French, they would be more successful at accurately representing their usage in dialogues.

Sociolinguistically oriented activities in the corpus of French Language Arts materials

One reason we have examined the treatment of sociolinguistic variation in the French Language Arts materials used in French immersion programs was Lyster's (1994a, 1994b, 2007) finding that pedagogical materials centered on specific sociolinguistic variables significantly improved the sociolinguistic competence of French immersion students. Specifically, Lyster (1994a) designed a set of materials that are based on the following teaching strategies: (1) the comparison of speech acts in formal and informal contexts; (2) role plays and peer correction; (3) structural exercises; (4) writing activities where students produce letters in formal and informal registers; (5) reading activities to sensitive students to geographic variation; and (6) cooperative activities involving project work with a focus on the difference between oral and written French. Since the materials that we have chosen to examine are based on the communicative approach, we did not expect to find an overwhelming number of activities involving analysis or practice of linguistic forms. Still, assuming that the materials would include certain mildly marked informal variants, we were curious to find out if these variants would be the object of special emphasis, either in the form of information about their sociostylistic status or of activities meant to develop the students' receptive or productive abilities to use such variants, such as those discussed by Lyster (2007). However, our analysis of the materials has revealed that the French Language Arts materials do not include any activities offering students opportunities to become aware of and practice sociolinguistic variation, whether it be lexical, morphological, phonological, etc. Furthermore, we found only two instances where sociolinguistic variation is acknowledged, first *ne* non-use, which, as we pointed out above, is mentioned under the heading of 'faulty ellipsis of particle *ne*' and is described as a potential source of error in written French and, second, use of *on* for *nous*, which is merely presented as another subject pronoun expressing the first person plural. The fact that sociolinguistic variation is not the object of any explicit attention or practice cannot be accounted for by the absence of sociolinguistic variation in the materials, since we have seen that certain mildly marked informal variants are used with varying levels of frequency. For instance, in an extract of a novel by a Quebec writer, one finds the very few instances of schwa non-use included in the entire series. Yet, the students are not made aware of these cases of non-use in any explicit way, nor are they told that they are commonplace in spoken French. Furthermore, in both series of materials, two of the rare instances of *ne* non-use that we found were in the speech of either drug dealers or individuals of lower-than-average intelligence!

The above-mentioned findings are in keeping with those previously reported in the research (e.g. Lyster & Rebuffot, 2002; O'Connor Di Vito, 1991) which found that FL2 teaching materials are devoid of activities designed to familiarize students with the socio-stylistic value of variants or to develop their mastery of such forms. Like us, these authors have also found that FL2 teaching materials contain incomplete or misleading clues about the sociostylistic status of the variants on which they focused.

Our examination of the French Language Arts materials used to teach in French immersion programs has revealed that, by and large, French immersion students are not being exposed to a variety of French that will enable them to become aware of and eventually internalize and use appropriately a range of French variants that reflects the sociolinguistic requirements of a variety of communicative situations. Further, we have found no evidence of activities specifically designed to target sociolinguistic variation in the materials we have examined (see Lyster, 2007).

Comparison of the Frequency and Treatment of Variants in Teachers' Classroom Discourse and the Teaching Materials

Frequency

To gain a sense of the degree to which the teachers' treatment of sociolinguistic variation is in line with or differs from that of the French Language Arts materials, we have tabulated the frequencies of each variant as a function of their sociostylistic status in each of the components of the educational input (see Tables 4.12 and 4.13).

The comparison of the teachers' speech and the French Language Arts materials reveals that the latter are even more closely aligned with formal Standard French usage than is the French immersion teachers' speech. For each of the sociolinguistic variables where we were able to compare the frequency of variant use displayed by the teachers with those found in

Table 4.12 Distribution (%) of marked and mildly marked informal variants in L1 Canadian French, immersion teachers' French, French Language Arts materials (dialogues) and French Language Arts materials (texts)

Variant	L1 Canadian French	Immersion teachers	Materials: dialogues	Materials: texts
Marked informal				
rien que	33	1	0	0
(ça) fait que	55	1	0	0
M'as	30	0	0	0
nous-autres on	4	0	0	0
avoir	33	5	0	0
su'	28	0	0	0
job	29	–	0	–
ouvrage	14	–	0	–
rester	64	0	–	0
Singular verbs	2	0	0	0
char	23	0	0	0
machine	19	0	0	0
Mildly marked informal				
ne non-use	99	29	1	0
juste	41	15	0	3
je vas	64	1	0	0
on	94	83	48	17
schwa non-use	68	n/a	0.1	0
/l/ non-use (in subject pronouns)	93	n/a	0	0

Table 4.13 Distribution (%) of neutral, formal and hyper-formal variants in L1 Canadian French, immersion teachers' French, French Language Arts materials (dialogues) and French Language Arts materials (texts)

Variant	L1 Canadian French	Immersion teachers	Materials: dialogues	Materials: texts
Neutral				
Periphrastic future	73	79	30	5
Futurate present	7	3	0	0
Plural verbs	98	100	100	100
chez 1	67	32	100	27
Other	5	12	0	0
chez 3	66	100	100	100
Other	6	0	0	0
à la maison	31	56	0	73
vivre	10	0	–	54
travail	35	–	0	–
auto	42	33	75	19
Formal				
seulement	25	79	0	11
alors	43	76	17	75
Inflected future	20	18	70	95
je vais	6	99	100	100
être	67	95	100	100
emploi	14	–	100	–
demeurer	20	0	–	4
schwa use	32	n/a	99.9	100
automobile	14	0	0	55
Hyper-formal				
ne use	1	71	99	100
ne ... que	1	5	100	86
donc	2	23	83	25
nous	1	17	52	83

(Continued)

Table 4.13 *Continued*

Variant	L1 Canadian French	Immersion teachers	Materials: dialogues	Materials: texts
voiture	2	67	25	20
véhicule	Unattested	0	0	6
/l/ use (in subject pronouns)	7	n/a	100	100

the teaching materials, we found substantially higher rates of use of the formal and hyper-formal variants in the materials than in the French immersion teachers' classroom speech. For a number of sociolinguistic variables the difference is quite spectacular. For instance, while in the teachers' speech hyper-formal *nous* is used only 17% of the time, in the two types of written materials that we analyzed, this variant is used 83% and 53% of the time. Similarly, in the teachers' speech hyper-formal variant *ne ... que* is used only 5% of the time, and in the materials it is used 86% and 100% of the time! As for the inflected future (also a variant associated with the formal register), it is used only 18% of the time in the teachers' speech while it is used 95% and 70% of the time in the materials. Finally, while in the teachers' speech hyper-formal variant *donc* is used between clauses only 23% of the time, in the materials, *donc* is used in this position 83% and 25% of the time.

In sum, the magnitude of the differences between variant frequencies in the teaching materials and those found in the classroom speech of the French immersion teachers leads us to temper somewhat our characterization of the classroom speech of the French immersion teachers. While it is true that the latter tends to under-expose French immersion students to the variants that are frequently used by FL1 speakers, it does not, with only three exceptions (i.e. *ne* use, *habiter* and *voiture*), over-expose them to hyper-formal variants to the same extent as do the French Language Arts materials.

Treatment

As we have seen, the teacher corpus contains no evidence of strategies designed to make students aware of variation, for example: explicit feedback on the appropriate use of variants, nor does it provide examples of activities whose purpose is to increase students' productive use of sociolinguistic variants. That said, the teachers' corpus to which we have access is somewhat limited and may not represent the full range of classroom-based activities in which the teachers and students engage in the immersion program under study.

As for the French Language Arts materials, they are also devoid of activities that focus explicitly on the teaching/learning of sociolinguistic variation, such as activities to increase production of or awareness of specific sociolinguistic variants, for example: activities centering on register variation, etc.

In sum, it would appear that neither the classroom nor the French Language Arts materials provide the immersion students with suitable activities and/or feedback necessary for them to develop their sociolinguistic competence. Furthermore, we have seen in the preceding section that, overall, the students are not exposed to a full range of variants in the classroom and in the French Language Arts materials. We have also noted that both the teachers and the materials under-use informal variants and, conversely, over-use (hyper)-formal ones.

These findings are a major concern for at least two reasons. Firstly, French immersion students are primarily dependent on teachers' speech, classroom activities and French Language Arts materials for exposure to sociolinguistic variation in French. Secondly, we have seen that the Ontario Ministry of Education has now explicitly recognized the importance of mastering the informal and formal registers of French by the end of secondary school immersion programs. As such, it would seem that both the immersion classroom and the French Language Arts materials are far removed from the pedagogical approach described by Lyster (2007) for the development of sociolinguistic competence and that the attainment of the goals established by the Ontario Ministry of Education are unlikely to be achieved under the current circumstances.

Types and Frequency of Variants Used by the French Immersion Students

According to the general hypotheses on the types and frequency of variants used by the French immersion students, presented in Chapter 2, we expect that the French immersion students will do the following:

(1) make infrequent use of marked informal variants;
(2) use mildly marked informal variants less often than would FL1 speakers;
(3) use certain forms that look like marked or mildly marked informal variants, but which are, in fact, symptomatic of their incomplete mastery of difficult standard variants;
(4) use non-native forms that also betray their imperfect mastery of difficult standard variants;
(5) over-use hyper-formal and formal variants, unless there were intervening factors that caused them to under-use such variants (e.g. in-class input and inherent complexity of the forms); and
(6) use some neutral variants, but not others, depending on their specific properties (e.g. English equivalent, structural complexity, etc.).

Marked informal variants

Concerning the first hypothesis, namely the expected rarity of marked informal variants in the French immersion students' speech, Table 4.14 shows that variants *m'as*, *(ça) fait que*, *ouvrage* and *rester* are entirely absent and that *rien que* and *nous-autres on* are practically non-existent (for further details see Mougeon & Rehner, 2001; Nadasdi & McKinnie, 2003; Nadasdi *et al.*, 2003; Rehner, 1998; Rehner *et al.*, 2001, 2003).

Examples (126) (129) illustrate the use of marked informal variants by the French immersion students.

(126) heu non **rien que** les émissions et c'est tout
'um no only programs and that's all'
(127) les autres prend l'autobus et **nous-autres** marche après
'the others take the bus and we walk later'
(128) oui j'**ai** allé avec ma famille
'yes I went with my family'
(129) tu dois avoir une bonne éducation pour avoir une **job**
'you have to have a good education to have a job'

Table 4.14 Frequency (%) of marked informal variants in the speech of immersion students compared to L1 Canadian French, French immersion teachers, written dialogues and texts

Variants	L1 French	Teachers	Dialogues	Texts	Students
rien que	33	1	0	0	0.1
(ça) fait que	55	1	0	0	0
m'as	30	0	0	0	0
nous-autres on	4	0	0	0	0.1
avoir	33	5	0	0	22
su'	28	0	0	0	0
job	29	–	0	–	6
ouvrage	14	–	0	–	0
rester	64	0	–	0	0
Singular verbs	2	0	0	0	19
char	23	0	0	0	0
machine	19	0	0	0	0

As Table 4.14 shows, our first hypothesis has been clearly confirmed by our research for 9 of the 12 variants examined since these variants are either never used or only marginally used by the students. Among those factors that explain these findings, one can mention (1) the relatively limited contacts that the French immersion students have had with FL1 speakers outside school; (2) the high likelihood that the students have not or have rarely been exposed to these variants in the school context (as suggested by the French immersion teachers' classroom speech); (3) the absence of these marked informal features in the French Language Arts materials; and (4) the marked informal status of these variants that may have caused the Francophones with whom the French immersion students have interacted to avoid these forms in the students' presence.

That said, the data in Table 4.14 remind us of the fact that FL1 speakers use seven of these 12 marked informal variants at levels of frequency above 25%. Therefore, while the quasi-total absence of these seven variants in the speech of the immersion students is accounted for by the factors mentioned above, it remains problematic from the point of view of sociolinguistic competence in that it suggests that the students would lack the features needed to converge toward their potential fellow Canadian interlocutors in the informal registers.

Finally, Table 4.14 highlights three apparent exceptions to the general absence of marked informal variants in the students' speech, namely auxiliary *avoir*, *job* and the 'singular' verb forms. We will be dealing with these three variants further down when we discuss forms that resemble marked or mildly marked informal variants. Suffice it to say here that they can be looked upon as developmental features in the students' speech, rather than as genuine marked informal variants.

Mildly marked informal variants

As for the second hypothesis, namely the expected use of mildly marked informal variants at levels of frequency below FL1 norms, Table 4.15 shows that it holds true for five of the six variants focused on in our research: non-use of /l/, schwa and *ne* and the use of *je vas* and *on* (for further details see Nadasdi *et al.*, 2001, 2003; Rehner & Mougeon, 1999; Rehner *et al.*, 2003; Uritescu *et al.*, 2004; and Tables D1, D7 and D8 in appendix).

Examples (130)–(135) illustrate the use of mildly marked informal variants mentioned above.

(130) *c'(ø)est pas cinq dollars c'est cinquante dollars*
         'it's not five dollars it's fifty dollars'
(131) *je pense que je vais maintenant **juste** pour médecin*
         'I think I will go now just for doctor'

Table 4.15 Frequency (%) of mildly marked informal variants in the speech of immersion students compared to L1 Canadian French, French immersion teachers, written dialogues and texts

Variant	L1 French	Teachers	Dialogues	Texts	Students
ne non-use	99	29	1	0	27
juste	41	15	0	3	54
je vas	64	1	0	0	10
on	94	83	48	17	55
schwa non-use	68	n/a	0.1	0	15
/l/ non-use (in subject pronouns)	93	n/a	0	0	2

(132) à l'université je **vas** prendre un cours de français
 'at university I'm going to take a French course'
(133) oh oui **on** échange les cadeaux le matin
 'ah yes we exchange presents in the morning'
(134) j**(e)** pense oui
 'I think so'
(135) dans le Canada i**(l)** y a beaucoup de différents langues
 'in Canada there are lots of different languages'

Furthermore, for five of the six mildly marked informal variants, the students' frequency of use is considerably below that of the FL1 speakers. However, the degree of this discrepancy varies according to the sociolinguistic variable under consideration. Specifically, the students' rate of /l/ non-use falls 91% below that of the FL1 speakers, *ne* non-use 72% below, *je vas* 54%, schwa non-use 53% and *on* use 40%. These differences likely reflect the complex influence of several factors and it would be interesting to identify them through further research. For instance, why is it that the French immersion students almost never delete /l/ in subject pronouns *il(s)*, whereas they delete schwa more often? This question is even more intriguing when one bears in mind the fact that FL1 speakers (and probably the immersion teachers as well[51]) do the reverse: they delete /l/ almost categorically in pronouns *il(s)* and delete schwa frequently, but less often than /l/. One possible answer to this question may lie in the influence of English phonology. To our knowledge, there are no dialects of English where /l/ can be deleted in word final position, while the non-use of mid vowels is a frequent phenomenon (e.g. *for instance* [fəɹinstəns/foɹinstəns > fɹinstəns]). In other words, the phonological rule of schwa non-use would appear to be easier to learn than the morphophonological rule of /l/ non-use. Furthermore, certain English cognates of French words do not feature a schwa where the French words have one (e.g. *exactly – exactement; government – gouvernement*) and, hence, it is possible that these English cognates might reinforce schwa non-use in the pronunciation of their French counterparts. Finally, in the audio French Language Arts materials we examined, schwa non-use is, as we have mentioned, more frequent than /l/ non-use (8% versus 2%, respectively), a difference that seems to be mirrored by the dialogues in the materials that include marginal occurrences of schwa non-use, but no instances of /l/ non-use. A further question would be, 'Why is the mildly marked informal variant *on* more easily learned than *ne* non-use'? One possible answer to this question may lie in the fact that, as we have seen in the preceding section, the French immersion teachers and the French Language Arts materials use *on* considerably more often than they delete *ne* (see Table 4.15). A further explanation may lie in the ease of verb conjugation that accompanies the choice of *on* in that this pronoun is always used with unmarked singular verb forms, whereas *nous* requires a special plural ending and may involve verb stem changes.

To sum up, while the immersion students make infrequent use of the five mildly marked informal variants mentioned above, they are somewhat closer to native norms than in relation to marked informal variants. This likely reflects the fact that these mildly marked informal variants are used to varying extents in the educational input of the students, which is what one might expect given that they are only weakly sociostylistically marked. Still, given that the frequency of these variants in the educational input is generally well below that observed in FL1 speech, the students' frequency of use of these variants also falls considerably short of approximating the native norms. Consequently, the infrequent use of these mildly marked informal variants by the immersion students is even more problematic from the point of view of sociolinguistic competence than is their lack of marked informal variant use in that these variants are commonplace in FL1 speech, and hence are part of the sociostylistic repertoire that fellow Canadian interlocutors would expect advanced L2 learners to use.

Finally, there is one mildly marked informal variant, however, whose frequency in the immersion students' speech is not below but above that of FL1 speakers, namely *juste* (see Table 4.15). As with the apparent exceptions for the marked informal variants examined above, we would argue that this mildly marked informal variant only appears to be an exception, but in fact, as we will see in the next section, is likely the result of a process of inter-systemic transfer, rather than the successful learning of a mildly marked informal FL1 variant.

Forms that resemble marked or mildly marked informal variants

Let us now examine the third hypothesis, namely that the French immersion students would use certain forms that look like marked or mildly marked informal variants, but which are, in fact, symptomatic of their incomplete mastery of difficult standard variants. As Table 4.16 shows, there are five variants that support this hypothesis, namely marked informal variants *job*, auxiliary *avoir* and singular verb forms in the third person plural and mildly marked informal variants *je vas* and *juste* (for further details see Knaus & Nadasdi, 2001; Nadasdi, 2001; Nadasdi & McKinnie, 2003; Nadasdi et al., 2003 and Tables D2, D7 and D11 in appendix).

For each of these variants we will now discuss the reasons why they are more likely the manifestation of incomplete learning of their difficult standard counterparts by the French immersion students, rather than the result of the students learning marked or mildly marked informal variants. Three main reasons can be mentioned in relation to the variant *job*. First, in the students' speech, the noun *job* is used half of the time as a one-word switch to English, as in example (1). Second, all but one of the seven students who used this variant never stayed in a Francophone family in Quebec or elsewhere. Third, the students do not assign a consistent gender to the word *job*, whereas FL1 speakers of Quebec French use this word in the feminine.[52] Thus, we suggest that if the immersion students use *job*, it is not because they have learned it as the result of interactions with FL1 speakers, but rather because they have a less than perfect mastery of the French equivalents.

(136)   *non pas ahm comme ah [n] **job** ah/je ne sais pas comment dire ahm//*
        'no not um like um a **job** um/I don't know how to say um//'

As for the French immersion students' use of the auxiliary *avoir* with verbs that require auxiliary *être* in Standard French, it can be pointed out that during the initial stages of learning French, French immersion students quite frequently use the auxiliary *avoir* with the '*être* verbs' (cf. Harley, 1982).

Table 4.16 Frequency (%) of forms that resemble marked and mildly marked informal variants in the speech of immersion students compared to L1 Canadian French, French immersion teachers, written dialogues and texts

Variant	L1 French	Teachers	Dialogues	Texts	Students
job	29	–	0	–	6
avoir	33	5	0	0	22
Singular verbs	2	0	0	0	19
je vas	64	1	0	0	10
juste	41	15	0	3	54

This mistake reflects the fact that, as pointed out in Chapter 3, the rules of use of auxiliary *être* are more complex than those of auxiliary *avoir*. Indeed, auxiliary *être* is used with only a small set of verbs (reflexive verbs and a small number of verbs of motion or state) and only when the latter verbs are used intransitively. In other words, auxiliary *avoir* is the default auxiliary of compound past tenses in French and it would therefore seem that the students are over-generalizing its use, in spite of the fact that they are massively exposed to the standard variant in their educational input.

As for the use of singular verb forms in the third person plural, we have pointed out in Chapter 3 that the distinctive third person plural verb forms represent a major difficulty in the French verbal system, since they are morphologically irregular and not entirely predictable. This explains why, in the speech of advanced FL2 learners, these third person verb forms are often replaced by default singular forms (cf. Bartning, 1997). Further, as a marked informal form in FL1 speech, the use of the default singular verb forms is very infrequent and highly constrained by syntactic rules (i.e. they occur only after *qui* and *ils*), whereas, as we will see further down, this is not the case for the French immersion students. Hence, this marked informal usage is unlikely to be at the root of the French immersion students' use of singular verb forms in place of their distinctive third person plural counterparts. In fact, the use of the 'singular' verb forms by the immersion students is yet another case where the students' frequency of use of forms that resemble marked or mildly marked informal variants far outweighs that found in FL1 speech and the educational input.

In the case of *je vas*, it is interesting to point out that this variant is used mostly by students who have had no or only limited contacts with FL1 speakers in a Francophone environment outside the school context (see Table D7 in Appendix D). These findings tie in with Harley's (1992) attestation of uses of *je vas* for *je vais* in the speech of very young French immersion students, an error that can be looked upon as the over-generalization of the /va/ form to all singular persons (cf. Chapter 3). It is therefore reasonable to hypothesize that the occasional use of *je vas* by the immersion students under study here can be attributed to the fact that they have not completely mastered the use of the irregular variant *je vais*, rather than having learned the mildly marked informal variant *je vas*. The case of *je vas* is, therefore, reminiscent of that of the auxiliary variant *avoir* discussed above.

The fact that the French immersion students' incomplete mastery of French can lead them to produce forms that are the same as marked or mildly marked informal variants is not particularly surprising, given that many of the sociolinguistic variables that have been documented in FL1 speech involve an alternation between structurally non-optimal (irregular, redundant, infrequent, etc., such as *je vais* and auxiliary *être*) and optimal variants (regular, non-redundant, frequent, etc., such as *je vas* and auxiliary *avoir*). During the long history of French, these structurally optimal variants have been introduced by speakers who were/are not greatly influenced by the norms of Standard French (cf. Chaudenson *et al.*, 1993). It is therefore to be expected that on certain non-optimal points of the structure of French, FL2 learners will produce some of the same alternatives that were once introduced into French by FL1 speakers. It is also noteworthy that, contrary to the marked and mildly marked informal variants we have discussed above, the students' frequency of use of these forms resembling marked or mildly marked informal variants does not mirror that found in the educational input, since the teachers and the French Language Arts teaching materials make no or marginal use of these variants.

Finally, concerning *juste*, it can be pointed out that English can express the notion of restriction with the cognate term *just* and so it is not unreasonable to posit that the immersion students would consciously or unconsciously favor the use of *juste* on account of its morphological and semantic similarity to English *just*. Another hypothesis is that the immersion students have extended the meaning and function of the French adjective *juste* (e.g. *ce n'est pas juste* 'it is not fair') to include its use as an adverb of restriction on the model of English *just* that functions as both an adjective (e.g. *it was a just decision*) and an adverb of restriction (e.g. *he was here for just three minutes*). While these two hypotheses partially account for the students' frequent use of *juste*, it should also be pointed out that the students are likely exposed to this variant to some extent in their educational input, as indicated by the data on the teacher in-class speech and the materials provided in Table 4.11. Consequently, the processes of inter-systemic transfer mentioned above and the presence of this variant in the educational input may reinforce each other and hence would explain why the immersion students use this variant more often than FL1 speakers.

Non-native forms

The fourth hypothesis, namely that the French immersion students would use non-native forms that betray their imperfect mastery of certain standard variants, has been confirmed in relation to seven of the sociolinguistic variables under study (for further details see DiCesare, in progress; Knaus & Nadasdi, 2001; Mougeon & Rehner, 2001; Nadasdi *et al.*, 2003; Rehner & Mougeon, 1999, 2004). An overview of the non-native features found for the variables under study is presented in Table 4.17.

Use of these non-native variants by the French immersion students is exemplified in examples (137)–(147).

(137) *parce qu'elle **ne** parle (ø) en français alors*
 'because she doesn't speak in French so'
(138) *je **juste** regarde ce qui est dans la télévision*
 'I just watch what's in TV'

Table 4.17 Frequency of non-native variants in the speech of immersion students

Variable	Non-native variant	%
Use versus non-use of *ne*	Deletion of *pas*	3
Restrictives	Pre-verbal *juste*	47
Expressions of consequence	*So*	7
Future verb forms	Infinitive, conditional, etc.	13
être versus *avoir*	Use of *avoir* with *aller*	12
Expressions of movement toward or location at the speaker's home (*chez* 1)	*chez la maison*, *dans* + possessive + *maison*, etc.	15
Expressions of movement toward or location at someone else's home (*chez* 3)	*dans la maison de, au la maison de*, etc.	20

(139) *ses parents peut aller pour trois jours après le Noël (pause)* **so** *nous allons aller à sa maison*
'her parents can go for three days after Christmas (pause) so we can go to her house'
(140) *dans l'année prochaine ah* **prendre** *le cours d'espagnol*
'next year ah I'll take the Spanish course'
(141) *je pense qu'il y* **aurait** *toujours des conflits moraux*
'I think that there will always be moral conflicts'
(142) *il* **a** *allé dans/l'hôpital*
'he went to the hospital'
Chez 1 (the speaker or subject lives in the house in question; the complement of *chez* is an object pronoun)
(143) *j'ai juste resté* **la maison** *et aide mes parents*
'I just stayed home and helped my parents'
(144) *elle a habité* **chez la maison**
'she lived at home'
(145) *l'école proche* **à moi**
'the school close to my home'
Chez 3 (the speaker or subject does not live in the house in question; the complement of *chez* is a full noun phrase)
(146) *nous allons* **dans la maison de** *ma grande mère*
'we are going in my grandmother's house'
(147) *tout la famille all[e]* **au la maison de** *ma grand-mère*
'the whole family went to my grandmother's home'

It should be pointed out that the above non-native features were not found in the educational input of the students, nor of course in the French of the FL1 speakers.[53] Let us consider each of these features in turn. First, the French immersion students have been found to delete the post-verbal negator *pas* 3% of the time.[54] An interesting property of the two-pronged negative construction of French (*ne* + verb + *pas*) is that both *ne* and *pas* are synonymous and hence the notion of negation is expressed redundantly. Consequently when they delete *pas*, the French immersion students simplify the morphosyntax of negation without a loss of meaning.[55] Still, the fact that this non-native feature appears in only 3% of contexts indicates that the immersion students have, by and large, figured out that the post-verbal negator in French is obligatory.

Second, the French immersion students have been shown to use the restrictive adverb *juste* to the left of a verb in 47% of the contexts where they use *juste* to restrict a verb. French syntax does not allow leftward movement of restrictive *juste*. The latter word is always used after the verb or the auxiliary (e.g. *je regarde juste la télévision anglaise* 'I just watch English TV' and *j'ai juste eu assez d'argent* 'I just had enough money'). Thus, the very high frequency of this non-native syntactic usage by the students underscores the strong effect that the syntax of English adverb *just* has on the students' placement of *juste* when restricting a verb.

Third, the French immersion students use conjunction *so* 7% of the time to mark a consequence between two clauses. As Table 4.17 demonstrates, *so* is not a variant present in FL1 Quebec speech and its presence in the French immersion students' speech is therefore not a result of exposure to this variety of French. Having said this, it is important to point out that in the speech of some of the French immersion students this form shows signs of being automatized. In fact, in approximately 70% of occurrences this conjunction is used without a preceding pause. Furthermore, in the students' speech, *so* is not only used to express the notion of consequence, but also fulfills a variety of discursive functions (e.g. turn yielder, clarification marker – see Rehner, 2004).

Fourth, the French immersion students have been found to use non-native verb forms to express the notion of futurity 13% of the time (e.g. infinitives, conditional-like forms, etc.). Although, strictly speaking, such forms are not cases of simplification, as is the deletion of *pas*, they are certainly indicative of the persistent difficulties that the French immersion students have in mastering the correct use of future verb forms (see Harley, 1992, for similar findings on the less-than-perfect learning of the future tenses by French immersion students close to the end of high school).

Fifth, the finding that the French immersion students use auxiliary *avoir* with *aller* 12% of the time, whereas the FL1 speakers in Montreal use it 0.7% of the time, is in line with the fact, see below, that these students have not mastered the linguistic constraints that condition the variable use of auxiliary *avoir* in L1 speech.

Finally, the French immersion students have been found to use non-native alternatives to preposition *chez* and its analytic counterpart *à la maison* 15% of the time in *chez* 1 and 20% of the time in *chez* 3. This finding underscores the French immersion students' difficulty in mastering the specialized preposition of French *chez* and its analytic counterpart *à la maison*, a difficulty that leads them to produce non-native forms that may be looked upon as a form of transfer from English (at/to [one's] home) and/or an approximation of *à la maison* (e.g. *à maison, au la maison* and *dans la maison*) or an extension of forms based on *à la maison* to the *chez* 3 context.

Formal, hyper-formal and neutral variants

The hypothesis that the French immersion students would over-use formal and hyper-formal variants has been largely confirmed. Indeed, it is noteworthy that the high frequencies found for the variants in Table 4.18 (except for *demeurer, ne ... que,* inflected future, *poste* and *automobile*) contrast sharply with the much lower frequencies of these variants in FL1 speech.

The French immersion students' use of these formal and hyper-formal variants is provided in examples (148)–(160).

Formal Variants

(148) *je restais là pendant **seulement** deux mois*
'I stayed there for only two months'
(149) *elle a sept frères et sœurs **alors** il y a comme trente-trois cousins*
'she has seven brothers and sisters so there are like thirty-three cousins'
(150) *l'air **sera** très difficile à respirer*
'the air will be very difficult to breathe'
(151) *je **suis** restée avec elle*
'I stayed with her'
(152) *c'est assez difficile de trouver un bon **emploi** maintenant*
'it's fairly difficult to find a good job now'
(153) *oh oui j[ə] pense*
'ah yes I think'
(154) *il était frappé par une **automobile***
'he was hit by a car'

Hyper-Formal Variants

(155) *je **ne** peux pas les trouver*
'I can't find them'

Table 4.18 Frequency (%) of formal and hyper-formal variants in the speech of immersion students compared to L1 Canadian French, French immersion teachers, written dialogues and texts

Variant	L1 French	Teachers	Dialogues	Texts	Students
Formal					
seulement	25	79	0	11	46
alors	43	76	17	75	78
Inflected future	20	18	70	95	20
je vais	6	99	100	100	90
être	67	95	100	100	78
emploi	14	–	100	–	38
demeurer	20	0	–	4	0
schwa use	32	n/a	99.9	100	85
automobile	14	0	0	55	5
Hyper-formal					
ne use	1	71	99	100	70
ne ... que	1	5	100	86	0
donc	2	23	83	25	15
nous	1	17	52	83	45
poste	8	–	0	–	0
habiter	6	100	–	42	60
voiture	2	67	25	20	21
/l/ use (in subject pronouns)	7	n/a	100	100	98

(156) *elle vit à Edmonton **donc** euhm elle quelque fois on fait*
'she lives in Edmonton so she eh sometimes we do'
(157) *quand **nous** parlons ensemble*
'when we speak together'
(158) *où j'**habite** il a un Walmart*
'where I live there's a Walmart'
(159) *c'était un vieille **voiture** c'est presque pourri*
'it was an old car it is almost rotten'
(160) *i[l] faut que tu prennes*
'you have to take'

Two principal explanations can be offered to account for the prevalence of formal and hyper-formal variants in the immersion students' speech: (1) the French immersion students have mostly been exposed to French in the classroom context and we have seen in the preceding section that the French immersion teachers, and the educational materials to an even greater extent, favor formal variants; and (2) the French immersion students have lacked opportunities to be exposed to the spoken French of L1 speakers outside this context, which might otherwise have reduced the standardization of their speech.

However, as we have seen above, there are five exceptions to this pattern, namely variants that are either absent from the French immersion students' speech or used at rates below that of the FL1 speakers. Let us consider each of these in turn. The absence of *demeurer* can be ascribed to its low frequency in the educational input. This same explanation applies to the absence of *poste* in the students' speech. As for *ne ... que*, it is not surprising that this variant is not used by the immersion speakers since it is a morphosyntactically complex variant involving the placement of two separate morphemes, one on each side of the verb. Concerning the inflected future, its relatively low frequency may be ascribed to the infrequency of this variant in the teachers' speech, as well as to the morphologically complex nature of this form, as pointed out above. Finally, in the case of *automobile* the infrequency of this variant in the students' speech is likely the result of several factors: (1) infrequency of this variant in the teachers' speech; (2) absence of this variant in the dialogues included in the teaching materials; and (3) the possibility that the students equate this form with the English word *automobile*, which is marked in spoken English, and therefore avoid the use of its French equivalent.

Let us now consider the variants that we have categorized as neutral. Uses of such variants are presented in examples (161)–(169).

(161) *après le Noël donc je **vais** être seule*
 'after Christmas so I'm going to be alone'
(162) *à Noël cette année on **reste** à la maison*
 'for Christmas this year we are going to stay home'
(163) *tous les parents **disent** quelque chose que les enfants n'aiment pas*
 'all parents say something that children don't like'
(164) *mes amis vient **chez** moi*
 'my friends come to my house'
(165) *on aime rester **à la maison***
 'we like to stay at home'
(166) *elle habite **chez** mon père*
 'she lives at my father's house'
(167) *j'aime mon **travail***
 'I like my job'

(168) je vais **vivre** en Afrique
'I am going to live in Africa'
(169) le conducteur de l'autre **auto** était ivre
'the driver of the other car was drunk'

The reader will recall that, according to our hypotheses, the frequency of neutral variants will be related to the following factors: (1) English equivalence; (2) structural complexity; and (3) frequency in the educational input. Results for the neutral variants are presented in Table 4.19.

As Table 4.19 shows, the immersion students use *vivre* much more often than do FL1 speakers. This result can be attributed to the existence of the English verb *live* which functions as both a verb of existence and residency. It is therefore not surprising that the immersion students make frequent use of this form with the meaning 'to reside' in French. In the case of *chez* 1 and 3, the fact that the immersion students use these two variants significantly less often than FL1 speakers undoubtedly reflects in part the complexity of these forms and, in the case of *chez* 1, the existence of a semantically more transparent and easier to understand variant (*à la maison*). An additional explanation may lie in the fact that the immersion teachers use *chez* 1 only sparingly. Structural complexity can also be invoked to explain why the immersion students make less frequent use of the plural verb forms than the immersion teachers and materials or, for that matter, the FL1 speakers. The fact that the immersion students' use of

Table 4.19 Frequency (%) of neutral variants in the speech of immersion students compared to L1 Canadian French, French immersion teachers, written dialogues, and texts

Variants	L1 French	Teachers	Dialogues	Texts	Students
Periphrastic future	73	79	30	5	67
Futurate present	7	3	0	0	10
Plural verbs	98	100	100	100	19
chez 1	67	32	100	27	20
Other	5	12	0	0	23
chez 3	66	100	100	100	23
Other	6	0	0	0	57
à la maison	31	56	0	73	42
travail	35	–	0	–	56
vivre	10	0	–	54	40
auto	42	33	75	19	74

the periphrastic future and the futurate present is in line with the FL1 speakers can be attributed to the fact that the teachers' use of these variants is on a par with that of FL1 speakers and the fact that these variants are alternatives to a relatively complex variant, namely the inflected future. Finally, the noteworthy finding that the immersion students strongly prefer *auto*, in spite of its limited use in classroom teacher speech deserves an explanation. Here again, it is possible to invoke the influence of intersystemic factors. Specifically, the morpheme *auto* is widely used in English in the same semantic field, even though it does not function as a noun (e.g. *the auto-industry, auto-workers* and *automotive*) and this may have triggered a process of convergence toward the French variant *auto* on the part of the immersion students. That said, it is also plausible to hypothesize that such convergence may have been reinforced by the fact that, as we have seen, in the dialogues included in the teaching materials *auto* is clearly preferred over *voiture*.

Let us now summarize the main findings of our examination of variant use frequency in the speech of the French immersion students. We have seen that the students practically never use marked informal variants. However, they use certain forms that coincide with marked or mildly marked informal variants in FL1 speech, but that reflect their imperfect mastery of difficult standard variants. We have also found that the difficulty of such variants may also be a source of errors and that the French immersion students substitute non-native forms for these difficult variants. We have seen that the French immersion students almost always use mildly marked informal variants at rates of frequency below those of FL1 speakers. We have also found that the French immersion students overuse formal and hyper-formal variants in comparison with FL1 speakers. Finally, our research has shown that the immersion students' use of neutral variants depends on the specific systemic properties of a given variant and its frequency in the educational input.

Comparison of results with previous research

Let us now consider the contributions of the findings reported in the section 'Types and Frequency of Variants Used by the French Immersion Students' to research on the sociolinguistic competence of advanced L2 learners. First, our review of the literature has shown that it is only when L2 learners have extensive contacts with L1 speakers that one observes marked informal variants in their speech (cf. Bayley, 1996; Nagy & Blondeau, 1998; Nagy *et al.*, 2003; Sankoff *et al.*, 1997). However, Dewaele and Regan (2001) remind us that even extensive contacts will not bring about the internalization of certain marked informal variants. By having investigated no less than 12 marked informal variants, our research has clearly confirmed that without significant contacts with L1 speakers FL2 learners are very unlikely to master the features of marked informal speech.

Second, Kenemer (1982) and Mannesy and Wald (1984) documented, in the speech of their FL2 learners, instances in which the learners used variants that coincided with FL1 marked informal variants, but that were, in fact, reflections of the problems the learners faced in mastering difficult standard variants. As we have seen, our research has also documented the presence of four forms in the speech of the French immersion students that coincide with marked or mildly marked informal variants in FL1 speech. These findings lend support to the idea that this coincidence is a prevalent feature of the interlanguage of FL2 learners in an educational setting.

Third, Dewaele's (1998) and Lealess' (2005) research documented the tendency for FL2 learners to produce non-native forms in place of difficult standard variants. Our research has also documented seven sociolinguistic variables where the French immersion students use non-native variants. Thus, the use of non-native variants by FL2 learners in educational settings is also a trend that now rests on solid empirical evidence.

Fourth, the fact that FL2 learners use mildly marked informal variants at rates of frequency below those of FL1 speakers, documented by Dewaele (1992, 2004b), Howard et al. (2006), Nagy et al. (1996), Regan (1996, 2004), Regan et al. (2009), Sax (2003), and Thomas (2002a), and has received further support by our research in all six of the mildly marked informal variants we have examined. This pattern is also now well-established for FL2 learners in an education setting.

Fifth, our research has provided ample support for the findings of Dewaele (1992, 2004b), Regan (1996, 2004, 2005), Regan et al. (2009), Sax (2003) and Thomas (2002a), which document a trend for FL2 learners in an educational setting to over-use formal and hyper-formal variants. Specifically, in our research we have attested this trend in 14 of the 18 sociolinguistic formal and hyper-formal variants that we have investigated. It should be noted, however, that like Harley and King (1989), Lyster (1994a), Lyster and Rebuffot (2002) and Swain and Lapkin (1990), we found several unexpected instances of the under-use/absence of a formal or hyper-formal variant in the speech of the French immersion students. It is interesting that, in these instances, just like in the exceptions documented by the above-mentioned authors, the students' under-use/non-use can be ascribed to the fact that the formal or hyper-formal variant is either difficult, or not in keeping with the structure of English.

Finally, with regard to neutral variants we have seen that the immersion students use three of the eight neutral variants at rates of frequency similar to that of FL1 speakers. In contrast, the four variants they use with less frequency are either complex, or not reinforced by English. This finding is in line with that of Lealess (2005) who found that FL2 learners in

Montreal used the modal construction *falloir* + verb in the subjunctive less often than did FL1 speakers. We have also documented an interesting case where the immersion students were found to use a neutral variant (*auto*) more frequently than FL1 speakers.

Learning of the Linguistic and Stylistic Constraints of Sociolinguistic Variation

The reader will recall that we had expected the French immersion students not to master the stylistic constraints on variation, due to the subtlety of such constraints, and the fact that we were not certain whether they would observe all of the linguistic constraints on sociolinguistic variation that are observed by FL1 speakers, due to the their less than native-like mastery of spoken French.

Linguistic constraints

Data pertaining to the effect of linguistic context on the French immersion students' and FL1 speakers' patterns of sociolinguistic variation are given in Table 4.20. As can be seen, it is indeed the case that the French immersion students only partially master the linguistic constraints of sociolinguistic variation (for further details on the learning of such constraints, the reader is referred to Tables D1, D2, D5, D8, D9, D11, D13–17, D19 and D21 in Appendix D that present the results of the GoldVarb regression analyses of variation). Specifically, we found that (1) for five sociolinguistic variables (*seulement* versus *juste*, *nous* versus *on*, use versus non-use of schwa and of /l/ and *chez 1/à la maison*), the French immersion students observe the same constraints as do the FL1 speakers; (2) for two sociolinguistic variables (future verb forms and auxiliary *avoir* versus *être*), the French immersion students observe only one of the constraints documented in L1 French; and (3) for two sociolinguistic variables (use versus non-use of *ne* and use versus non-use of third person plural verb forms), the French immersion students do not observe the linguistic constraints found in L1 French. Finally, Table 4.20 shows that in the case of *seulement* versus *juste* and use versus non-use of third person plural verb forms, the French immersion students observe constraints that are particular to them.

Let us examine these results in more detail. In the sociolinguistic variable involving the use versus non-use of *ne*, we examined only one of the linguistic constraints attested in L1 French, namely, the effect of the type of post-verbal negator (e.g. *pas* 'not', *rien* 'nothing', *plus* 'no more', etc.; cf. Rehner & Mougeon, 1999). Contrary to the FL1 speakers, the French immersion students do not delete *ne* more often in negative sentences involving *pas*. In fact, they do the opposite; they delete *ne* less often in

Table 4.20 Linguistic constraints on the use of variants found in the speech of L1 speakers and French immersion students

	Linguistic variables										
	ne	*seulement*	*donc;* *aller +* *inf. 1sg.*	*future* *(all persons)*	*nous*	*Third plural* *verb forms*	*Auxiliary*	*chez 1*	*chez 3;* *emploi;* *habiter*	*auto*	*schwa; /l/*
Constraints observed in L1 French	*pas* > deletion	Infinitive > *juste*; COD > *rien que*	*donc*[a]; *aller* + inf. 1sg.[b]	Specific adverb > present; negative sentences; +/− fixed expressions; polite *vous* > infl. Future	Specific and restricted referent > *nous*	*qui* and *ils* > singular verb forms	Frequent verbs > *être*; transitive usage; adjectival usage of past part. > *avoir*	Movement > *chez* 1	*chez* 3[b]; *emploi*[b]; *habiter*[b]	*en* > *auto*	cf. Table footnotes 1 and 2
Constraints respected by students	No	Yes		No, except with specific adverbs	Yes	No	No, except verb frequency	Yes		No	Yes
Constraints unique to French immersion students	None	Use of restrictive adverb to the left of the verb > *juste*		None	None	Infrequent verbs; presence of an object clitic; presence of a plural marking on the subject > singular verb forms	None	None		None	None

> = favorable to.

[a]Case where the linguistic factors investigated by the L1 studies were found to have no effect.
[b]Cases where the L1 studies did not investigate the effect of any linguistic factors; ? constraints not yet examined.

Notes: (1) Schwa non-use is more frequent in clitic sequences (e.g. *je me* 'I me') and word internally (e.g. *maintenant* 'now') than in word initial syllables (e.g. *venir* 'to come').
(2) /l/ non-use is more frequent in impersonal *il* than in personal *il(s)*; it is more frequent when *il* is followed by a consonant.

these sentences than in negative sentences involving the other adverbs. The likely explanation for this is that in the educational input of the French immersion students, negative utterances featuring *pas* are far more frequent than those featuring the other post-verbal negators. Since we have seen that the French immersion students are considerably more exposed to *ne* use than *ne* non-use, it is not surprising that it is first and foremost with *pas* that *ne* is retained.

In the case of *seulement* versus *juste*, we can see that the French immersion students observe the constraint that is found in FL1 speech for *juste*, namely the higher frequency of this variant before an infinitive. As for the FL1 association of *rien que* with direct objects, the absence of this variant in the French immersion students' speech made it impossible to investigate this constraint. However, we did find one constraint in their speech that does not exist in FL1 speech (see Mougeon & Rehner, 2001). Specifically, the French immersion students occasionally use restrictive adverbs to the left of the verb. As we have pointed out, this is a non-native usage that is likely due to transfer from English. When an adverb is used to the left of a verb, the French immersion students almost always use the variant *juste*.

As concerns the sociolinguistic variable involving future verb forms, it can be pointed out that FL1 speakers use the inflected future more often than the other variants in negative sentences, in fixed expressions (e.g. proverbs) and in sentences involving the use of the polite subject pronoun *vous*. These same FL1 speakers also use the futurate present more often than the other variants with time-specific adverbs. This latter constraint is the only one that is observed by the French immersion students and is likely not particular to the French language (see Nadasdi *et al.*, 2003).

In the case of *nous* versus *on*, we found that the degree of specificity and restriction of the group of individuals to whom the pronoun refers influences variant choice: the more specific and restricted the group, the more the French immersion students tend to use *nous* (see Rehner *et al.*, 2003). Interestingly, this effect is much more clear-cut in the speech of the French immersion students than in FL1 speech. This difference reflects the fact that in FL1 speech, *nous* has been almost fully replaced by *on*, even in the context in which *nous* was once used exclusively (i.e. specific and restricted groups of individuals, cf. King *et al.*, 2009).

As we have already pointed out, the use of a singular verb form in the third person plural is strongly associated in FL1 speech with sentences whose subject is either *qui* or *ils*. The French immersion students do not observe this constraint. 'Singular' verb forms appear in their speech in all syntactic contexts and with the same level of frequency in these different contexts. Furthermore, in their speech, the use of 'singular' verb forms is conditioned by several linguistic constraints that have no effect in FL1 speech. More precisely, unlike FL1 speakers, the French immersion students use 'singular' verb forms more often with (1) infrequent verbs; (2) sentences where the subject is separated from the verb by an object clitic; and (3) subjects bearing an overt marker of plurality (see Nadasdi, 2001). The attestation of these non-native constraints suggests that the use of these 'singular' forms by the French immersion students reflects a grammar different from that of FL1 speakers and suggests that the French immersion students have not completely mastered the system of ending and stem alternations of third person plural verbs and that they use 'singular' verb forms by default.

The findings concerning the use of auxiliaries *avoir* and *être* in compound tenses are reminiscent of those for future verb forms. The French immersion students observe only one of the three linguistic constraints that have been found in FL1 speech, namely, the constraint associated with verb frequency. The more frequent the verb, the more often speakers will use auxiliary *être* (see Knaus & Nadasdi, 2001).

As for the linguistic constraint of *chez* 1 versus *à la maison*, FL1 speakers favor variant *chez* 1 more often in utterances involving movement to one's home than in utterances not involving such movement and to favor *à la maison* more often in utterances of the latter type than in those of the former. While the French immersion students differ from the FL1 speakers insofar as, overall, they favor *à la maison* rather than *chez*; they nonetheless observe the FL1 constraint on this sociolinguistic variable. This is a somewhat surprising finding given the general difficulty the French immersion students display in mastering the use of preposition *chez*.

In the case of words meaning 'automobile', the strong association between *en* and *auto* is not found in the spoken French of the immersion students. This suggests that students are unaware of the collocational status of *en auto* in Canadian French.

Finally, in the sociolinguistic variables involving use versus non-use of schwa and of /l/, the French immersion students observe the same constraints on sociolinguistic variation that have been found in FL1 speech (see footnotes to Table 4.20). As with *chez 1/à la maison*, these results are somewhat unexpected since the French immersion students rarely delete these two phonemes (Nadasdi *et al.*, 2001; Uritescu *et al.*, 2004).

In summary, our investigation of the learning of linguistic constraints on sociolinguistic variation by French immersion students has revealed that, for approximately half of the sociolinguistic variables where linguistic constraints were examined, such students display all of the constraints documented in FL1 speech. Concerning the other half, the immersion students display only a partial knowledge (or none at all) of such constraints. If we add to this the finding that, for two variables, these same students observe constraints that are unique to them, one can conclude that as we had expected the students display less than native-like mastery of the linguistic constraints of sociolinguistic variation.

Regarding the findings of previous FL2 research, the reader will recall that in their respective analysis of a given variable researchers such as Blondeau and Nagy (1998), Dion and Blondeau (2005), Goldfine (1987), Howard et al. (2006), Nagy et al. (2003), Nagy et al. (1996), Regan (1996, 2004, 2005), Regan et al. (2009), Sax (2003) and Thomas (2002a) found that FL2 learners display almost all of the linguistic constraints of variation. This latter finding may be a reflection of the fact that the FL2 learners examined by these researchers were more advanced in their learning of French than the immersion students focused upon in our own research. However, one must bear in mind that comparison across studies is problematic for at least two reasons. First, in their respective studies, the above-mentioned researchers did not provide a global picture on the mastery of the linguistic constraints of several sociolinguistic variables by their learners and thus we cannot tell if their findings are exceptional or indicative of a general trend. Second, few of the studies that examined the mastery of linguistic constraints by different groups of FL2 learners focused on the same sociolinguistic variables. The only variable that was investigated by more than two studies (including one carried out by us) is /l/ non-use in subject pronoun *ils*. In all three studies the FL2 learners displayed the same phonetic constraints observed in FL1 speech. Obviously, more comparative research focused on the same sociolinguistic variables and different groups of FL2 learners is needed before one can arrive at solid generalizations on this particular aspect of the sociolinguistic competence of FL2 learners.

Stylistic constraints

The effect of level of (in)formality on sociolinguistic variation has been the object of only limited research in FL1 speech. As such, there are few FL1 studies available to use as benchmarks. In our research, as Table 4.21 shows, we have focused on the non-use of *ne*, schwa and /l/ (for further details on the learning of such constraints, the reader is also referred to Tables D1, D8, D17 and D19 in Appendix D that present the results of the GoldVarb regression analyses of variation). The immersion students do not display significantly different patterns of *ne* use when speaking about formal topics compared to informal ones (74% versus 70%, respectively) (see Rehner & Mougeon, 1999). Our study of /l/ non-use in pronouns *il(s)* has arrived at a similar result. We found that the French immersion students maintain this phoneme as frequently during the interview as in the reading passages (98% versus 99%; see Nadasdi et al., 2001). As for phoneme schwa, we found that the French immersion students delete this vowel somewhat less often during the reading passages (4%) than during the interview (15%) and hence seem to display incipient learning of the style constraint (see Uritescu et al., 2002). However, when we examined the frequency of schwa non-use as a function of topic formality, we found

Table 4.21 Effect of stylistic parameters in the speech of French immersion students and L1 speakers of French

	Linguistic variables												
	Ne	seulement	donc	aller + inf. (1sg.)	Future (all pers.)	nous	Third plural verb forms	Auxiliary	chez 1, chez 3	emploi habiter	auto	schwa	/l/
Effect of formality (L1 speakers)	Formal topics > ne use?[a]	?	?	?	Formal topics > inflected future	Formal topics > nous	?	?	?	?	?	Reading passage > use	?
Effect of formality (French immersion students)	No	?	?	?	?	Formal topics > nous	?	?	?	?	?	Reading passage slightly > use[b]	No

> = favorable to; ? = the effect of this parameter was not examined.
[a] Previous research on the significance of this factor are inconsistent (see the section 'Use/non-use of the negative particle ne').
[b] Two measures of formality were used, one associated with topics and another reflecting the differences between interviews and reading passages. On the measure associated with topics, the French immersion students did not display differential levels of schwa use according to (in)formality.

that the French immersion students did not display significantly different patterns of sociolinguistic variation (formal topics 22% versus informal topics 19%; see Uritescu *et al.*, 2004).

In sum, our somewhat limited study of the effect of level of (in)formality on sociolinguistic variation in the speech of the French immersion students suggests that they have only a minimal mastery of stylistic constraints. Past research on the effect of (in)formality on sociolinguistic variation in the speech of FL2 learners in an education setting found that such learners observed certain stylistic constraints on sociolinguistic variation and that opportunities to interact with FL1 speakers outside the educational setting had a positive effect on the mastery of such constraints (Kinginger, 2008; Regan, 1996; Regan *et al.*, 2009; Sax, 2003; Thomas, 2000, 2002a, 2002b). In contrast, when opportunities to interact with FL1 speakers are lacking, however, previous research (Dewaele, 2002, 2004c; Lyster, 1994a; Swain & Lapkin, 1990) has found that learners' mastery of the stylistic constraints of variation is quite limited.

Further, we pointed out earlier that research on the acquisition of the stylistic constraints of variation by learners of languages other than French (e.g. Adamson & Regan, 1991; Barron, 2003; Major, 2004; Marriott, 1995) suggests that extensive contact with native speakers of the target language in naturalistic settings does not guarantee that L2 speakers' mastery of such constraints will necessarily be close to or on a par with native norms. This leads us to hypothesize that future research on the mastery of stylistic variation by FL2 learners who lack opportunities to interact with FL1 speakers outside the educational setting will confirm that this particular aspect of sociolinguistic variation is especially difficult to learn.

Effect of Independent Variables on the Learning of Sociolinguistic Variation

In addition to measuring the frequency with which the French immersion students use specific variants, our research has also examined the effect of independent variables on such frequency: (1) the French immersion students' sex and social class, (2) the French immersion students' exposure to French outside the school and (3) the language(s) they speak at home. The results of this examination appear in Table 4.22 (for further details on the learning of such constraints, the reader is also referred to Tables D1–4, D6, D8, D10, D12–15, D18 and D21 in Appendix D that present the results of the GoldVarb regression analyses of variation).

Sex and social class

As regards the variable of sex, Table 4.22 shows that, as we had expected, the female French immersion students use hyper-formal and formal

Table 4.22 Effect of independent variables on variant choice in the speech of the French immersion students

	Linguistic variables												
	ne	seulement	donc	aller + inf. (1sg.)	future (all pers.)	nous	Third plural verb forms	Auxiliary	chez 1[a]	emploi	habiter	auto	Schwa /l/
Effect of sex and/or social class	Middle class > ne use	Female > seulement	Male, middle class > donc	No	Female > inflected future	Female and middle class > nous	No	Middle class > être	No	No	No	No	?
Effect of increased exposure to French outside the school	> Non-use of ne	> juste	> donc	< je vas	> aller + infinitive; < non-native forms	> on	> Third plural verb forms	No	> chez; < non-native forms	No	No	No	> Non-use of schwa
Effect of home language	Romance language > ne use	Romance language > seulement; English > juste	Romance language > alors	?	No	Romance language > nous	?	No	No	Romance language > travail		Romance language > auto	?

> = favorable to; < = unfavorable to; ? = the effect of this parameter was not examined.
[a]Due to a low number of tokens for chez 3, it was not possible to run a GoldVarb.

variants more often than do male students: (1) *seulement* (Rehner & Mougeon, 2003); (2) inflected future (Nadasdi *et al.*, 2003); and (3) *nous* (Mougeon & Rehner, 2001). At first blush, this finding might be looked upon as only a modest confirmation of our initial hypothesis; however, it should be borne in mind that in the case of four of the six variables where no effect of sex was found, all the variants used by the students are part of Standard French (namely, *chez* 1, *chez* 3, *habiter* and *auto*) and hence one would not expect to find the hypothesized effect of sex. Furthermore, there are two sociolinguistic variables for which we did not examine the effect of speakers' sex. Thus, in the final analysis, our finding of the expected effect of learners' sex is supported by our results.

The reader will recall that other than our research, several studies examined the learning of sex-based constraints on variation by FL2 learners who had significant opportunities to interact with FL1 speakers in naturalistic settings and that nearly all of these studies found that such learners had acquired the sex-based constraints (e.g. Blondeau & Nagy, 1998; Regan *et al.*, 2009). Further, research that focused on languages other than French arrived at similar findings (e.g. Adamson & Regan, 1991; Major, 2004). To explain their finding these authors hypothesized that the L2 learners had internalized the sex effects on variation due to extensive interactions with native speakers of the target language. We cannot invoke this explanation in relation to the immersion students examined in our research, since their contacts with FL1 speakers are quite limited. Rather, we hypothesize that the explanation for our own finding of the expected correlation with learners' sex may lie in the classroom discourse of French immersion teachers or in the course materials that they use for the teaching of French Language Arts. This hypothesis receives support from the findings that the French immersion teachers use *seulement* 79% of the time and *nous* 71% (see Table 4.12).[56] As for the materials, they use *nous* close to 70% of the time and the inflected future 83% of the time. In other words, the strong preference evidenced by immersion teachers and the authors of teaching materials for the three formal variants mentioned above may lead the female students to use such variants more often than the male students, just as in research on sociolinguistic variation in L1 speech, female speakers have often been found to prefer standard variants over their non-standard counterparts (Labov, 1990).

That said, we need to explain why, in relation to hyper-formal variant *donc*, we found the opposite correlation with learners' sex, namely, male students use it more often than female students. One explanation for this contradictory pattern may lie in the fact that the French immersion students cannot properly infer the sociostylistic value of *donc* due to the paucity of their exposure to these forms both in the teachers' classroom speech and in the pedagogical materials. Specifically, in the educational input of the students we found a total of 113 tokens of the variants expressing the notion of consequence, as opposed, for instance, to over 1000 tokens of the variants expressing the future (all persons). Another explanation for the French immersion students' contradictory patterns of sex may lie in the fact that the frequency of variant use found in the teachers' classroom speech and in the pedagogical materials contradicts each other, namely the teachers favor *alors*, while the materials favor *donc* and, if this was not confusing enough; in the teaching materials *donc* is much more frequent than *alors* in the dialogues whereas in the texts *alors* is much more frequent than *donc* (see Table 4.12).

In sum, the results of our research and those of other studies that examined the learning of the sex-based constraints of variation suggest that, overall, L2 learners are successful in their acquisition of such constraints. This may reflect the fact that gender-based constraints are easier to learn than the multifaceted stylistic constraints of variation discussed above.

Turning now to the variable of social class, Table 4.22 shows that the expected effect was found for negative particle *ne* (Rehner & Mougeon, 1999), subject pronoun *nous* and auxiliary *être* (Knaus & Nadasdi, 2001). As has been shown by research on sociolinguistic variation in L1 speech, the variable of social class and sex often go hand in hand (i.e. when one finds the effect of social class, it is usually the case that speaker sex is also associated with variation). This is precisely what we found for the variant *nous*. It is true that in the case of auxiliary *être* and negative particle *ne* only the expected social class effect was found. Still this finding reinforces the notion that the basic social characteristics of FL2 learners (i.e. sex and social class) can have an influence on the learning of variants that involve a contrast between standard versus non-standard usage, since the examination of these two variables has confirmed their expected effect for 5 out of the 10 variables where such a contrast obtains. However, when such a contrast does not obtain, as in the case of sex, social class does not correlate with variant choice.

To explain our finding of the expected effect of social class, we can invoke the same factor that we discussed in the preceding section, namely the use of variants in the educational input of the students. Specifically, it is noteworthy that auxiliary *être* is used 90% of the time by the teachers and categorically in the teaching materials, and that *ne* is used 71% of the time by the teachers and almost categorically in the teaching materials. Further, it can be pointed out that the materials consider ellipsis of particle *ne* as a mistake, and present it as such to the students and teachers. Thus, we would like to hypothesize that the strong normative preference for the above-mentioned variants displayed by the teachers and the authors of teaching materials leads the students to infer that such variants are part of correct usage, and hence the fact that those students who hail from the middle class show a tendency to prefer these variants.[57]

As we pointed out in the review of the literature, no other research has examined the effect of social class on the learning of sociolinguistic variation by FL2 learners in an educational setting. Thus, it is hoped that further research will continue the investigation of what has up to now remained a relatively under-researched topic.

Exposure to French outside the school

In relation to the influence of exposure to French outside the school, we expected that an increase in such exposure would be associated with the French immersion students' increased use of mildly marked or marked informal variants. We have used three measures of the French immersion students' exposure to French outside the school: (1) use of spoken French media, (2) stays with Francophone families and (3) stays in a Francophone environment. The effects of these three measures were assessed separately in the GoldVarb analysis (cf. Appendix D), but are represented in Table 4.22 under the general heading of exposure to French outside the school. Thus, when an association with this factor is reported in Table 4.22, it may mean that any or all of these separate measures is/are at play.

As Table 4.22 shows, increased exposure to French outside the school was found to favor the following mildly marked informal variants: *ne* non-use (Rehner & Mougeon, 1999), *juste* (Mougeon & Rehner, 2001), *on* (Rehner *et al.*, 2003) and schwa non-use (Uritescu *et al.*, 2002, 2004). These four variants are used frequently in FL1 speech (see Table 4.15). It is therefore understandable that those French immersion students who have had the highest levels of contact with these speakers would use these variants most often. The only remaining mildly marked informal variant not associated in the French immersion students' speech with increased exposure to French outside the school is *je vas*, a frequent variant in FL1 speech. In fact, we found an inverse correlation between this factor and the use of *je vas*, with the highest levels of exposure to French outside the school being associated with nil use of this variant. We have pointed out earlier that the form *je vas* has been reported in the speech of students in the early stages of SLA, including early French immersion students (Harley, 1982, 1992). Thus, the presence of this form in the speech of the current French immersion students is likely a remnant of this developmental stage. What is interesting, however, is that increased exposure to French outside the school setting where *je vas* is frequent does not lead to the persistence of this form, or even the increased use of it. One possible explanation for this may be that the difference between *je vas* and *je vais* is not phonetically salient enough for the French immersion students to become aware of the frequent use of *je vas* by FL1 speakers and, hence, increased exposure does not promote its learning.

Thus, in general, our hypothesis concerning the effect of increased exposure on mildly marked informal variants is supported. However, this is not the case for marked informal variants, as we had originally anticipated, since, as we have seen, these variants are almost entirely absent from the French immersion students' speech. This likely reflects the fact that the exposure to French outside the school is simply not great enough to bring about the learning of marked informal features that are not present in their educational input. Note also that for forms that coincide with marked informal variants (such as use of auxiliary *avoir* for auxiliary *être*), increased exposure to French outside the school setting does not lead to increased use of these forms on the part of the French immersion students who display the highest levels of such exposure.

Interestingly, in examining the effect of increased exposure to French outside the school, we discovered that this independent variable also has an effect on the French immersion students' use of certain formal variants. For instance, a favorable effect of this independent variable has been found for their use of *donc*. This variant is marginal and highly formal in L1 Quebec French. Hence, this association may appear, at first sight, difficult to explain. However, if we assume that the French immersion students with the highest levels of exposure to French outside the school also have higher levels of French language proficiency, then their greater use of *donc* could be an indication of a more expanded lexicon.

Further, we found that increased exposure to French outside the school was also associated with more frequent use of *chez* 1 and the use of distinctive third person plural verb forms and concomitant less frequent use of non-native alternatives to *chez* 1 and the use of regularized third person 'singular' verb forms. The reader will recall that both *chez* 1 and the third person plural distinctive verb forms are difficult for the French immersion students to learn. Therefore, it makes sense that French immersion students with greater exposure to French outside the school, and presumably greater proficiency, would be better able to master this highly specialized preposition and these irregular verb forms. Further, it should be borne in mind that the non-standard use of third person singular verb forms instead of irregular third person verb forms is quite infrequent in FL1 speech. Thus it is likely that the immersion students who have had contacts with FL1 speakers have been only marginally (if at all) exposed to such non-standard forms. In other words, exposure to FL1 speech would have provided students with additional opportunities to hear the third plural verb forms, and not the other way around.

We also found that increased use of the periphrastic future was associated with higher levels of exposure to French outside the school. Given that the periphrastic future is frequently used by French immersion teachers, it makes sense that students with increased exposure to FL1 speech, which also features frequent use of this variant, would display the highest rates of use of this variant.

In sum, our research has indicated that as one moves up the scale of exposure to French outside the classroom setting, there is an effect on sociolinguistic variation. This effect translates into a greater use of mildly marked informal variants, of native (as opposed to non-native) and even of certain formal variants.

Our finding of a positive effect on the learning of mildly marked informal variants exerted by exposure to French outside the FL2 classroom context reinforces the findings of many studies that documented this same pattern (e.g. the works of Dewaele, 1992, 2004b; Dewaele & Regan, 2002; Lapkin et al., 1995; Nagy et al., 1996; Regan, 1996, 2005; Regan et al., 2009; Sax, 2003; Thomas, 2000, 2002a, 2002b). While our research has found that the limited exposure to L1 French outside the educational setting experienced by several of the immersion students does not result in their learning marked informal variants, other studies focused on French or on other languages have found that such learning will occur when L2 learners have extensive interactions with L1 speakers (e.g. Bayley, 1996; Blondeau & Nagy, 1998; Dewaele & Regan, 2001; Major, 2004; Nagy et al., 2003; Sankoff, 1997; Sankoff et al., 1997).

The finding that increased exposure to FL1 speech brings about a decrease in the use of non-native forms coexisting with native variants is an original contribution of our research since previous work did not document such a correlation. This may reflect in part the fact that the FL2 learners examined in previous research were for the most part more advanced than the learners in our own research. But it also likely reflects the fact that non-native usages were not considered in previous research.

Influence of the students' L1s

As Table 4.22 shows, our research has confirmed the influence of English or Italian and Spanish on the learning of sociolinguistic variation in five cases where we expected to find such an influence, namely, *ne* use versus *ne* non-use (Rehner & Mougeon, 1999), *seulement* versus *juste* (Mougeon & Rehner, 2001), *donc* versus *alors* (Rehner & Mougeon, 2003), *on* versus *nous* (Rehner et al., 2003) and *travail* versus *emploi* versus *job* (Nadasdi & McKinnie, 2003).

More specifically, we found that the students who speak Spanish or Italian at home use much more frequently the negative particle *ne*, *seulement*, *alors*, *nous*, *travail* and *auto* than do the rest of the students. These results reflect the following facts. In these two languages, the pre-verbal negative particle *non* is never deleted; the notion of restriction is expressed with adverb *solamente*; consequence is commonly expressed via *allora*; first person singular is expressed via only one pronoun, namely *noi* or *nosotros*; the notion of 'paid work' can be expressed by the words *travaglio* or *trabajo*;[58] and the notion of 'automobile' can be conveyed by forms in Italian and Spanish that are closely related to variant *auto*, namely *auto* for both languages and *automobile*, and *automóvil* respectively for Italian and Spanish. Thus, it can be assumed that the presence of these closely related counterparts in Italian and Spanish leads the students who speak these languages at home to favor the corresponding French expressions.

As for the influence of English, this was evidenced by our findings related to *juste*, a variant that is similar to the English restrictive adverb *just*. As can be seen in Table 4.22, the French immersion students, in fact, make more frequent use of *juste* than do the FL1 speakers, despite the fact that their teachers have in all likelihood rarely used this variant (see Table 4.4). Further, we also found that those French immersion students who speak only English at home exhibit the highest levels of *juste* use (Mougeon & Rehner, 2001 and Table D2 in Appendix).

These results suggest that L1 transfer can play an important role in the learning of sociolinguistic variation, in the same way that it has been shown to influence the learning of invariant usages (Gass & Selinker, 2001; Harley, 1992, 1989a). Still, one should not lose sight of the fact that, as Table 4.22 shows, there were four sociolinguistic variables where the relationship between the home language and French is not as straightforward as those we have seen above. For instance, in the case of the simple future, both Italian and Spanish have inflected and periphrastic futures. It should be pointed out that the periphrastic futures are available in certain Italian dialects and, notably, in those spoken in the Southern regions from where the French immersion students' parents are likely to have come.[59] In the case of auxiliary *avoir* versus *être*, both Italian and Spanish have a simple past that, unlike its French counterpart, is still very much alive in current speech. Further, when speakers of these languages use 'perfect' tenses, the auxiliary *avoir* is either the only option, as in Spanish, or the more common option, as in the dialects of Southern Italy. As for *habiter* and its variants, Italian, which is the language spoken by most of the French immersion students from Romance-speaking homes, uses both *abitàre* and *vivere*. Finally, in the case of *chez*, there are two options in Italian, namely preposition *da* and the analytic locution *a casa, in/en casa*.

What seems to be happening in these four sociolinguistic variables is that the presence of more than one option in the home language that either maps directly onto the options available in French or that are at variance with the French variants is diluting the effect of L1 transfer on the Romance-speaking French immersion students' patterns of sociolinguistic variation.

In summary, our research has found that, when the French immersion students' home language possesses a variant that has a morphophonetically and semantically equivalent counterpart in French, the French immersion students' spoken French features more frequently use of the French variant in question, in accordance with the students' home language background. Similar findings have been arrived at for FL2 learners in an educational setting by Dewaele (1999), Rehner (2004) and Trévise and Noyau (1984), and even for FL2 learners, or L2 learners of other languages, outside of educational settings (Barron, 2003; Blondeau *et al.*, 1995, 2002; Sankoff, 1997). That said, in our research we have also highlighted the fact that when there are several competing variants with counterparts in the students' home language, the influence of L1 transfer is much less obvious.

Chapter 5
The Potential Benefits of Increased FL1 Input in an Educational Context

Introduction

As was pointed out by Tarone and Swain (1995) and Lyster (2007), immersion students use their L2 mostly in the context of the immersion classroom and hence have very limited opportunities to be exposed to L1 speakers of the target language. These authors surmised that, were it otherwise, immersion students would be in a better position to learn informal features of the target language, a desirable outcome according to some of the immersion students they interviewed. To this we can add that such exposure might also have the concomitant benefit of reducing the percentage of formal and hyper-formal variants in the immersion students' speech to levels that approach those found in the taped speech of L1 speakers. Tarone and Swain's findings echo those of Hart *et al.* (1989), who found that French immersion students have the desire to speak like same-aged FL1 speakers, those of MacFarlane and Wesche (1995), who found that French immersion students are of the opinion that French immersion programs could do more to promote contacts with FL1 speakers both within and outside such programs and those of Auger (2002) to whom graduates of French immersion programs expressed frustration at not being able to use their French in real-life settings.

In several countries around the world (e.g. Australia, the USA), immersion programs have been specifically designed to foster contacts between L1 and L2 speakers. For instance, two-way immersion programs in the USA (Lindholm-Leary, 2001; Rhodes *et al.*, 1997) admit students from linguistic minorities who speak as an L1 the language used as a medium of instruction, as well as students who speak this language as an L2. Such programs would be an ideal setting where one could test the hypothesis that increased exposure to L1 speakers in the educational environment would have a beneficial effect on the sociolinguistic competence of immersion students. However, no such research has yet been carried out on students enrolled in two-way immersion programs, or for that matter in immersion programs outside of Canada.

We cannot turn to Canadian French immersion programs to assess this hypothesized beneficial effect, since Canada does not currently have two-way French immersion programs and the regular French immersion programs do not include sufficiently high proportions of FL1 students, primarily because they generally exercise their right to enroll in French-medium schools. This is the case, for instance, in the school district where our corpus of French immersion students' speech was gathered. FL1 students are primarily enrolled in the local French medium schools and, hence, only a limited number of FL1 students enroll in the French immersion programs. Recall that we found these programs to include only 12% of students who speak French at home at least half of the time.

However, we can turn to Ontario's French language schools, which constitute an interesting setting that provides the kind of evidence we seek. Specifically, these schools include, on the one hand, students who are not unlike the French immersion students in that they use French almost exclusively in a classroom setting (i.e. restricted speakers of Ontario French) and, on the other hand, unrestricted speakers of Ontario French who use French at school, at home and in the community on a regular basis. These latter students are proficient in the formal, informal and marked informal registers of French (see Mougeon & Beniak, 1991, for further information on these schools and their students). Thus, Ontario's French language schools and their students allow us to take the first step in verifying the yet untested hypothesis that exposure to FL1 speakers in an educational context is beneficial to the acquisition of sociolinguistic competence by students who are highly restricted in their use of this language. In addition to exposure to the speech of unrestricted schoolmates, other factors promote greater in-school exposure to FL1 speech on the part of restricted speakers. Ontario's French language schools constitute full-fledged French-medium establishments where the entire ambiance is French (e.g. all the subjects are taught in French, the school staff are French-speaking and most of the teachers are FL1 speakers). This opens up the possibility that such French-medium schools would have a beneficial effect on the (socio)linguistic development of students who are restricted in their use of French. This possibility is of potential interest to those who organize and administer not only Canada's French immersion programs, but also other types of immersion programs in other countries. While the influence of same-aged peer exposure and that of the use of French by teachers and staff in the school cannot be easily disentangled, the importance of the comparative research contained in this chapter should not be underestimated as it paves the way for future studies on this topic.

In summary, there are several important differences between the educational environment of the French immersion students and that of the restricted speakers of French, since only the latter (1) have extensive opportunities to interact with same-aged Francophones at school; (2) study all school subjects in French; (3) interact exclusively in French with their instructors; and (4) study in an environment where French is the dominant school language outside the classroom (i.e. in the hallways and in interactions with all school staff).[60] One further potential difference between the educational input of the immersion students and restricted speakers could be the variety of French spoken by the teachers themselves. For example, it is possible that in their interactions with students, teachers in French-medium schools make greater use of mildly marked informal variants than do teachers in French immersion programs. If this is the case, it could perhaps be attributed to the fact that French is used in all school-related activities and that the teachers assume a certain familiarity with such variants on the part of students. In order to gain insight into the variants use by teachers in French-medium schools, we will present data from a preliminary corpus of 12 teachers from a French-medium high school in Cornwall, Ontario, gathered in 2005. This community is one of four where we have twice gathered corpora of Franco-Ontarian students' speech (1978, 2005).

To test the hypothesis that increased exposure to L1 in an educational environment would improve immersion students' sociolinguistic competence, we will undertake in this chapter a comparison of the sociolinguistic competence of three categories of speakers: (1) unrestricted speakers of Ontario French; (2) restricted speakers of Ontario French; and (3) French immersion students. The data on the speech of the Franco-Ontarian students come from the 1978 corpus collected in four Franco-Ontarian communities (see Chapter 2) and the data on the speech of the French immersion students are that used throughout this present volume. Should this comparison reveal that the restricted speakers are much more closely aligned with the unrestricted speakers than with the French immersion students, it will be possible to make two inferences. Firstly, we could infer that intensive exposure to FL1 French in a school setting has had a beneficial effect on the sociolinguistic competence of the restricted Franco-Ontarian students. Secondly, we could infer that, were the French immersion students to have greater exposure to FL1 speakers in a school setting, their sociolinguistic competence, too, would benefit from such exposure. It should be noted that we are by no means suggesting that mere exposure to the speech of L1 peers in an educational settings is the only factor that will improve students' sociolinguistic competence. As noted in the previous chapters, immersion students also need to be provided with explicit feedback concerning the appropriateness of their use of variants and opportunities to engage in activities designed to improve their receptive knowledge and productive use of sociolinguistic variants (cf. Lyster, 2007).

Our three-way comparison of the speech of the unrestricted speakers of Ontario French, the restricted speakers of Ontario French and the French immersion students will focus on the sociolinguistic variables discussed in Chapters 3 and 4. More specifically, it will examine the use of mildly marked and marked informal variants since, as we have seen, such variants are either lacking or highly infrequent in the immersion students' speech. We will also examine formal and hyper-formal variants since the immersion students use such forms much more frequently than do FL1 speakers. Note that we will not consider neutral variants since, overall, the differences between the immersion students' and FL1 speakers' use of such variants are less problematic than is the case for the other four kinds of variants (cf. Nadasdi *et al.*, 2004). Finally, we will examine the mastery of stylistic constraints on sociolinguistic variation by all three speaker groups.

Effects of Increased Exposure to FL1 Speakers in an Educational Context

In order to consider the potential effects of FL1 speakers on the immersion students' speech, we will consider variants examined in Chapter 4.[61] These potential effects will be categorized as to whether they are beneficial (i.e. the immersion students' sociolinguistic competence is brought more in line with that of FL1 speakers) or detrimental (i.e. the immersion students' sociolinguistic competence is moved further away from that of FL1 speakers).

Beneficial effects

Mildly marked informal variants

Our three-way comparison of the use of mildly marked informal variants (see Table 5.1) suggests that interaction with FL1 speakers would result in the French immersion students making greater use of the following variants: (1) *ne* non-use; (2) *je vas*; (3) *on*; (4) schwa non-use; and (5) /l/ non-use.

As can be seen in Table 5.1, the Franco-Ontarian restricted students' frequency of use of mildly marked informal variants is, by and large, only slightly lower than that of their unrestricted counterparts and markedly higher than that of the French immersion students. The marginal difference between the restricted and unrestricted students' frequency of use of mildly marked informal variants likely reflects the fact that the unrestricted students present in the French-medium schools use these forms extensively and, hence, provide ample opportunities for the restricted students to be exposed to these forms.

Table 5.1 Mildly marked informal variants for which beneficial effects are likely to obtain

Variants	Unrestricted students	Restricted students	French immersion students
ne non-use	99.6	97.3	28
je vas	64	60	10
on	99	99	56
Schwa non-use	68	57	15
/l/ non-use (in subject pronouns)	96.4	87.9	2

As mildly marked informal variants, the five forms in question are also likely to be used by other individuals in the French-medium schools (e.g. the teachers and the support staff). Preliminary analysis of the Cornwall teachers' corpus supports such a claim. For example, these teachers use informal *je vas* more frequently than *je vais* (55% versus 45%) in the classroom.

The marked difference between the restricted students' and the French immersion students' frequency of use of mildly marked informal variants likely reflects the fact that the French immersion students have not had this same type of exposure (with perhaps the exception of *on* use). As we have seen, there are few same-aged Francophone students in the French immersion programs under study. Further, we have seen that these mildly marked informal variants are not frequent in the French immersion teachers' in-class speech or in the French Language Arts materials. Taken together, these two findings on the learning of mildly marked informal variants provide the first indication that if the French immersion students were to have greater exposure to unrestricted FL1 French in a school setting, there would be a beneficial effect on their sociolinguistic competence.

Marked informal variants

Let us turn now to the marked informal variants to see if we can document a similar effect. These variants are particularly interesting because they are less likely to be heard in the formal context of the school than are the mildly marked informal variants discussed above, although, as we have seen, these marked informal variants are not marginal in spoken Quebec French (see Table 5.2).

A comparison of the use of marked informal variants in the three populations (see Table 5.2) suggests that the French immersion students would benefit from greater interaction in the case of the following marked

Table 5.2 Marked informal variants for which beneficial effects are likely to obtain

Variants	Unrestricted students	Restricted students	French immersion students
nous-autres on	7	3	0
m'as	30	27	0
rester	62	21	0
rien que	18	6	0
(ça) fait que	70	5	0
su'	28	9	0
char	26	15	0

informal variants: (1) *nous-autres on*; (2) *m'as*; (3) *rester*; (4) *rien que*; (5) *(ça) fait que*; (6) *su'*; and (7) *char*. All of these variants are found in the speech of both the restricted and unrestricted students, but are never used by the French immersion students. It is true that they are used less frequently by the restricted students than by the unrestricted ones. However, the restricted students are clearly aware of these forms and are able to produce them.

One explanation for these findings is that these variants are not reinforced by intra- or inter-systemic processes that would promote their use in the French of the restricted and French immersion students. Another likely explanation is that these variants are more sociostylistically marked than the mildly marked informal variants and, hence, are, by and large, more likely to be under-used in the school setting. This is likely to be true not only for the unrestricted students, but also for the teachers and other school staff. As far as the teachers are concerned, it is interesting that such under-use does not seem to lead to categorical avoidance, since in the Cornwall teachers' corpus we found examples of the following marked informal variants: *char*, *(ça) fait que*, *rien que* and *rester*. Concerning the unrestricted students, it should be borne in mind that the frequency results in Table 5.2 reflect the use of these marked informal variants during sociolinguistic interviews specifically designed to tap the students' formal and informal registers. Consequently, in the formal setting of the school, the unrestricted students' use of these marked informal variants is likely to be less frequent than that noted in Table 5.2. One final point is the startlingly large gap between the restricted and unrestricted students' use of *(ça) fait que* (a difference of 93%). This gap can be attributed, in part, to the fact that *(ça) fait que* happens to be in competition with another marked informal variant, namely *so*, which, as we have seen in previous chapters, is reinforced by inter-systemic transfer from English.[62]

Table 5.3 Formal variants for which beneficial effects are likely to obtain

Variants	Unrestricted students	Restricted students	French immersion students
je vais	6	13	90
seulement	16	14	46
être	67	54	78
demeurer	18	37	0
schwa use	32	43	85

As the above findings show, as far as marked informal variants are concerned, overall the French immersion students would benefit from greater exposure to FL1 speakers in a school setting. However, the degree of this beneficial effect would depend on the markedness of the specific marked informal variants.

Formal variants

Table 5.3 reveals that there are four formal variants (i.e. *je vais, seulement*, auxiliary *être* and schwa use) used more or less frequently by both the unrestricted and restricted students, but which are used by the immersion students at frequencies that surpass these levels. It is therefore likely that greater contact with FL1 speakers in an educational setting would result in the immersion students using these forms at a rate more in line with FL1 usage. Interestingly, the comparison of formal variants also reveals that there is one variant, namely the verb *demeurer* (meaning 'live'), used by the restricted and unrestricted students that is absent from the immersion students' repertoire. This finding suggests that greater contact with FL1 speakers in an educational setting may not only bring about a decrease in the frequency of formal variants on the part of immersion students, but also a widening of the range of variants used by such students reflected in the learning of certain formal variants that are not part of their repertoire.

Hyper-formal variants

Our comparison of the use of hyper-formal variants appears in Table 5.4. The results show clearly that, like the unrestricted students, the restricted students make only marginal use of the following hyper-formal variants: *ne, donc, nous, habiter, voiture* and /l/.[63] This finding contrasts sharply with what is found in the speech of the immersion students who use such variants considerably more frequently. We can therefore infer from these results that greater exposure to FL1 speakers in a school setting would result in the immersion students making significantly less frequent use of these hyper-formal variants.

Table 5.4 Hyper-formal variants for which beneficial effects are likely to obtain

Variants	Unrestricted students	Restricted students	French immersion students
ne use	1	3	70
donc	2	7	15
nous	2	1	45
habiter	3	0	60
voiture	7	1	21
/l/ use [in subject pronouns *il(s)*]	2	9	98

Style constraints

Only limited data exist concerning style constraints on variation in the speech of the unrestricted, restricted and French immersion students. These data pertain to phonetic variation, namely variable non-use of /l/ in subject pronouns *il(s)* and variable schwa non-use. The results of the three-way comparison for these two sociolinguistic variables are displayed in Figures 5.1 and 5.2. As can be seen, the restricted students, for both /l/ and schwa non-use, display a marked contrast between their rates of non-use in the interview and the reading passage and they do so to a degree that is not that far from the unrestricted students' norm. In contrast, the French immersion students almost never delete /l/ in subject pronouns *il(s)*, both in the interview and in the reading passage, and, hence, they are

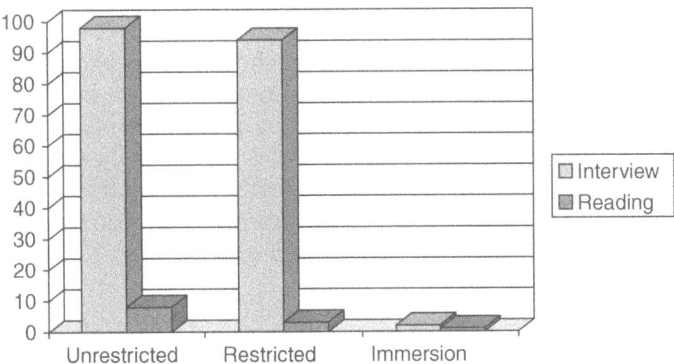

Figure 5.1 Rates of /l/ non-use (%) in interviews versus reading passages by unrestricted speakers, restricted speakers and French immersion students

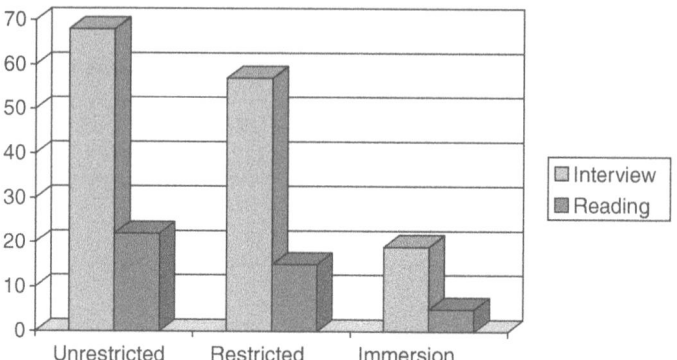

Figure 5.2 Rates of schwa non-use (%) in interviews versus reading passages by unrestricted speakers, restricted speakers and French immersion students

considerably below the unrestricted students' norm in relation to this sociolinguistic variable. However, the French immersion students do evidence a stylistic contrast between the interview and the reading passage in relation to schwa non-use, although this contrast is not as pronounced as that displayed by the unrestricted students, since the French immersion students' non-use of schwa in the more informal context of the interview is even less frequent than the non-use of schwa by the unrestricted students in the more formal context of the reading passage.

In sum, as far as stylistic constraints on variation are concerned, these preliminary results suggest that increased exposure to FL1 speech in a school setting would be of great benefit to the French immersion students.

Negative effects

In this section we will discuss variants where it is less likely that greater exposure to FL1 speakers would result in more native-like patterns of sociolinguistic variation on the part of the French immersion students. These variants fall into two general categories: (1) cases where the restricted students use a variant much more frequently than do their unrestricted counterparts and (2) cases where the restricted speakers do not use a given variant. These results are presented in Table 5.5.

Mildly marked informal variants

As Table 5.5 shows, there is one mildly marked informal variant where the French immersion students are unlikely to benefit from greater exposure to FL1 speakers, namely *juste*, since the restricted students use this adverb more often than do their unrestricted counterparts. Furthermore, the French immersion students use *juste* at a level of frequency that

Table 5.5 Variants for which negative effects are likely to obtain

Variants	Unrestricted students	Restricted students	French immersion students
Mildly marked informal			
juste	66	80	54
Marked informal			
avoir	33	46	22
so	8	19	7
job	5	30	6
ouvrage	12	0	0
Singular verbs	2	19	19
Formal			
automobile	12	0	5
alors	21	70	78
emploi	60	32	38

approaches that of the unrestricted students. The high frequency of *juste* in both the restricted students' and the French immersion students' spoken French is likely the result of a process of inter-systemic transfer from English (see Chapter 4). Therefore, if the students had greater interaction with FL1 speakers in the school setting, it is likely that their use of *juste* would surpass that of FL1 speakers.

Marked informal variants

As Table 5.5 shows, there are four marked informal variants that the restricted students use more often than do their unrestricted counterparts, namely auxiliary *avoir*, *job*, *so* and 'singular' verb forms. Furthermore, for three of these variants (i.e. auxiliary *avoir*, *job* and *so*), the French immersion students' frequency use of these variants is similar to that of the unrestricted students, and in the case of 'singular' verb forms is considerably higher and on a par with the restricted students. One possible explanation for these patterns has been discussed in the previous chapter, namely that in the speech of the French immersion students these variants are the result of either transfer from English or a process of intra-systemic regularization, and not necessarily the result of exposure to marked informal French. This explanation holds, to some degree as well, for the restricted students and this may account for why they use these marked informal variants more frequently than do their unrestricted counterparts. Hence, it can be safely inferred that greater exposure to FL1 speech in a school setting would cause the French immersion students to surpass native norms. What is of equal interest is that the French immersion students likely do not realize that these forms that they use spontaneously carry currency in native speech as marked informal variants. This is clearly something about which the French immersion students should be made aware of.

In the case of *ouvrage*, the restricted students never use this variant. In addition, this variant is also absent from the Cornwall teacher corpus we examined. One likely reason for these findings is that the sociolinguistic variable involving *ouvrage* is not frequent and this variant itself is highly infrequent and stylistically marked. Therefore, this greatly diminishes the opportunities for exposure to it within the school setting. In addition, *ouvrage*, like *(ça) fait que*, also competes with another marked informal variant, namely *job*, a variant that, as we have seen, is reinforced to some extent by transfer from English. As such, it is unlikely that greater exposure to FL1 speakers at school would result in the immersion students using *ouvrage*.

Formal variants

Finally, we can see from Table 5.5 that there is one formal variant that the immersion students do not over-use, namely *automobile*. In fact, they under-use this variant in comparison with the unrestricted students. Interestingly, the restricted students do not use this variant, despite potentially hearing it in the speech of their unrestricted classmates. Therefore, in the case of this variant, even if the immersion students had greater exposure to FL1 speakers in a school setting, it is doubtful whether this would lead to an increase in their use of this variant.

Conversely, both the restricted students and the immersion students use the formal variant *alors* at rates far greater than the unrestricted students. Here too, it is unlikely that greater exposure to FL1 speakers in the school would result in a decrease in use of this formal variant. The reverse pattern obtains for variant *emploi* since this form is used in a majority of occurrences by only the unrestricted students. The restricted and immersion students use this variant with similar frequency (32% and 38%, respectively).

Conclusion

The purpose of this chapter has been to gain insight into what the French immersion students' sociolinguistic competence would be like if they had greater exposure to FL1 speakers in a school setting. In order to do so, we have compared the use of mildly marked informal, marked informal, formal and hyper-formal variants in the speech of the French

The Potential Benefits of Increased FL1 Input 151

immersion students, students who are restricted users of Ontario French and students who are unrestricted users of this language variety. Table 5.6 synthesizes the findings of this comparison.

From this synthesis, we can see in Table 5.6 that, for the great majority of variants studied, the French immersion students would benefit from greater exposure to FL1 speakers in a school setting, in that their patterns

Table 5.6 Expected effects on French immersion students' speech of greater interactions with FL1 speakers in a school setting

Variants	Become more like FL1 speech	Surpass FL1 speech	Change would be unlikely
on	×		
ne non-use	×		
schwa non-use	×		
je vas	×		
/l/ non-use (in subject pronouns)	×		
nous-autres on	×		
m'as	×		
rester	×		
rien que	×		
(ça) fait que	×		
su'	×		
char	×		
je vais	×		
seulement	×		
être	×		
demeurer	×		
travail	×		
ne use	×		
donc	×		
nous	×		
habiter	×		
voiture	×		

(*Continued*)

Table 5.6 Continued

Variants	Become more like FL1 speech	Surpass FL1 speech	Change would be unlikely
/l/ use (in subject pronouns)	x		
juste		x	
avoir		x	
job		x	
so		x	
Singular third person plural verb forms			x
ouvrage			x
automobile			x
alors			x
emploi			x

of variant use would be more native-like. Since they would use mildly marked informal variants at rates closer to that of FL1 speakers, they would increase their repertoire of marked informal variants and decrease their use of formal and hyper-formal variants. However, there are also several variants where this general beneficial effect may not obtain, in that the French immersion students may end up becoming less native-like by overusing some of them or experiencing no change in their use of others.

Concerning the likelihood that greater contacts with FL1 speakers would result in the French immersion students' speech being less native-like for some variants, we need to consider characteristics of the variety of FL1 speech that French immersion students would be exposed to. For instance, in relation to *so*, the hypothesis that greater exposure to FL1 speech in a school setting would lead the French immersion students to over-use this variant is predicated on the assumption that they would be exposed to a variety of French that would feature this word as part of the marked informal register, which happens to be the case in Ontario French. However, if the French immersion students were to be exposed to Quebec French, a variety that does not feature the variant *so*, the French immersion students' use of this variant would likely not increase and could, potentially, even decrease.

In a setting like the USA, where two-way immersion programs exist and include local L1 speakers of the target language, these kinds of considerations would be important to bear in mind, since it is likely that certain varieties of Spanish will display some of the features that second language learners of Spanish might use because of transfer from English or processes of simplification. For instance, Lynch (2002) compared the spoken Spanish of second- and third-generation native-Spanish-speaking university students residing in Miami with that of L2 speakers of Spanish. His findings revealed that all three groups of speakers had features in their speech that were different from standard unilingual Spanish and that could be traced either to structural simplification (e.g. blurring of the distinction between *ser* and *estar*, both meaning 'to be', but the former conveying the notion of a permanent state or attribute) or to transfer from English (e.g. use of English discourse markers). Lynch concluded that it was not always possible to differentiate clearly between the L1 and L2 speakers and called for a revisiting of the concept of the native speaker in minority speech communities. These findings suggest that if L2 learners of Spanish in two-way immersion programs were exposed to L1 speakers of Spanish like those examined by Lynch, their tendency to use variants due to the influence of English or structural simplification might be amplified, just as we have seen is the case with the restricted speakers of French in the Franco-Ontarian schools. On the other hand, they would also benefit from being exposed to features of Spanish that are typical of L1 Spanish (e.g. Spanish discourse markers or features of informal Spanish). Regardless of what varieties of the target language the L2 learners are exposed to in a school setting, it would be advisable to examine the speech of both the L1 and L2 speakers of the target language to identify potential aspects of the competence of the L2 speakers that would or would not benefit from such exposure. In addition to such an examination, one might also investigate the possibility of special pedagogical interventions in relation to those aspects of their competence where no beneficial effect is expected.

One potential problem of implementing the suggested integration of L1 and L2 students in immersion programs, is, as Rhodes *et al.* (1997) point out, striking the right balance between the number of L1 and L2 speakers. As our research suggests, the presence of only 12% of FL1 students in the French immersion programs we examined does not seem to have had an obvious beneficial effect on the sociolinguistic competence of the French immersion students, since the latter do not use marked informal variants, under-use mildly marked variants, etc. In other words, a higher proportion of FL1 students would need to be present for such beneficial effects to occur. However, from the perspective of FL1 students, one may also rightfully question whether programs that include a disproportionately high number of L2 learners do not run the risk of doing a disservice to the L1 speakers in those programs insofar as the language maintenance benefit of such programs would be diluted. This risk to L1 speakers in programs bringing together speakers of minority and majority languages has been documented by Hickey (2001) in relation to Irish-medium schools in the Gaeltacht region. According to Rhodes *et al.*, in order to avoid the type of problems focused on by Hickey, an equal ratio of L1 and L2 speakers is needed to 'achieve the full benefits of two-way bilingual education' (Rhodes *et al.*, 1997: 266). This is an important pedagogical matter that needs to be fully investigated.

In summary, our three-way comparison of variant usage by unrestricted/ restricted speakers of Ontario French and same-aged French immersion students suggests that the latter would clearly benefit from increased exposure to L1 speech in school settings that resemble the Franco-Ontarian schools we have investigated, since this would bring their frequency of use of sociolinguistic variants more in line with L1 norms and it would also significantly broaden their range of variants. Having said this, we should remind the reader that such improvements would be all the more likely if increased exposure to L1 speech in a school setting was coupled with a pedagogical approach that specifically focuses on sociolinguistic variation. Indeed, the two-way immersion classroom would be an ideal setting for peer-based collaborative activities designed to raise students' awareness of linguistic variation in the target language and engage in the productive use of sociolinguistic variants (see Lyster, 2007: 77 for a description of such collaborative activities).

Chapter 6
Conclusion

Introduction

As we have pointed out in our review of previous research on the learning of sociolinguistic variation by advanced FL2 learners, most of the studies that examined this topic focused on learners who, while they initially learned French in an educational setting, subsequently had significant opportunities to interact with FL1 speakers outside such a setting. Thus, it is not surprising that these studies have found that, in such circumstances, FL2 learners eventually develop a sociolinguistic repertoire that includes many of the same variants that are used by FL1 speakers, tend to use some of these variants at levels of frequency comparable to those found in FL1 speech and tend to observe the linguistic and extra-linguistic constraints that govern variant choice in FL1 speech. Obviously, these studies have also found that the sociolinguistic competence of these advanced FL2 learners is not entirely the same as that of FL1 speakers, since there are variants that such learners either do not learn or use considerably less often than FL1 speakers (e.g. various informal marked variants). However, one can surmise that with continued opportunities to interact with FL1 speakers, such FL2 learners will eventually make progress in their learning of these less-easily learned variants.

While these studies have certainly underscored the important role of extra-curricular opportunities to interact with FL1 speakers to improve their sociolinguistic competence, one may wonder if they have not had the effect of detracting from the needed investigation of the sociolinguistic competence of FL2 learners who learn the target language almost entirely in an educational context and of the extent to which the educational input of the learners influences the acquisition of such competence. By examining FL2 learners who have learned French in an immersion program and who have had no or only limited interactions with FL1 speakers, and by investigating their educational input, we have, in a sense, shifted the focus of research on the sociolinguistic competence of FL2 learners and brought forward considerable empirical data that advance our understanding of this aspect of SLA in an educational context.[64]

In this final chapter, we will first provide a comprehensive overview of our research on sociolinguistic variation in the educational input of French immersion students and on the sociolinguistic competence of such students. Secondly, we will discuss various aspects of the educational implications of the findings of our research, focusing notably on the curricular measures that could be taken to improve the sociolinguistic competence of immersion students. Finally, we will address issues related to the limitations of our research and to some of the gaps that could be bridged in order to move forward in future research on the learning of sociolinguistic variation by advanced L2 learners in an educational context.

Sociolinguistic Variation in the Educational Input of French Immersion Students

Our investigation of sociolinguistic variation in the educational input of French immersion students is perhaps one of the most original contributions of our research, since, apart from our research, only three studies with a focus on sociolinguistic competence have examined the educational input of FL2 learners. Further, the two studies that examined variation in French Language Arts materials (Auger, 2002; O'Connor Di Vito, 1991) did not undertake a systematic assessment of the frequency of variants in such materials and, more crucially, did not relate their findings to the other major component of the educational input of learners, namely teacher classroom speech. In contrast, Lyster and Rebuffot (2002) were primarily focused on the latter component of the educational input of immersion students. However, while Lyster and Rebuffot's fine-grained approach provided very interesting insights into the complex ways in which teacher–student interactions in the classroom can affect the development of students' sociolinguistic competence, their study was centered on only one sociolinguistic variable.

In our own investigation of the educational context of French immersion students, in order to provide a backdrop for our investigation of 15 sociolinguistic variables in the spoken French of immersion student, we measured the frequency of use of the variants associated with the variables under study in both components of the educational input of students. Further, such measurement was related to data on the frequency of the same variants in FL1 speech. For greater convenience, we have presented together in a single table the findings of our investigation of variant frequency in the educational input of the students, in the spoken French of the students and in FL1 spoken Canadian French (see Table 6.1). Our

Conclusion

Table 6.1 Sociostylistic status of the variants and their frequency (%) in the immersion students' speech and their educational input and in FL1 speech

Variants	Sociostylistic status of variants	FL1 speakers	FLA materials		French immersion teachers	French immersion students	
			Text	Dialogue		Native variants	Non-native usages
ne use	hyper-formal	00.5	100	99	71	70	3 = deletion of *pas*
ne non-use	mildly marked informal	99.5	0	1	29	27	
ne...que	hyper-formal	<1	86	100	5	0	*juste* used to the left of the verb[a]
seulement	formal	17	11	0	79	46	
juste	mildly marked informal	52	3	0	15	53.9	
rien que	marked informal	31	0	0	1	0.1	
donc	hyper-formal	2	25	83	23	15	7 = *so*
alors	formal	43	75	17	76	78	
(ça) fait que	marked informal	55	0	0	1	0	
je vais	formal	6	100	100	99	90	
je vas	mildly marked informal	64	0	0	1	10	
m'as	marked informal	30	0	0	0	0	

(*Continued*)

Table 6.1 Continued

Variants	Sociostylistic status of variants	FL1 speakers	FLA materials		French immersion teachers	French immersion students	
			Text	Dialogue		Native variants	Non-native usages
inflected	formal	20	95	70	18	10	13 = infinitive, conditional, etc.
periphrastic	neutral	73	5	30	79	67	
futurate present	neutral	7	0	0	3	10	
nous	hyper-formal	2	83	52	17	45	
on	mildly marked informal	94	17	48	83	55	
nous-autres on	marked informal	4	0	0	0	0	
plural verbs	neutral	98	100	100	100	81	
singular verbs	marked informal	2	0	0	0	19	
être	formal	66	100	100	95	78	Use of *avoir* with *aller*[a]
avoir	marked informal	34	0	0	5	22	

Conclusion

							15 = *chez la maison*, *à* + strong pronouns, etc.
chez 1	neutral	67	27	100	32	20	
à la maison	neutral	28	73	0	56	42	
other[b]	neutral	5	0	0	12	23	
chez 3	neutral	66	100	100	100	23	20 = *dans la maison de*, *au la maison de*, etc.
other	neutral	6	0	0	0	57	
su'	marked informal	28	0	0	0	0	
poste	hyper-formal	8	No data	0	Insufficient data	0	
travail	neutral	35		0		56	
emploi	formal	14		100		38	
job	marked informal	29		0		6	
ouvrage	marked informal	14		0		0	
habiter	hyper-formal	6	42	No data	100	60	
demeurer	formal	20	4		0	0	
vivre	neutral	10	54		0	40	

(*Continued*)

Table 6.1 Continued

Variants	Sociostylistic status of variants	FL1 speakers	FLA materials		French immersion teachers	French immersion students	
			Text	Dialogue		Native variants	Non-native usages
rester	marked informal	64	0	0	0	0	
/ə/ use	formal	32	100	99.9	c	85	
/ə/ non-use	mildly marked informal	68	0	00.1	c	15	
/l/ use	hyper-formal	7	100	100	c	98	
/l/ non-use	mildly marked informal	93	0	0	c	2	
voiture	hyper-formal	2	20[d]	25	67	21	
automobile	formal	14	55	0	0	5	
auto	neutral	42	19	75	33	74	
char	marked informal	23	0	0	0	0	
machine	marked informal	19	0	0	0	0	

[a] *Juste* was used to the left of the verb in 36% of instances and *avoir* was used with *aller* in 12% of instances.
[b] It is not obvious what sociostylistic one can ascribe to these 'other' variants. We have placed them in the 'neutral' category by default.
[c] We did not have access to the teachers' in-class speech recordings.
[d] In the French Language Arts materials, the texts included 6% of occurrences of the variant *véhicule*.

review of the findings of our examination of variant frequency will therefore be limited to general points, which readers can relate back to specific findings in previous chapters, if they so wish.

Finally, it should be pointed out that in our examination of variation in the French Language Arts teaching materials, we distinguished the texts that were dialogic from those that were meant to be read as written French and, in a related vein, we looked for evidence that the sociolinguistic variants under study had been explicitly acknowledged as such and were the object of sociostylistically oriented pedagogical activities.

Sociolinguistic variation in the French Language Arts materials of French immersion students

- The French Language Arts materials make no use of the marked informal variants in their textual components or even in the dialogic ones.
- The French Language Arts materials make very infrequent use of the mildly marked informal variants and do not use such variants significantly more often in the dialogues than in the texts (except for variant *on*).
- The French Language Arts materials make very frequent use of the formal and hyper-formal variants under study, although only a minority of such variants are used significantly more often in the textual components of the materials than in the dialogic ones and for a few hyper-formal variants the difference in frequency goes against sociolinguistic expectations.
- No clear pattern has emerged from our measurement of the frequency of neutral variants in the French Language Arts materials. That said, all but one of the neutral variants are used in the teaching materials – a finding that is in keeping with the fact that neutral variants are part of standard French usage.[65]
- The French Language Arts materials do not include sociolinguistically oriented activities that focus on the variants under study or explicit acknowledgments of their sociostylistic status.[66]

In sum, our examination of sociolinguistic variation in the French Language Arts materials used in the immersion programs in Ontario suggests that the production of a new generation of French Language Arts materials, which would be sociolinguistically realistic and which would include pedagogical activities to improve the sociolinguistic competence of students, along the lines of Lyster (1994a, 2007), would be a welcome addition to the FL2 teaching resources used in Ontario and elsewhere.

Sociolinguistic variation in the classroom speech of French Immersion teachers

In their classrooms, the French immersion teachers

- Never use or only marginally use the marked informal variants focused on in our research.
- Make only modest use of the mildly marked informal variants under study (variant *on* is the only exception, which teachers use much more often than *nous*).
- Make frequent use of the formal and hyper-formal variants under study, although, generally, they do so at levels of frequency that are not as high as those found in the teaching materials.
- Use of the neutral variants under study in a way that is essentially in keeping with that of other FL1 speakers.
- Do not provide students with feedback concerning the appropriateness of sociolinguistic variants and do not engage in specially designed activities to raise students' awareness of variation or to offer them opportunities to use variants in a range of contexts.

While the teachers' strong preference for formal and hyper-formal variants may be looked upon as sociostylistically appropriate, since the classroom is a formal communication setting, it along with the absence of feedback and sociolinguistically oriented activities under-exposes the students to the informal variants that are part and parcel of everyday spoken Canadian French and hinders the development of their acquisition of sociolinguistic competence.

Sociolinguistic variation in the spoken French of French immersion students

Apart from our research, only three studies have been devoted to the sociolinguistic competence of French immersion students (Harley & King, 1989; Lyster, 1994a; Swain & Lapkin, 1990). Furthermore, unlike our research, these studies did not follow a sociolinguistic variationist methodology. Their data were collected, in part, via language proficiency tests and were focused on both written and spoken language. Inasmuch as our research is focused on no less than 15 sociolinguistic variables and the 44 variants that actualize them, and insofar as it examines the students' use of variants from the perspective of Labovian variationist sociolinguistics, our research has contributed in a major way to the advancement of studies on the learning of sociolinguistic variation by L2 learners in an educational context.

Our main findings of this research are summarized below.

Conclusion

Frequency of the variants

In the context of a semi-directed taped interview, the French immersion students

- Never use or use only marginally the marked informal variants under study.
- Use the mildly marked informal variants under study at levels of frequency well below FL1 norms, but somewhat closer to native norms than their use of marked informal variants.
- Use several marked and mildly marked informal variants that are in all likelihood developmental forms (e.g. singular verb forms in the third person plural, auxiliary *avoir*, *job*, *je vas* and restrictive adverb *juste*), rather than exceptional informal variants that the student would have learned. In most instances, such developmental forms underscore the structural markedness of their standard equivalents.
- Tend to over-use formal and hyper-formal variants that are strongly favored in their educational input.
- Use neutral variants in a way that reflects the systemic properties of these forms rather than their frequency in the educational input.
- Use some 'variants' that are not found in the speech of the FL1 speakers. Such non-native variants reflect the fact that certain variants that are part of the students' educational input are difficult to master.

In sum, our examination of the frequency of variant use in the spoken French of immersion students has brought to light the paucity of informal variants in their speech and the concomitant over-use of formal and hyper-formal variants. This finding reflects to a large extent the infrequency or absence of informal variants in the educational input of the students and, in contrast, the predominance of formal and hyper-formal variants in such input. The fact that many of the informal variants under study are used extensively by FL1 speakers and the prevalence of formal and hyper-formal variants in the immersion students' speech suggests that they might experience receptive and productive difficulties when interacting in French with FL1 speakers. Such a hypothesis is in line with immersion students' actual acknowledgment of the disconnect between their speech and that of FL1 speakers (Auger, 2002; Segalowitz, 1976; Tarone & Swain, 1995).

Mastery of the linguistic constraints of variation

The French immersion students observe some of the linguistic constraints on sociolinguistic variation documented in FL1 speech and also observe some linguistic constraints not found in FL1 speech.

Mastery of the stylistic constraints of variation

The French immersion students' ability to style shift, as indicated by frequency fluctuations reflecting the level of (in)formality of the various topics touched upon in the interview, seems to be limited.

Effect of independent variables on variant use frequency

The following independent variables were examined in our research: (1) frequency of interactions with FL1 speakers; (2) the students' home language(s); (3) the students' sex; and (4) the students' social background. To our knowledge, the effect of this latter variable has only been examined in our research.

- The French immersion students with greater exposure to L1 French outside the classroom use mildly marked informal variants more often than do the other students. Consequently, even a modest amount of additional exposure to L1 French outside the school context will make a difference in the students' internalization of such variants. With marked informal variants such exposure is clearly insufficient to bring about such internalization since our research shows that the immersion students never use these variants or use them only marginally.
- The French immersion students who speak Italian or Spanish at home are likely to use French variants that have morphologically and semantically similar counterparts in Italian or Spanish more often than immersion students who do not speak such languages at home. In a similar vein, we found that immersion students who speak only English at home use the restrictive adverb *juste* (whose English counterpart is the adverb *just*) more often than the other students. These findings underscore the fact that inter-systemic factors can influence the learning of sociolinguistic variants.
- Female French immersion students use hyper-formal and formal variants more often than do male students, when such variants alternate with non-standard informal counterparts. Students from the upper social strata use hyper-formal and formal variants more often than do students from the lower social strata when such variants alternate with non-standard informal counterparts.

Educational Implications of Results

As we have mentioned, the French Language Arts materials used in French immersion programs never use the marked informal variants under study, never or marginally use almost all of the mildly marked informal variants under study and conversely use the formal or hyper-formal counterparts of these informal variants categorically or very frequently. Furthermore, when we compared the textual components with the dialogic ones, it was found that for a majority of variants there was little difference and in several instances there was a tendency to over-use formal and hyper-formal variants in the dialogues. Thus, the students would not be able to infer the sociostylistic status of variants from differential frequency of use in the texts and dialogues. Finally, the materials we examined contain no activities whatsoever which would lead the students to become aware of the sociostylistic status of variants or to use them in sociolinguistically appropriate ways. Similar patterns of variant use were found in the classroom speech of immersion teachers. The teachers never use the marked informal variants and tend to avoid the mildly marked informal variants, although not to the same extent as do the teaching materials. Conversely, the teachers mostly use the formal, and some of the hyper-formal, counterparts of the informal variants. Further, they do not provide feedback on the sociolinguistic appropriateness of variants, nor do they engage in activities designed to raise students' awareness of sociolinguistic variants or enable students to use them. As such, the pedagogical approach found in the French Language Arts materials and the teachers' classroom discourse is far removed from the multifaceted sociolinguistically sensitive pedagogical approach to second language teaching advocated by Lyster (2007). In other words, the shortcomings of the French immersion students' sociolinguistic competence cannot be attributed solely to the input to which they are exposed, but rather results from a combination of input and pedagogical practice.

As was shown by our analysis of the spoken French of immersion students, on the one hand there is a startlingly close match between the patterns of variant use found in the students' speech and the patterns of variant use in the educational input summarized above and, on the other, there is a clear mismatch between the students' range of variants and frequency of use of variants and those of FL1 speakers.

The above findings suggest two main pedagogical implications. Firstly, there needs to be a general 'rethinking' of the pedagogical approaches and the content of the educational materials used in immersion programs in relation to the treatment of sociolinguistic variation. Students need to be exposed to a broader range of variants than is currently the case, in particular marked and mildly marked informal variants that are frequent in FL1 speech. Students also need to be provided with detailed information on the sociostylistic status of variants and engage in appropriate activities that would allow them the opportunity to develop both receptive and productive abilities that are as close to native-like norms as possible (Lyster, 1994a, 2007; Nadasdi et al., 2005). This is particularly the case for mildly marked informal and hyper-formal variants. More specifically, students need to improve their ability to produce mildly marked informal variants and to reduce their use of hyper-formal ones in spoken discourse. While one may not expect students to make frequent use of marked informal variants, one can nonetheless hope that they would be able to understand such forms when they encounter them. This is particularly true for marked informal variants that are found frequently in L1 spoken discourse (e.g. *ça fait que* and *rester*). One means of achieving such an outcome would be to present students with activities that underscore the variation that exists between written and spoken language. Secondly, the variants that pose significant learning problems for the French immersion students would need to be the object of explicit form-focused pedagogical interventions that are sociolinguistically relevant. This could take the form of either specially designed teaching materials or specialized classroom practices, since it has been found that such forms of pedagogical interventions are an effective way to overcome these problems within the classroom context (Day & Shapson, 1991; Harley, 1989b; Lapkin & Swain, 2000; Lyster, 1994a, 1994b, 1998).

Because of the findings reported in this volume and those of Swain and Lapkin (1990) and Harley and King (1989), French immersion teachers will have at their disposal a substantial body of results that will allow them to target the variants used in L1 Canadian French that the students need to learn first and foremost. These findings will also provide them with valuable information concerning the social and stylistic connotations of the variants that will be indispensable for the development of a syllabus for the teaching of sociolinguistic variation in French (for information on the development of such syllabi see Critchley, 1994; Cuq, 1994; Lyster, 1994a, 2007; Lyster & Rebuffot, 2002; Nadasdi et al., 2005; Offord, 1994). Teaching of this type would have the advantage of providing students with a sociolinguistic repertoire that could allow them to converge toward the norms of L1 speakers of Canadian French in both formal and informal communicative situations and to have more natural interactions (see Segalowitz, 1976).

As mentioned in Chapter 1, according to Hart et al. (1989), Tarone and Swain (1995) and Auger (2002), French immersion students are eager to familiarize themselves with marked and/or mildly marked informal usages. Moreover, in the guidelines for the teaching of French in immersion programs issued by the Ontario Ministry of Education (2000), it is explicitly stated that students should be able to express themselves in both formal and informal registers by the end of secondary school. This would have the added benefit of offering French immersion students opportunities to familiarize themselves with variants that are reflective of the sociostylistic rules of French as it is spoken in Canada. Such a result would also be in keeping with another curriculum goal of the Ontario Ministry of Education which stresses the need for French immersion students to develop familiarity with the local norms of French, including different regions in Canada (see Appendix C). Let us hope that our call for the development of new pedagogical materials for the teaching of sociolinguistic variation will be heeded and that French immersion students will have the opportunity to learn the kinds of sociolinguistic skills that they clearly need and desire.

Another way of developing the sociolinguistic competence of French immersion students would be to provide them with opportunities to interact with FL1 speakers in the educational setting. This is a possibility that we have examined in Chapter 5 via the ternary comparison of the patterns and frequency of variant use in the speech of restricted and unrestricted adolescent speakers of Ontario French and French immersion students. This comparison revealed that for the majority of variants studied, the French immersion students would indeed benefit from greater contacts with FL1 speakers in an educational setting. Such a beneficial effect does not preclude the value of pedagogical interventions focused on sociolinguistic variation. This pedagogical focus might also target variants where the restricted students display frequency rates that are considerably below those of the unrestricted speakers e.g. *(ça) fait que* and *ouvrage* and hence where the French immersion students would only benefit marginally from exposure to FL1 speech in a school setting.

We also identified in Chapter 5 a number of variants where this general beneficial effect of interaction with FL1 speakers may not obtain in that the French immersion students may end up over-using some of them (e.g. *juste, job*, auxiliary *avoir* and *so*) or experiencing no change in their use of others (e.g. use of third person plural verb forms). In cases like these, it is all the more important that students receive explicit information regarding these variants' sociostylistic status.

In Chapter 5 we also raised the important issues of the characteristics of the variety of FL1 speech that French immersion students would be exposed to and of the ratio of FL1 to French immersion students necessary to obtain the beneficial effects summarized above. We believe that these are delicate issues that school authorities contemplating the implementation of two-way immersion programs should consider carefully, since they are related to both the linguistic and cultural needs and aspirations of both sets of students and their parents.

Finally, our preliminary analysis of the speech of teachers from the French-medium schools of Ontario undertaken in Chapter 5 suggests that there is a correspondence between student usage and that of the teachers, even for L1 speakers of French. For example, like the teachers the restricted students make use of a number of marked informal variants. Also, in the case of *je vas*, there is a close statistical parallel between the teachers' use of this form (55%) and that of the restricted speakers (60%). These preliminary results suggest that were the French immersion teachers to make greater use of these marked or mildly marked informal variants, the French immersion students' sociolinguistic competence would become more native-like. This would be all the more likely if it was complemented with a pedagogical approach that involves teacher feedback concerning the sociolinguistic appropriateness of variants and activities to raise awareness and production of these variants.

Limitations and Directions for Future Study

In spite of the fact that our research has investigated a broad range of sociolinguistic variants pertaining to the main components of language (phonology, morphology, morphosyntax and lexicon), it is subject to several limitations that should be spelled out for the benefit of researchers who may contemplate conducting similar research on the learning of sociolinguistic variation by L2 learners of French or of other languages in an educational setting.

First, our research has not delved deeply into the investigation of the learning of stylistic variation. We have studied this topic in relation to only three sociolinguistic variables. The main reason for this lies in the paucity of variationist studies that have examined stylistic variation in the speech of FL1 speakers of Canadian French. Put differently, there is a lack of comparative baseline data on stylistic variation in FL1 speech that we can turn to in order to assess the style shifting competence of the French immersion students. This means that in our future research on this topic we will likely have to analyze our own corpora of Ontario French in order to extract this kind of comparative data. In a related vein, one should bear in mind that the topic of the learning of stylistic variation by advanced FL2 learners in various settings has been investigated with an overly heterogeneous set of methodologies, making it difficult to compare results across studies. Clearly this is something that future research will need to address.

Second, we have not been able to gather a corpus of French immersion teachers' classroom speech in the school district where we collected our own corpus of French immersion students' spoken French. Consequently, we used the Allen *et al.* corpus of classroom French immersion teachers' speech, which presented a number of drawbacks. As stated earlier, the corpus was gathered approximately ten years before our corpus of French immersion students' spoken French. Further, not all of the teachers worked in the Toronto area and they taught French immersion in Grades 3 and 6. No information on the teachers' geographical provenance, years of experience, and other characteristics was gathered. Finally, we had access only to the orthographic transcriptions of the teachers' speech. Clearly, in our future studies, we will need to take steps to gather a teacher classroom speech corpus that is free from the above-mentioned limitations. Obviously, such considerations would also apply in relation to future research on the learning of sociolinguistic variation by other advanced L2 learners.

Third, our research has focused on a type of French immersion program (late partial immersion) that provides students with significant exposure to French in an educational setting, but is below the amount of exposure to French that students receive in an early total immersion program. Thus, it is possible that French immersion students who are enrolled in the latter type of program would achieve a slightly higher level of mastery of sociolinguistic variation than the students focused upon in our research.

In a similar vein, we have pointed out that the French immersion students under study come from less affluent families than is the case in other immersion programs in neighboring school districts and that this has had a limiting impact on their stays in Francophone settings. Consequently, since such stays have a beneficial impact on the learning of sociolinguistic variation, it is possible that if we had gathered our speech corpus in these other school districts we might have arrived at somewhat different results. Obviously this is a topic that also needs to be further investigated.

The reader will also recall that the student questionnaire survey revealed that the students display a range of more or less favorable attitudes toward French Canadians and French Canadian culture, and of motivations to learn French. These factors would appear to be good candidates for assessing the effect of independent variables on the learning of sociolinguistic variation and this is a topic we are currently investigating.

A further limitation to our research is that we did not differentiate among what we termed the 'other' languages spoken at home by the French immersion students (i.e. languages other than English, French, Italian and Spanish). The primary reason for this is that these 'other' languages are represented by too few students to support a detailed statistical analysis of their possible effect on the learning of sociolinguistic variation. Thus, there is a clear need for this type of statistical analysis to be conducted on corpora including enough speakers from a range of linguistic backgrounds to further advance research on the influence of the students' home language on the learning of sociolinguistic variation.

Finally, it would have been interesting to compare the results of our research with those of similar research focused on the immersion programs established in the USA and elsewhere and, especially, to compare our findings concerning the role of educational input on the learning of sociolinguistic variation. However, to our knowledge, no such research has yet been carried out. It is true that several studies on the learning of the patterns of sociolinguistic variation by L2 learners of other languages have been undertaken (e.g. English – Adamson & Regan, 1991; Bayley, 1996; Major, 1999; German – Barron, 2003; Japanese – Hashimoto, 1994; Marriott, 1995). However, they are focused, for the most part, on languages that are learned in the target-language community, rather than in educational settings, and, hence, are not directly comparable to our own. Thus, by providing a systematic investigation of the learning of sociolinguistic variation by French immersion students, with a special focus on the role of educational input, our research offers a blueprint for future research on the learning of sociolinguistic variation by advanced L2 learners who rely primarily on the educational setting.

Appendix A: Semi-Directed Taped Interview Schedule – Including Reading Passages

Entrevue avec les élèves

Nom de l'interviewé(e)

1. Où habites-tu? Comment est-ce-que tu fais pour te rendre de chez toi à l'école? Est-ce que ça prend longtemps? Est-ce que tu aimes l'endroit où tu habites? Si oui ou si non: pourquoi?
2. Quelle sorte de program de télévision est-ce que tu aimes regarder? Quel est ton program préféré? Pourquoi? Quand est-ce que tu l'as vu la dernière fois? Peux-tu m'en parler? Est-ce qu'il y a des programs de télévision que tu n'aimes pas ou que tu trouves stupides? Pourquoi?
3. Est-ce que tu vas au cinéma? Quel(s) genre(s) de films est-ce que tu préfères? Est-ce que tu as vu un bon film récemment? Est-ce que tu peux me raconter ça brièvement?
4. La religion, est-ce que c'est important pour toi? Crois-tu que c'est important dans la vie d'aujourd'hui? Pourquoi? Quelles sont les différences entre les écoles catholiques et les écoles publiques?
5. On dit que les jeunes ne s'entendent pas toujours très bien avec leurs parents. Pourquoi d'après toi? Est-ce que tu penses que certains parents ne laissent pas leurs enfants assez libres de faire ce qu'ils veulent? Est-ce que c'est parce que les enfants ne parlent pas assez avec leurs parents?
6. Pourrais-tu me raconter un bon tour joué à un de tes professeurs ou à un(e) de tes ami(e)s de classe (à l'élémentaire ou au secondaire)?
7. Qu'est-ce que tu as fait pendant les dernières vacances de l'été? Quel a été le meilleur ou le pire moment de tes vacances? Raconte un peu.
8. Est-ce que tu penses faire quelque chose de spécial pendant les prochaines vacances de Noël? Est-ce que Noël est un événement

spécial chez vous? Qu'est-ce que vous faites? Allez-vous visiter des gens?
9. As-tu lu ou vu quelque chose de comique récemment ou est-ce qu'il t'est personnellement arrivé quelque chose de comique récemment? Pourrais-tu raconter?
10. Prévois-tu des changements pour le monde d'après l'an 2000? Quelles sortes de changements? Es-tu pessimiste ou optimiste face à l'avenir? Pourquoi?
11. Pourrais-tu me raconter un moment de ta vie où tu as une grande peur? Par exemple, tu as peut-être déjà vu un accident ou un feu. Peux-tu raconter ce qui s'est passé?
12. Si tu avais la possibilité de voyager à l'étranger, où aimerais-tu aller? Pourquoi? Qu'est-ce que tu aimerais voir? Combien de temps voudrais-tu y rester?
13. Si tu gagnais un million de dollars à Loto Canada ou à Wintario, qu'est-ce que tu ferais avec tout cet argent? En donnerais-tu aux autres? À qui et pourquoi?
14. Aimes-tu la politique? Crois-tu que le Québec va se séparer du reste du Canada? S'il se sépare, comment, d'après toi, cela va affecter l'Ontario et le Canada? Quelle serait la réaction des autres provinces? Est-ce que l'on devrait faire quelque chose pour empêcher la séparation du Québec?
15. Est-ce que tu aimes les livres ou les revues? Si oui quel(s) genre(s) de livre/revue préfères-tu? As-tu lu un bon livre récemment? Peux-tu me parler de ce livre?
16. Est-ce que tu aimes la musique? Si oui quel genre de musique? As-tu un groupe/un musicien préféré? Pourquoi aimes-tu cette musique/ce groupe/ce musicien?
17. As-tu un petit animal chez toi, un chien, un chat, etc.? Est-ce que tu l'aimes? Est-ce que tu t'en occupes. Pourquoi?
18. Quels sont tes jeux ou sports préférés? Où et quand les pratiques-tu? As-tu d'autres activités ou passe-temps? Pourquoi les pratiques-tu?
19. Il y a des gens qui disent que le français parlé au Québec est moins bon que le français parlé en France. Es-tu d'accord avec cette opinion? Pourquoi? As-tu déjà entendu des gens qui parlent le français québécois et des gens qui parlent le français de France? Peux-tu mentionner des différences entre ces deux français? Toi, comment essaies-tu de parler? Comme un francophone du Québec ou comme un Français de France? Pourquoi?
20. Peux-tu m'expliquer comment on enseigne le français à ton école? Aimes-tu ça? Pourquoi? Est-ce qu'il y a des choses que tu aimerais apprendre et que l'on ne t'enseignes pas?
21. Maintenant que tu as presque complété ton secondaire, est-ce que tu te considères bilingue? Pourquoi? (13e année)/Est-ce que tu penses

que tu seras bilingue quand tu auras complété ton secondaire? (10e année)
22. Est-ce que tu écoutes la radio française ou la télévision française? Souvent? Pourquoi? Quels sont tes programs favoris? Pourquoi?
23. As-tu une idée du travail que tu aimerais faire plus tard? Pourquoi as tu choisi ce genre de travail?

PASSAGE À LIRE À HAUTE VOIX POUR LES ÉLÈVES DE LA 9e ET 12e ANNÉE

- Salut Marc. Comment ça va? – Ca va bien, puis toi?
- O.K. Ca ne va pas trop pire, merci.
- Viens faire un tour à la maison pour voir mon nouveau char. – Tu as acheté un char!
- Oui, je l'ai acheté la semaine passée. C'est un Mustang noir, convertible avec deux gros pneus d'hiver, Good Year; pour 3,500 piastres. Tu ne peux pas trouver mieux.
- 3,500 piastres!
- Je l'ai acheté à crédit, 150 piastres par mois.
- Veux-tu bien me dire où c'est tu peux trouver l'argent toi. Moi j'arrive tout juste à joindre les deux bouts. Ce n'est pas avec l'argent que je fais avec ma job que je pourrais acheter un char pareil. J'aime bien mieux sauver mon argent qu'acheter des affaires à crédit puis de m'endetter.
- Tu sais, de l'argent quand tu en as, tu es bien mieux de la dépenser. J'aime mieux acheter les choses qui me tentent que de m'en passer. De toute façon, les prix n'arrêtent pas de monter et ça sert à rien de mettre son argent de côté, parce qu'elle perd de sa valeur.

LISTE DES PHRASES HORS CONTEXTE POUR LES ÉLÈVES DE LA 9e ET 12e ANNÉE

Le plancher est dur.
On y va demain mardi
Dis-moi quand c'est ta fête.
Le gros singe monte sur la branche.
C'est pas vrai.
C'est de la belle laine.
Le mur est tout en brique.

Je suis né au Canada.
C'est une rose rouge.
Vous y allez.
Il s'est cassé une hanche.
Ma soeur est grosse.
Il y a cinq anglais.
Deux pintes de vin.

Appendix B: Student Questionnaire Survey

1. Name/Nom:

2. Sex(e):   M ____   F ____

3. Date of birth/Date de naissance (day/jour/ month/mois/ year/année):

4. Grade/Année:

5. Place of birth/Lieu de naissance: Country/pays
   Province
   City/town/ville

6. Mother's occupation (be specific, e.g. if teacher, indicate what type of school; if manager, indicate what type of business, etc.)/Emploi de la mère (sois précis, ex.: si enseignante, indiquer le type d'école; si gérante, indiquer le type d'entreprise, etc.)

7. Father's occupation (be specific, e.g. if teacher, indicate what type of school; if manager, indicate what type of business, etc.)/Emploi du père (sois précis, ex.: si enseignant, indiquer le type d'école; si gérant, indiquer le type d'entreprise, etc.)

8. What language(s) does your father speak fluently?/Quelle(s) langue(s) est-ce que ton père parle couramment?
   1.   2.   3.   4.

9. What language(s) does he speak at home?/Quelle(s) langue(s) parle-t-il à la maison?
   1.   2.   3.   4.

10. What language(s) does your mother speak fluently?/Quelle(s) langue(s) est-ce que ta mère parle couramment?
    1.   2.   3.   4.

11. What language(s) does she speak at home?/Quelle(s) langue(s) parle-t-elle à la maison?
    1.   2.   3.   4.

Appendix B

Circle the number that best describes what you do/Encercler le numéro que décrit le mieux ce que tu fais

12. At home I speak English/A la maison je parle anglais:

always/toujours	often/souvent	1/2 the time/la moitié du temps	rarely/rarement	never/jamais
1	2	3	4	5

13. At home I speak French/A la maison je parle français:

always/toujours	often/souvent	1/2 the time/la moitié du temps	rarely/rarement	never/jamais
1	2	3	4	5

14. At home I speak another language/A la maison je parle une autre langue (please specify/s.t.p. préciser):

always/toujours	often/souvent	1/2 the time/la moitié du temps	rarely/rarement	never/jamais
1	2	3	4	5

15. Outside my home I speak English/A l'extérieur de la maison je parle anglais:

always/toujours	often/souvent	1/2 the time/la moitié du temps	rarely/rarement	never/jamais
1	2	3	4	5

16. Outside my home I speak French/A l'extérieur de la maison je parle français:

always/toujours	often/souvent	1/2 the time/la moitié du temps	rarely/rarement	never/jamais
1	2	3	4	5

17. Outside my home I speak another language/A l'extérieur de la maison je parle une autre langue : (please specify/s.t.p. préciser):

always/toujours	often/souvent	1/2 the time/la moitié du temps	rarely/rarement	never/jamais
1	2	3	4	5

18. In the chart below, please indicate what schools have you attended/Dans le tableau ci-dessous indiquer s.t.p. les écoles que tu as fréquentées:

Name and location of school/Nom et lieu de l'école	Year(s) attended/ Année(s) de fréquentation	Language of instruction (circle the appropriate number)/Langue d'enseignement (encercler le numéro approprié)					
		French only/ Seulement en français	Mostly in French/Surtout en français	Half English/ anglais 1/2 French/ français	Mostly in English/ Surtout en anglais	Only in English/ Seulement en anglais	Other (specify)/Autre (préciser)
		1	2	3	4	5	
		1	2	3	4	5	
		1	2	3	4	5	
		1	2	3	4	5	
		1	2	3	4	5	

Appendix B

19. Do you feel that you receive a sufficient amount of instruction in French in your high school?/D'après toi, reçois-tu suffisamment d'instruction en français à ton école secondaire?

   Yes/Oui _____ No/Non _____ (if no, indicate how much more would be necessary)/(si ce n'est pas le cas, combien d'instruction supplémentaire en français te serait nécessaire)

a little more than what I now receive/ un peu plus que ce que je reçois maintenant	a great deal more than what I now receive/ beaucoup plus que ce que je reçois maintenant
1	2

20. Most days, I watch television/La plupart des jours je regarde la télé:

never/jamais	less than 1 h/moins d'une heure	1–2 h/1 à 2 heure(s)	2–3 h/2 à 3 heures	3 h+/plus de 3 heures
1	2	3	4	5

21. When I watch television, I watch programs/Quand je regarde la télé, je regarde des programs:

always in English/ toujours en anglais	often in English/ souvent en anglais	as often in English as French/ aussi souvent en anglais qu'en français	often in French/ souvent en français	always in French/ toujours en français
1	2	3	4	5

   Other (specify)/autre (préciser):

22. Most days, I listen to the radio/La plupart des jours j'écoute la radio:

never/jamais	less than 1 h/moins d'une heure	1–2 h/1 à 2 heure(s)	2–3 h/2 à 3 heures	3 h+/plus de 3 heures
1	2	3	4	5

23. When I listen to the radio, I listen to programs/Quand j'écoute la radio, j'écoute des programs:

always in English/	often in English/	as often in English as French/	often in French/	always in French/
toujours en anglais	souvent en anglais	aussi souvent en anglais qu'en français	souvent en français	toujours en français
1	2	3	4	5

Other (specify)/autre (préciser):

24. I listen to music/J'écoute de la musique:

often/souvent	fairly often/assez souvent	rarely/rarement	never/jamais
1	2	3	4

25. When I listen to music, I listen/Quand j'écoute de la musique, je l'écoute:

always in English/	often in English/	as often in English as French/	often in French/	always in French/
toujours en anglais	souvent en anglais	aussi souvent en anglais qu'en français	souvent en français	toujours en français
1	2	3	4	5

Other (specify)/autre (préciser):

26. I read books/Je lis des livres:

often/souvent	fairly often/assez souvent	rarely/rarement	never/jamais
1	2	3	4

Appendix B

27. When I read books, I read/Quand je lis des livres:

always in English/	often in English/	as often in English as French/	often in French/	always in French/
toujours en anglais	souvent en anglais	aussi souvent en anglais qu'en français	souvent en français	toujours en français
1	2	3	4	5

Other (specify)/autre (préciser):

28. I read magazines/Je lis les revues:

often/souvent	fairly often/assez souvent	rarely/rarement	never/jamais
1	2	3	4

29. When I read magazines, I read/Quand je lis les revues, je les lis:

always in English/	often in English/	as often in English as French/	often in French/	always in French/
toujours en anglais	souvent en anglais	aussi souvent en anglais qu'en français	souvent en français	toujours en français
1	2	3	4	5

Other (specify)/autre (préciser):

30. If you have the choice, in the future, in which kind of community would you like to live?/Si tu as le choix, dans l'avenir, dans quel genre de communauté aimerais-tu habiter?:

French only/	mosty French/	as much French as English/	mostly English/	English only/
seulement française	surtout française	aussi française qu'anglaise	surtout anglaise	seulement anglaise
1	2	3	4	5

31. How often do you use French in the following situations? Please circle the number that best describes you/ Utilises-tu le français dans les situations suivantes? S.V.P., encercler le numéro qui décrit le mieux ce que tu fais.

	Never have the chance/L'occasion ne se présente jamais	Sometimes have the chance, but never or rarely use French/L'occasion se présente parfois, mais je n'emploie jamais ou rarement le français	Sometimes have the chance and usually use French/L'occasion se présente parfois, et j'emploie d'habitude le français	Often have the chance but never or rarely use French/L'occasion se présente souvent, mais je n'emploie jamais ou rarement le français	Often have the chance and usually use French/ L'occasion se présente souvent et j'emploie d'habitude le français
In stores, restaurants/Dans les magasins et restaurants	1	2	3	4	5
In class with teacher/En classe avec le professeur	1	2	3	4	5
With friends in class/Avec mes amis en classe	1	2	3	4	5
With friends at school (outside of class)/Avec mes amis en dehors de la classe	1	2	3	4	5
With friends outside of school/Avec mes amis en dehors de l'école	1	2	3	4	5
With family members/Avec les membres de ma famille	1	2	3	4	5

	1	2	3	4	5
On the street with strangers/Dans la rue avec des inconnus	1	2	3	4	5
Other situations?/Autre(s) situation(s)?					
1.	1	2	3	4	
2.	1	2	3	4	
3.	1	2	3	4	

32. If you know someone's first language is French do you try to speak to them in French?/Si tu sais que la première langue de quelqu'un est le français, est-ce que tu essaies de lui parler en français:

    always/toujours   often/souvent   fairly often/assez souvent   rarely/rarement   never/jamais
    1   2   3   4   5

33. Do you belong to a club, team or other group where most or all of the other members are French-speaking?/Est-ce que tu fais partie d'un club, d'une équipe ou d'un groupe où la plupart des membres parlent français?

    Yes/Oui _____   No/Non _____   Name of club/nom du club: _____

34. Would you be interested in joining such a club?/Serais-tu intéressé(e) à faire partie d'un tel club, équipe, etc.?

    Yes/Oui _____   No/Non _____

35. In the last 3–5 months, how many English movies have you seen?/Durant les derniers 3 à 5 mois, combien de films anglais as-tu vu?

36. In the last 3–5 months, how many French movies have you seen?/Durant les derniers 3 à 5 mois, combien de films français as-tu vu?

38. Name three French Canadian singers or musical groups/Indiquer 3 chanteur(s) ou groupes musicaux Canadien-Français:

   1.
   2.
   3.

39. Please indicate how you feel about each of the following statements. Circle the number under the answer that best describes your feelings/S.VP., indiquer tes sentiments par rapport aux affirmations suivantes. Encercler le numéro des réponses qui décrivent le mieux tes sentiments.

   I think that it is important to learn French/je pense qu'il est important d'apprendre le français:

40. Because it is nice to know other languages/Parce que c'est bien de connaître d'autres langues:

very unimportant/	fairly unimportant/	neutral/	fairly important/	very important/	no opinion/
très peu important	assez peu important	neutre	assez important	très important	sans opinion
1	2	3	4	5	6

41. Because you need it more and more for most things you do in Canada/Parce qu'on en a de plus en plus besoin pour la plupart des choses qu'on fait au Canada:

very unimportant/	fairly unimportant/	neutral/	fairly important/	very important/	no opinion/
très peu important	assez peu important	neutre	assez important	très important	sans opinion
1	2	3	4	5	6

42. Because it is an official language of Canada/Parce que c'est une langue officielle au Canada:

very unimportant/	fairly unimportant/	neutral/	fairly important/	very important/	no opinion/
très peu important	assez peu important	neutre	assez important	très important	sans opinion
1	2	3	4	5	6

43. Because if we don't, the French language in Ontario might disappear/Parce que sinon, la langue française en Ontario pourrait disparaître:

very unimportant/ très peu important	fairly unimportant/ assez peu important	neutral/ neutre	fairly important/ assez important	very important/ très important	no opinion/ sans opinion
1	2	3	4	5	6

44. Indicate to what extent you agree or disagree with the following statements/Indique ton degrès d'accord ou de désaccord avec les affirmations suivantes:

45. I want to learn as much French as possible/Je veux apprendre autant de français que possible:

strongly agree/ fortement d'accord	moderately agree/ modérément d'accord	slightly agree/ un peu d'accord	neutral/ neutre	slightly disagree/ un peu désaccord	moderately disagree/ en modérément désaccord	strongly disagree/ en fortement en désaccord	no opinion/ sans opinion
1	2	3	4	5	6	7	8

46. Learning French is a waste of time/L'apprentissage du français est un perte de temps:

strongly agree/ fortement d'accord	moderately agree/ modérément d'accord	slightly agree/ un peu d'accord	neutral/ neutre	slightly disagree/ un peu désaccord	moderately disagree/ en modérément désaccord	strongly disagree/ en fortement en désaccord	no opinion/ sans opinion
1	2	3	4	5	6	7	8

47. The French-Canadian culture is an important part of our Canadian identity/La culture canadienne-française est un aspect important de notre identité canadienne:

strongly agree/ fortement d'accord	moderately agree/ modérément d'accord	slightly agree/ un peu d'accord	neutral/ neutre	slightly disagree/ un peu désaccord	moderately disagree/ en modérément désaccord	strongly disagree/ en fortement en désaccord	no opinion/ sans opinion
1	2	3	4	5	6	7	8

48. If Canada was to lose the French culture, it would certainly be a great loss/Si le Canada devait perdre la culture française, cela serait certainement une grande perte:

strongly agree/ fortement d'accord	moderately agree/ modérément d'accord	slightly agree/ un peu d'accord	neutral/ neutre	slightly disagree/ un peu désaccord	moderately disagree/ modérément désaccord	strongly disagree/ en fortement en désaccord	no opinion/ sans opinion
1	2	3	4	5	6	7	8

49. I really enjoy learning French/J'aime vraiment apprendre le français:

strongly agree/ fortement d'accord	moderately agree/ modérément d'accord	slightly agree/ un peu d'accord	neutral/ neutre	slightly disagree/ un peu désaccord	moderately disagree/ modérément désaccord	strongly disagree/ en fortement en désaccord	no opinion/ sans opinion
1	2	3	4	5	6	7	8

50. French-Canadians are very friendly, warm-hearted and creative people/Les Canadiens-Français sont des gens très amicaux, chaleureux, et créatifs:

strongly agree/ fortement d'accord	moderately agree/ modérément d'accord	slightly agree/ un peu d'accord	neutral/ neutre	slightly disagree/ un peu désaccord	moderately disagree/ modérément désaccord	strongly disagree/ en fortement en désaccord	no opinion/ sans opinion
1	2	3	4	5	6	7	8

51. When I leave school, I will give up the study of French entirely because I am not interested in it/Quand je terminerai l'école, j'abandonnerai l'étude du français complètement parcque cela ne m'intéresse pas:

strongly agree/ fortement d'accord	moderately agree/ modérément d'accord	slightly agree/ un peu d'accord	neutral/ neutre	slightly disagree/ un peu désaccord	moderately disagree/ modérément désaccord	strongly disagree/ en fortement en désaccord	no opinion/ sans opinion
1	2	3	4	5	6	7	8

Appendix B

52. Parisian French is better than Canadian French/Le français parisien est meilleur que le français canadien.

strongly agree/ fortement d'accord	moderately agree/ modérément d'accord	slightly agree/ un peu d'accord	neutral/ neutre	slightly disagree/ un peu désaccord	moderately disagree/ en modérément désaccord	strongly disagree/ en fortement désaccord	no opinion/ sans opinion
1	2	3	4	5	6	7	8

53. If there were French-speaking families in my neighbourhood (circle the appropriate answer)/S'il y avait des familles francophones dans mon voisinage (encercle la réponse qui convient):

    (1) I would speak French with them as much as possible/Je leur parlerais en français autant que possible.
    (2) I would never speak French with them/Je ne leur parlerais jamais en français.
    (3) I would speak French with them sometimes/Je leur parlerais parfois en français.

54. When people hear me speaking French I want them to think/Quand les autres m'entendent parler français, j'aimerais qu'ils pensent que:

    (1) I speak Quebec French/Je parle le français québécois.
    (2) I speak Parisian French/Je parle le français parisien.
    (3) I don't care/Cela m'est égal.

55. Have you ever spent time in a French-speaking city/town? Yes ___ No ___ If yes, please specify when and where:
    As-tu déjà séjourné dans une ville francophone? Oui ___ Non ___ Si oui, s.v.p. indiquer où et quand:

Where?/Où?	For how long?/Pendant combien de temps?	Which year?/En quelle année?	Did you enjoy this experience?/As-tu aimé cette expérience		
			Yes/Oui	Somewhat/Un peu	Not at all/Pas du tout
1.			1	2	3
2.			1	2	3
3.			1	2	3
4.			1	2	3
5.			1	2	3

56. Have you ever stayed with a French speaking family? Yes ____ No ____ If yes, indicate where, when and for how long:

   As-tu déjà passé du temps dans une famille francophone? Oui ____ Non ____ Si oui, indiquer où, quand et pendant combien de temps:

57. If it were entirely up to me whether or not to take French/Si j'avais le choix de prendre le français ou de ne pas prendre le français:

   (1) I would drop it/Je le laisserais tomber.
   (2) I would definitely take it/Je le prendrais sans aucun doute.
   (3) I don't know whether I would take it or not/Je ne sais pas si je le prendrais.

Appendix C: Objectives of the Ontario Ministry of Education Concerning the Development of Sociolinguistic Competence by Secondary School French Immersion Students

Students should have the following productive abilities: incorporate colloquialisms and idiomatic expressions into their speech; debate formally and informally issues arising from their reading of literary and other works; express clearly and confidently their personal point of view in informal discussions; and write letters in an appropriate style for a variety of purposes. Students should also have the following receptive abilities: demonstrate the ability to detect nuances of language in various forms of oral communication; identify and demonstrate an understanding of a range of accents as well as some dialects from the Francophone world (ex. accents and expressions from different regions of France and Canada); recognize the vocabulary variations typical of different geographical areas where French is spoken; and use regional dictionaries (ex. a dictionary of Canadian French) to become familiar with language diversities from region to region (Ontario Ministry of Education, 2000).

Appendix D: Results of the GoldVarb Analyses of the Sociolinguistic Variables Focused upon in the Current Research

Table D1 Effects of linguistic and extra-linguistic constraints on *ne* use versus non-use of *ne*

Factor groups	Use of ne (N)	Non-use of ne (N)	Use of ne (%)	Non-use of ne (%)	Total (N)	Factor effect on ne non-use
Post-verbal negator						
pas	1524	559	73	27	2083	0.48
others	38	42	48	52	80	0.77
Francophone family						
0 h	995	272	79	21	1267	0.40
1–13 days	223	130	63	37	353	0.42
2 weeks and over	344	199	63	37	543	0.75
Home language						
romance	366	74	83	17	440	0.30
english	800	286	74	26	1086	0.47
other	396	241	62	38	637	0.67
Francophone environment						
0 h–1 day	372	109	77	23	481	0.43
2–6 days	353	119	75	25	472	0.63

(*Continued*)

Table D1 *Continued*

Factor groups	Use of ne (N)	Non-use of ne (N)	Use of ne (%)	Non-use of ne (%)	Total (N)	Factor effect on ne non-use
1–3 weeks	588	254	70	30	842	0.54
over 3 weeks	249	119	68	32	368	0.31
Social class						
middle[a]	883	329	73	27	1212	0.44
upper-working	559	257	69	31	816	0.58
Grade						
9	686	295	70	30	981	0.56
12	876	306	74	26	1182	0.44
French media						
never	1013	323	76	24	1336	0.45
occasional	549	278	66	34	827	0.57
French schooling						
0–25%	337	99	77	23	436	0.49
26–38%	992	382	72	28	1374	0.47
over 38%	233	120	66	34	353	0.59
Formality						
formal	616	211	74	26	827	n.s.
neutral	276	104	73	27	380	
informal	670	286	70	30	956	
Sex						
female	1345	518	72	28	1863	n.s.
male	217	83	72	28	300	
total	1562	601	72	28	2163	

Significance = 0.04, input = 0.25.
[a] Students from the upper middle and middle class have been regrouped under the general category middle.

Table D2 Effects of linguistic and extra-linguistic constraints on *seulement* versus *juste*[a]

Factor groups	Seulement (N)	Juste (N)	Seulement (%)	Juste (%)	Total (N)	Factor effect on juste
Linguistic context						
left of verb	2	45	4	96	47	0.97
verb	34	51	40	60	85	0.56
complement	48	86	36	64	134	0.51
adjective	4	5	44	56	9	0.45
noun	118	91	56	44	209	0.29
Home language						
romance	53	13	80	20	66	0.19
english	69	191	27	73	260	0.76
other	84	74	53	47	158	0.22
French media						
never	138	117	54	46	255	0.33
occasionally	68	161	30	70	229	0.69
Francophone family						
0 h	69	71	49	51	140	0.36
1–6 days	18	16	53	47	34	0.43
7–13 days	52	101	34	66	153	0.44
2 weeks and over	67	90	43	57	157	0.69
Francophone environment						
0 h	156	163	49	51	319	0.53
1–6 days	3	38	7	93	41	0.65
7–20 days	5	17	23	77	22	0.85
3 weeks and over	42	60	41	59	102	0.27
Sex						
female	174	215	45	55	389	0.46
male	32	63	34	66	95	0.66

(*Continued*)

Table D2 *Continued*

Factor groups	Seulement (N)	Juste (N)	Seulement (%)	Juste (%)	Total (N)	Factor effect on juste
Social class						
middle	156	163	49	51	319	n.s.
upper-working	68	90	43	57	158	
Grade						
9	84	114	42	58	198	n.s.
12	122	164	43	57	286	
Total	206	278	43	57	484	

Significance = 0.01, input = 0.66.
[a]No tokens of *ne...que* and only one of *rien que* were found in the corpus.

Table D3 Effects of extra-linguistic constraints on *alors* versus donc

Factor groups	Alors (N)	Donc (N)	Alors (%)	Donc (%)	Total (N)	Factor effect on donc
Home languages						
romance	110	0	100	0	110	Knock out[a]
english	227	93	71	29	320	
other	147	3	98	2	150	
Francophone environment						
0 h	133	2	99	1	135	0.05
1–6 days	85	13	87	13	98	0.51
1–3 weeks	174	52	77	23	226	0.71
over 3 weeks	92	29	76	24	121	0.81
Francophone family						
0 h to 3 days	259	60	81	19	319	0.69
over 3 days	225	36	86	14	261	0.28
Social class						
middle	237	67	78	22	304	0.64

(Continued)

Table D3 Continued

Factor groups	Alors (N)	Donc (N)	Alors (%)	Donc (%)	Total (N)	Factor effect on donc
upper-working	218	29	88	12	247	0.32
Sex						
female	466	38	92	8	504	0.37
male	18	58	24	76	76	0.96
French media						
never	334	25	93	7	359	n.s.
occasional	150	71	68	32	221	
Total	484	96	83	17	580	

Significance = 0.00, input = 0.06.
[a]When a variant is used categorically, the effect of the factor associated with such usage is obviously quite strong, but GoldVarb cannot operate because there is no variation. This situation is referred to as a 'knock out'.

Table D4 Effects of extra-linguistic constraints on *alors* and *donc* versus *so*

Factor groups	Alors and donc (N)	So (N)	Alors and donc (%)	So (%)	Total (N)	Factor effect on so
Home languages						
romance	110	0	100	0	110	Knock out
english	320	28	92	8	348	
other	150	16	90	10	166	
Francophone environment						
0 h	135	26	84	16	161	0.66
1–6 days	98	3	97	3	101	0.30
1 week and over	347	15	96	4	362	0.47
Sex						
female	504	26	95	5	530	0.42
male	76	18	81	19	94	0.84

(*Continued*)

Table D4 *Continued*

Factor groups	Alors and donc (N)	So (N)	Alors and donc (%)	So (%)	Total (N)	Factor effect on so
French media						
never	359	38	90	10	397	0.65
occasional	221	6	97	3	227	0.25
Social class						
middle	304	18	94	6	322	n.s.
upper-working	247	26	90	10	273	
Francophone family						
0 h to 3 days	415	38	92	8	453	n.s.
over 3 days	165	6	96	4	171	
Total	484	96	83	17	580	

Significance = 0.00, input = 0.06.

Table D5 Effects of linguistic constraints on the use of three variants denoting future time reference[a]

Factor groups	Inflected future			Periphrastic future			Futurate present			Total
	N	%	Factor effect	N	%	Factor effect	N	%	Factor effect	N
Time adverb										
specific	17	13	n.s.	84	67	0.33	25	20	0.71	126
non-specific	8	15		38	70	0.40	8	15	0.64	54
no adverb	14	8		151	88	0.66	7	4	0.30	172
Temporal distance										
more than a week	3	18	n.s.	14	82	n.s.	0	0	n.s.	17
less than a week	19	9		154	76		30	15		203
continual	4	29		10	71		0	0		14
uncertain	13	11		95	81		10	8		118

(*Continued*)

Table D5 *Continued*

Factor groups	Inflected future			Periphrastic future			Futurate present			Total
	N	%	Factor effect	N	%	Factor effect	N	%	Factor effect	N
Negative sentences										
negative	5	17	n.s.	23	77	n.s.	2	7	n.s.	30
affirmative	34	11		250	78		38	12		322
Person										
first	23	13	n.s.	135	74	n.s.	24	13	n.s.	182
second	1	7		12	80		2	13		15
third	15	10		126	81		14	9		155
Contingency										
contingent	1	4	n.s.	25	89	n.s.	2	7	n.s.	28
non-contingent	38	12		248	77		38	12		324
Certainty										
certain	15	12	n.s.	88	72	n.s.	19	16	n.s.	122
uncertain	19	14		103	77		12	9		134
neutral	5	5		82	85		9	9		96
Total	39	11		273	78		40	11		352

[a]In this GoldVarb analysis, each variant was pitted against the other two. This means that the frequencies and factor effects for each variant are to be interpreted against the combined frequency and factor effect data for the other two variants.

Table D6 Effects of extra-linguistic constraints on the use of three variants denoting future time reference

Factor groups	Inflected future			Periphrastic future			Futurate present			Total
	N	%	Factor effect	N	%	Factor effect	N	%	Factor effect	N
Francophone environment										
0–1 day	22	24	0.77	57	61	0.29	14	15	0.59	93
1–7 days	7	22	0.58	43	68	0.31	13	21	0.74	63

(*Continued*)

Table D6 *Continued*

Factor groups	Inflected future			Periphrastic future			Futurate present			Total
	N	%	Factor effect	N	%	Factor effect	N	%	Factor effect	N
7 days to 3 weeks	9	7	0.44	115	85	0.60	11	8	0.42	135
over 3 weeks	1	2	0.16	58	95	0.79	2	3	0.29	61
Grade										
9	29	16	0.63	131	72	0.42	23	13	n.s.	183
12	10	6	0.36	142	84	0.59	17	10		169
Sex										
female	37	13	0.59	211	76	n.s.	28	10	n.s.	276
male	2	3	0.20	62	82		12	16		76
Home languages										
romance	7	11	0.54	46	73	0.41	10	16	n.s.	63
english	28	15	0.62	134	72	0.41	24	13		186
other	7	4	0.27	93	90	0.70	6	6		106
Francophone family										
0 h	28	14	n.s.	150	73	n.s.	27	13	n.s.	205
1–13 days	0	65		59	91		6	9		65
over 2 weeks	11	13		64	78		7	9		82
Social class										
middle	22	12	n.s.	146	78	n.s.	19	10	n.s.	187
upper-working	16	12		100	76		16	12		132
French media										
never	30	12	n.s.	192	78	n.s.	24	10	n.s.	246
occasional	9	8		81	76		16	15		106
Total	39	11		273	78		40	11		352

Table D7 Use of *je vais* versus *je vas* as a function of length of stay in a Francophone environment[a]

Length of stay	Je vais		Je vas		Total
	N	%	N	%	N
0–1 day	12	75	4	20	16
2–7 days	7	77	2	22	9
8–21 days	33	89	2	5	37
over 3 weeks	29	100	0	0	29
Total	81	85	8	15	95

[a]Due to paucity of data on *je vais* versus *je vas*, a GoldVarb analysis was not run.

Table D8 Effects of linguistic and extra-linguistic constraints on *nous* versus *on*

Factor groups	On (N)	Nous (N)	On (%)	Nous (%)	Total (N)	Factor effect on on
Specific/restricted						
specific/restricted	674	595	53	47	1269	0.47
non-specific/restricted	100	43	70	30	143	0.57
non-specific/unrestricted	36	4	90	10	40	0.85
French media						
never	434	436	50	50	870	0.43
occasional	376	206	65	35	582	0.60
Francophone environment						
0 h	148	195	43	57	343	0.41
1–6 days	78	175	31	69	253	0.46
7–20 days	361	252	59	41	613	0.45
over 3 weeks	223	20	92	8	243	0.74
Francophone family						
0 h	333	508	40	60	841	0.41
1–13 days	223	31	88	12	254	0.73
over 2 weeks	254	103	71	29	357	0.52
Sex						
female	608	558	52	48	1166	0.46
male	202	84	71	29	286	0.63

(*Continued*)

Table D8 *Continued*

Factor groups	On (N)	Nous (N)	On (%)	Nous (%)	Total (N)	Factor effect on on
Home language						
romance	56	152	27	73	208	0.14
english	526	286	65	35	812	0.66
other	228	204	53	47	432	0.39
Formality						
informal	521	269	66	34	790	0.73
formal	289	373	44	56	662	0.24
Social class						
middle	385	429	47	53	814	0.39
upper-working	401	185	68	32	586	0.68
Total	810	642	56	44	1452	

Significance = 0.00, input = 0.68.

Table D9 Effects of linguistic constraints on singular versus plural verb forms in the third person plural

Factor groups	Singular (N)	Plural (N)	Singular (%)	Plural (%)	Total (N)	Factor effect on singular form
Element separating subject and verb						
element present	44	78	36	64	122	0.65
no element present	74	396	16	84	470	0.46
Plural mark on subject						
overt	62	157	28	72	219	0.61
non-overt	56	317	15	85	373	0.44
Verb frequency						
high	33	425	7	93	458	0.33
low	85	49	63	37	134	0.92
Subject type						
lexical noun phrase	47	144	25	75	191	n.s.
ils	57	266	18	82	323	
qui	14	60	19	81	74	
Total	118	474	20	80	592	

Significance = 0.01, input = 0.19.

Table D10 Effects of extra-linguistic constraints on singular versus plural verb forms in the third person plural

Factor groups	Singular (N)	Plural (N)	Singular (%)	Plural (%)	Total (N)	Factor effect on singular form
French schooling						
25% or less	37	95	28	72	132	0.66
over 25%	81	379	18	82	460	0.45
Sex						
female	97	397	20	80	494	n.s.
male	20	77	21	79	97	
Social class						
middle	67	301	18	82	368	n.s.
upper-working	42	143	23	77	185	
Home language						
romance	23	63	27	73	86	n.s.
english	60	273	18	82	333	
other	35	138	20	80	173	
Francophone environment						
0 h	32	102	24	76	134	n.s.
1–7 days	31	107	22	78	138	
7 days to 3 weeks	35	179	16	84	214	
over 3 weeks	20	86	19	81	106	
Total	118	474	20	80	592	

Significance = 0.01, input = 0.19.

Table D11 Effects of linguistic constraints on auxiliaries *avoir* versus *être*

Factor groups	Avoir (N)	Être (N)	Avoir (%)	Être (%)	Total (N)	Factor effect on avoir
Verb type						
pronominal	0	15	0	100	15	Knock out
non-pronominal	78	269	22	78	347	
Tense						
compound past	78	268	23	77	346	Knock out
other	0	16	0	100	16	
Adjacency to past participle						
yes	72	279	21	79	351	0.49
no	6	5	55	45	11	0.87
Verb frequency						
frequent	27	204	12	88	231	0.35
infrequent	51	80	39	61	131	0.77
Transitive counterpart						
yes	8	13	38	62	21	n.s.
no	70	271	21	79	341	
Total	78	284	22	78	362	

Significance = 0.01, input = 0.20.

Table D12 Effects of extra-linguistic constraints on *avoir* versus *être*

Factor groups	Avoir (N)	Être (N)	Avoir (%)	Être (%)	Total (N)	Factor effect on avoir
Grade						
9	36	72	33	67	108	0.64
12	42	212	17	88	254	0.44
Francophone family						
0 h	46	172	21	79	218	0.527
1–13 days	22	28	44	56	50	0.753
over 2 weeks	10	84	11	89	94	0.301

(*Continued*)

Table D12 *Continued*

Factor groups	Avoir (N)	Etre (N)	Avoir (%)	Etre (%)	Total (N)	Factor effect on avoir
Social class						
middle	35	138	18	82	194	0.45
upper-working	34	103	28	72	123	0.58
Francophone environment						
0 h	19	60	24	76	79	n.s.
1–7 days	14	39	26	74	53	
7 days to 3 weeks	34	141	20	80	175	
over 3 weeks	11	44	24	76	55	
Sex						
female	56	233	19	81	289	n.s.
male	22	51	30	70	73	
Home language						
romance	11	52	17	83	63	n.s.
english	50	155	24	76	205	
other	17	77	18	82	94	
French media						
never	47	173	21	79	220	n.s.
occasional	31	111	22	78	142	
Total	78	284	22	78	362	

Significance = 0.03, input = 0.187.

Table D13 Effects of linguistic and extra-linguistic constraints on *chez 1* versus *à la maison*[a]

Factor groups	Chez 1 (N)	À la maison (N)	Chez 1 (%)	À la maison (%)	Total (N)	Factor effect on chez 1
Location/movement						
location	18	50	26	74	68	0.39
movement	16	20	44	56	36	0.69

(*Continued*)

Table D13 *Continued*

Factor groups	Chez 1 (N)	À la maison (N)	Chez 1 (%)	À la maison (%)	Total (N)	Factor effect on chez 1
Francophone family						
0 h	14	39	26	74	53	0.48
1–13 days	2	22	8	92	24	0.15
over 2 weeks	18	9	67	33	27	0.83
Francophone environment						
0 h	10	12	44	55	22	n.s.
1–6 days	5	14	26	74	19	
7–20 days	10	25	29	71	35	
over 3 weeks	9	19	32	68	28	
Social class						
middle	16	31	34	66	47	n.s.
upper-working	18	30	38	63	48	
Sex						
female	28	61	31	69	89	n.s.
male	6	9	40	60	15	
Grade						
9	15	38	28	72	53	n.s.
12	19	32	37	63	51	
French media						
never	17	47	27	73	64	n.s.
occasional	17	23	43	58	40	
French schooling						
0–25%	7	16	30	70	23	n.s.
26–38%	26	32	45	55	58	
over 38%	1	21	5	95	22	
Home language						
romance	7	14	33	67	21	n.s.
english	19	34	36	64	53	
other	8	22	27	73	30	
Total	34	70	33	67	104	

Significance = 0.02, input = 0.30.
[a]For *chez* 2, the immersion students used variant *chez* and several non-native forms. A GoldVarb analysis of *chez* 2 versus the non-native forms failed to find any significant factor groups.

Table D14 Effects of linguistic and extra-linguistic constraints on *travail* versus *emploi*[a]

Factor groups	Travail (N)	Emploi (N)	Travail (%)	Emploi (%)	Total (N)	Factor effect on travail
Priming[b]						
by *emploi*	2	9	18	82	11	0.14
unprimed	43	22	66	34	65	0.58
Home language						
romance	15	3	84	16	18	0.82
english	22	19	54	46	41	0.39
other	8	9	47	53	17	0.35
Grade						
9	22	12	65	35	34	n.s.
12	23	19	55	45	42	
Social class						
middle	22	24	48	52	46	n.s.
upper-working	16	7	70	30	23	
Sex						
female	32	25	56	44	57	n.s.
male	13	6	68	32	19	
Francophone environment						
0 h	17	17	50	50	34	n.s.
1–6 days	12	1	92	8	13	
7–20 days	12	8	60	40	20	
over 3 weeks	4	5	44	56	9	
French media						
never	33	25	57	43	58	n.s.
occasional	12	6	67	33	18	
Francophone family						
0 h	36	23	61	39	59	n.s.
1–13 days	2	1	67	33	3	
over 2 weeks	7	7	50	50	14	
Total	45	31	59	41	76	

Significance = 0.00, input = 0.59.
[a]The GoldVarb analysis was performed on the variants *travail* versus *emploi*. The third variant used by the immersion students, namely *job*, was too infrequent to lend itself to statistical analysis.
[b]'Priming' refers to the use of either or neither variant by the interviewer in a question to the students.

Appendix D

Table D15 Effects of linguistic and extra-linguistic constraints on *vivre* versus *habiter*

Factor groups	Habiter (N)	Vivre (N)	Habiter (%)	Vivre (%)	Total (N)	Factor effect on habiter
Priming						
by *habiter*	16	1	94	6	17	0.90
unprimed	50	38	57	63	88	0.43
by *vivre*	1	6	14	86	7	0.09
Home language						
romance	6	6	50	50	12	n.s.
english	40	22	65	35	62	
other	21	17	55	45	38	
Social class						
middle	38	24	61	39	62	n.s.
upper-working	25	20	56	44	45	
Sex						
female	48	36	58	42	84	n.s.
male	19	9	70	30	28	
Total	67	45	60	40	112	

Significance = 0.19, input = 0.60.
Note: 'Priming' refers to the use of either or neither variant by the interviewer in a question to the students.

Table D16 Effects of linguistic and extra-linguistic constraints on *auto* versus *voiture*

Factor groups	Auto (N)	Voiture (N)	Auto (%)	Voiture (%)	Total (N)	Factor effect on auto
Priming						
by *auto*	12	0	100	0	12	Knock out
by *voiture*	0	1	0	100	0	
unprimed	56	18	76	24	74	
Preceding element						
adjective	12	2	86	14	14	n.s.
preposition	14	2	88	13	16	
determiner	42	15	74	26	57	
Home language						
romance	14	1	93	7	15	0.97
english	26	11	70	30	37	0.27
other	28	7	80	20	35	0.45
Francophone environment						
0 h	17	1	94	6	18	0.75
1–6 days	11	7	61	39	18	0.07
7–20 days	33	2	94	6	35	0.86
over 3 weeks	7	9	44	56	16	0.11
Sex						
female	55	12	82	18	67	n.s.
male	13	7	65	35	20	
Grade						
9	32	4	89	11	36	n.s.
12	36	15	71	29	51	
French media						
never	39	5	89	11	44	n.s.
occasional	29	14	67	33	43	

(Continued)

Table D16 *Continued*

Factor groups	Auto (N)	Voiture (N)	Auto (%)	Voiture (%)	Total (N)	Factor effect on auto
French schooling						
0–25%	16	0	100	0	16	Knock out
26–38%	37	19	66	34	56	
over 38%	14	0	100	0	14	
Social class						
middle	43	12	78	22	55	n.s.
upper-working	22	7	76	24	29	
Total	68	19	78	22	87	

Significance = 0.01, input = 0.89.

Table D17 Effects of linguistic constraints on schwa use versus non-use

Phonetic context	Order for L1 speakers	Schwa use (N)	Schwa non-use (N)	Schwa use (%)	Schwa non-use (%)	Total (N)	Factor effect on schwa non-use
K.	C. F. E.	47	191	20	80	238	0.96
E.	K.	50	145	26	74	195	0.95
C.		123	62	66	34	185	0.76
A.	B.	108	21	84	16	129	0.55
B.	D.	598	72	89	11	670	0.43
G.	A.	79	8	91	9	87	0.39
L.	G.	124	11	92	8	135	0.36
D.	I.	652	38	94	6	690	0.27
I.	L.	42	2	95	5	44	0.23
J.	H.	309	7	98	2	316	0.12
H.	J.	18	0	100	0	18	Knock out
F.		142	0	100	0	142	Knock out
Total		2132	557	79	21	2689	

Significance = 0.00, input = 0.13.

Table D18 Effects of extra-linguistic constraints on schwa use versus schwa non-use

Factor groups	Schwa non-use (N)	Schwa use (N)	Schwa non-use (%)	Schwa use (%)	Total (N)	Factor effect on schwa non-use
Style						
formal	227	1211	16	84	1438	0.42
informal	330	939	26	74	1269	0.58
Sex						
female	488	1729	22	78	2217	0.53
male	69	421	14	86	490	0.35
French media						
never	274	1243	18	82	1517	0.47
occasionally	283	907	24	76	1190	0.53
Social class						
middle	321	1526	17	83	1847	n.s.
upper-working	236	624	27	73	860	
Francophone family						
0 h to 6 days	335	1204	22	78	1539	n.s.
1 week and over	222	946	19	81	1168	
Francophone environment						
0 h to 6 days	159	834	16	84	993	n.s.
1 week and over	398	1316	23	77	1714	
Total	557	2150	21	79	2707	

Significance = 0.03, input = 0.19.

Table D19 Effects of morphophonetic context on /l/ use versus non-use

Morphophonetic context	/l/ use (N)	/l/ non-use (N)	/l/ use (%)	/l/ non-use (%)	Total (N)
il y a	652	37	95	5	689
il (impersonal)	105	3	97	3	108
ils	825	17	98	2	842
il (personal)	833	1	99.88	0.12	834
elle(s)	703	0	100	0	703
Total	3118	58	98	2	3176

[a]Due to paucity of data, a GoldVarb analysis was not run.

Table D20 Effects of style on /l/ non-use in the speech of the French immersion students and Mougeon and Beniak's North-Bay Franco-Ontarian students

Corpora	Semi-directed taped interview (% /l/ non-use)	Reading passages (% /l/ non-use)
french immersion students	2	1
franco-Ontarian students	94	7

Notes

1. The listing of authors is alphabetical, reflecting an equal contribution by each.
2. The project is entitled *Research on Variation in the Spoken French of Immersion Students* and was funded by the Social Sciences and Humanities Research Council of Canada.
3. As pointed out by Kinginger (2008), the finding that students' understanding of colloquial words and reported ability to use such words benefited significantly from a study abroad in France is not in keeping with Dewaele and Regan's finding that after a one-year stay in France their own students made only modest use of French colloquial words. One explanation for these seemingly contradictory findings proposed by Kinginger is that reported ability to use colloquial terms may not exactly reflect the learners' actual ability to use such words, measured by production tasks.
4. While generic French pronoun *on* can be looked upon as formal in contrast to generic pronoun *tu* versus *vous* 'you', it is much less formal and marked than English generic pronoun *one*. The lesser level of formality associated with *on* is reflected in its non-negligible discursive frequency. For instance, in Montreal spoken French, generic pronoun *on* is used in 49% of occurrences and generic pronoun *tu* versus *vous* is used in 51% of them (Laberge, 1977).
5. The linguistic factors that constrain future variant choice in European versus Quebec or Ontario French are not identical. For instance, the Montreal Anglophone FL2 speakers examined by Dion and Blondeau (2005) master a polarity constraint (an association of the inflected future with negative sentences) that does not seem to obtain in European French. Conversely, in Regan *et al.* (2009), the Irish FL2 learners who spent one year in France master the association between the periphrastic future and proximal events, which was not documented in either Quebec or Ontario French (see Poplack & Turpin, 1999).
6. Interestingly, increased exposure to FL1 speech seems also to have a favorable effect on the learning of difficult formal variants (e.g. variable liaisons such as *les jeunes* (/z/) *enfants* 'the young children' – Thomas, 2000; Howard, 2005). This interesting topic is unfortunately under-researched.
7. The relevance of data on the sociolinguistic abilities of FL1 speakers in the development of FSL pedagogical norms has also been recently underscored by Lyster (1996), O'Connor Di Vito (1991) and Valdman (1998, 2003).
8. The teacher corpus we use has certain limitations that should be pointed out. First, it was gathered approximately 10 years before our corpus of French immersion students' spoken French, not all of the teachers who were taped

worked in the Toronto area, they taught French immersion in Grades 3 and 6, no information on their geographical provenance, years of experience and other characteristics was gathered, and, finally, we had access only to the orthographic transcriptions of their speech. Clearly, in our future studies, we will need to take steps to gather a teacher classroom speech corpus that is free from the above-mentioned limitations.

9. The series used in the school district where our French immersion corpus was collected is entitled *Portes ouvertes sur notre pays* and includes series 1A and B (Roy Nicolet & Jean-Côté, 1994) and 3A and B (Le Dorze & Morin, 1994). The other series is called *Capsules* (Deslauriers & Gagnon, 1995, 1997).
10. We would like to thank Kyle Conway for the treatment and preliminary analysis of the data yielded by the student survey.
11. It should be pointed out that Grade 13 in Ontario was phased out in September 2003.
12. At the time the data were collected, secondary education in Ontario included five grade levels (9–13). The approximate age of high school students ranged from 14 to 18 years.
13. The North York Board of Education is one of the school districts that amalgamated into the Toronto District School Board when various municipalities were brought together to form the mega city of Toronto.
14. The sample includes 20 students in Grade 9, 1 in Grade 10, 1 in Grade 11, 17 in Grade 12 and 2 in Grade 13. For the purposes of this present research focusing on Grades 9 and 12 students, those from Grade 10 are considered with the 9s and those from Grades 11 and 13 with the 12s.
15. Another reason for excluding students raised in Francophone homes was that numerous studies on variation in the spoken French of Ontario Francophone students have already been carried out (see, among others, Mougeon & Beniak, 1991; Mougeon & Nadasdi, 1998).
16. The fact that the average length of stay in a Francophone environment is the same as that found for length of stay with a Francophone family reflects the fact that the students' stays in a Francophone environment, while more numerous, were shorter than those with a Francophone family.
17. Ottawa is on the Ontario side of the Ottawa River and Hull is on the Quebec side. The decision to include Poplack's corpus within the category of Ontario corpora reflects the fact that the majority of the speakers in her corpus are from Ottawa.
18. The verification of this hypothesis is of special interest because as we pointed in our review of previous research only one study other than our research (Lealess, 2005) has examined the learning of a neutral variant by FL2 learners.
19. The decision to focus on English, Italian and Spanish should not be taken to mean that we believe that the other languages spoken by the immersion students do not also influence their learning of sociolinguistic variation. Rather this decision simply reflects the fact that these other languages are spoken by too few students in the corpus to sustain a statistical analysis that would demonstrate that such languages had an influence.
20. We have chosen not to make hypotheses concerning neutral variants since, by definition, they have no intrinsic sociostylistic properties that would lead teachers to favor or disfavor them.
21. Sociolinguistic variation typical of the Acadian varieties of French spoken in the Atlantic Provinces of Canada has also been the object of sociolinguistic research (e.g. King & Nadasdi, 2003). The patterns of sociolinguistic variation brought to light by this research have been found to differ considerably from

those observable in Quebec or Ontario French. For this reason and for the additional reason that the students in our sample have not been exposed to Acadian French, we could not use the findings of sociolinguistic research on this variety of Canadian French.
22. When *on* is used with either *nous-autres* or *nous*, it can occur to the right of these pronouns as in examples (3) and (4) or to the left of such pronouns as in: *on dit pas toi nous autres, là, on dit toé* 'we don't say *toi* twa [you] us, like, we say *toé* /twe/ [you]'.
23. Examples have been drawn from the Mougeon and Beniak corpus of spoken adolescent Ontario French whenever the studies on variation in Quebec French did not provide the necessary examples.
24. Willis (2000) also considered socioeconomic status. She found that there was a great deal of interaction between this category and education, and that education ultimately turned out to be a better predictor of variant choice.
25. Blondeau's (2006) study suggests that a contingency constraint may also exert a favorable effect on choice of the inflected future. However, given that her study was based on only 12 speakers, this finding needs to be confirmed by a study based on a larger speaker sample.
26. *M'as* is not used in Acadian French (King & Nadasdi, 1998). The varieties of French spoken in Canada also include another two variants, which are derived from the reflexive verb *s'en aller*, namely, *je m'en vais* and *je m'en vas*. Although these two variants were relatively frequent in the 17th century, they are almost extinct as future or habitual auxiliaries in contemporary spoken French on both sides of the Atlantic.
27. In marked informal French, adjectives are often not marked for gender after *être* 'to be'. This is why we find *français* instead of *française* in this example with the feminine noun *personne*.
28. In reference works on European French, *rien que* is not the object of proscriptive comments, or of any special comments for that matter. It is simply presented as an alternative to *seulement* and *ne...que*. We can infer from this that the association of *rien que* with lower class speech is particular to Canadian French.
29. We will see in Chapter 4 that in the French Language Arts materials used in the Ontario French immersion programs, *juste* is almost totally avoided. Such avoidance may be a further indication of a perception that *juste* is not a feature of standard French.
30. Throughout the text, we have placed the word singular between quotes when the singular verb form is used for a third person plural subject.
31. It should be noted that among these four variants, *(ça) fait que* is singled out by Le Nouveau Petit Robert (1996) as regional.
32. The brackets around *ça* indicate that this locution is often pronounced without *ça*.
33. As concerns this particular sociolinguistic variable, Mougeon *et al.* (1981) examined not only the Mougeon and Beniak corpus (see the section 'The Ontario corpora'), but also data from another corpus of Franco-Ontarian adolescent speech gathered in the towns of Rayside, Sudbury and Welland. The data on frequency of variant use reported in the present section and used as our FL1 benchmark, come from both this latter corpus and from the Mougeon and Beniak corpus. As in the case of the other variables where we used Franco-Ontarian adolescent speech as a substitute for FL1 Quebec French, we report frequency percentages calculated only for the speech of unrestricted users of Ontario French.
34. The subscript numbers in the examples below indicate coreferentiality or lack thereof between the subject and the dweller.

35. We will see in Chapter 5 that in the speech of the restricted Franco-Ontarian adolescents the frequency of variant *su'* falls to 9%.
36. Sankoff *et al.* (1978) also examined another lexical variable involving words meaning 'thing'. However, it has not been studied yet in the immersion corpus and will therefore be excluded from the present discussion.
37. The Sherbrooke corpus of 100 adult francophones was gathered in 1973 and followed a Labovian semi-directed interview protocol.
38. In European Standard French, the variant *job* is considered as an informal variant. *Job* is a masculine noun (e.g. *un job* 'a job'), whereas in Canadian French it is a feminine noun (e.g. *une job* 'a job').
39. Preliminary analysis of the Mougeon, Nadasdi and Rehner corpus of adolescent Ontario French gathered in 2005 in the same communities where Mougeon and Beniak gathered their corpus in 1978 suggests that the frequency of variant *voiture* has increased from 2% to 10%, primarily at the expense of *auto*.
40. As shown by examples (96) and (98) the gender of *auto* in Quebec spoken-French is variable.
41. We will see in Chapter 4 that in the written text component of the French Language Arts materials used in immersion programs, *automobile* is the most frequent variant. This finding suggests that *automobile* is associated with the formal registers of Quebec French.
42. Although no sociolinguistic study of schwa non-use in Quebec French is available, two studies attest its existence in Quebec French and examine its theoretical significance for phonology (Morin, 1978; Picard, 1991).
43. It should be noted here that the figures for the effect of topic (in)formality and interview versus reading passage were calculated for all three levels of French language use restriction.
44. Note that /l/ non-use does not occur in the definite article *le*.
45. Unlike Sankoff and Cedergren, Poplack and Walker found a sufficiently high number of occurrences of *elles* in their corpus to calculate a rate of /l/ deletion for that pronoun (33%) and they also documented /l/ deletion in pronouns *lui* (91%) and *leur* (4%).
46. As shown by Tables 4.5 and 4.6, the immersion teachers did not speak about 'remunerated work' in the classroom. Therefore we lack information on how frequently they use the different (in)formal or neutral variants that express this notion.
47. Schwa and /l/ non-use might also have revealed exceptional trends in view of the fact that they are quite frequent in FL1 speech. However, the fact that we were not able to analyze the teachers' pronunciation prevented us from verifying this hypothesis.
48. The teachers in our corpus used the word *travail* quite frequently in the classroom. However, they did so to express the notion of 'class' or 'homework'.
49. Given that these audio materials faithfully reflect all the words and usages included in the written textbooks, we limited our analysis of variation to the phonological variables.
50. We found only three instances of intra-sentential uses of *donc* in the teachers' classroom speech. Two were clearly instances in which the teacher was reading aloud sentences from a book. As for the third instance, it was more difficult to determine whether it reflected spontaneous speech or reading aloud.
51. Recall that we have not been able to analyze pronunciation features of the French immersion teachers since we do not have access to the tape recordings of their classroom speech.

52. While this third explanation is reasonable, it is not as convincing as the first two, since the immersion students in the present study, like other immersion students (cf. Carroll, 1999; Harley, 1979), have an incomplete mastery of grammatical gender.
53. It should be noted that the only 'exception' to this is the sporadic use of *avoir* with *aller* found in Montreal French (0.7%).
54. It can be pointed out that in formal literary French negative sentences sometimes appear without post-verbal negator *pas*. This construction is a relic of old French and, while it is used marginally in the French Language Arts materials we have analyzed, it is not used by the French immersion teachers in the Allen *et al.* (1987) corpus. As such, this literary construction is an unlikely source for the French immersion students' deletion of *pas*. A more likely explanation is that these instances of *pas* deletion represent a remnant of a quasi-universal developmental stage where the learners expressed sentence negation via only a pre-verbal element.
55. In a similar vein, it could be argued that the trend to delete the pre-verbal negative particle *ne* documented in the students' speech also reflects, to some extent, a form of simplification. Still, given the fact that the immersion teachers delete *ne* some of the time and that the immersion students who have had contacts with FL1 speakers must have been exposed to *ne* non-use, simplification cannot be the only explanation.
56. We saw earlier that in relation to the *seulement* variable the materials use both *ne...que* and *seulement* and that they show a strong preference for the former. However, due to the morphosyntactic complexity of *ne...que* the immersion students fail to learn this variant. Thus, it could be argued that through the materials the students are exposed to only one 'learnable' variant, namely, *seulement*.
57. As is shown by Table 4.22, in relation to the variant *donc*, our research found the reverse correlation with social class, namely the students from the upper working class used this variant more often than the students from the other social classes. To explain this finding we can invoke the very same factors that we discussed in relation to the contrary effect of learners' sex.
58. The word *travaglio* is a feature of the dialects of Italian spoken in the South of Italy, an area from where the great majority of Italians residing in Toronto have emigrated.
59. For instance, in Sicilian, the inflected future is very much a formal option that alternates with two periphrastic futures, one with the verb *to want* + infinitive and the other with the verb *to have* + infinitive.
60. We should also point out that yet another potential difference concerns possible exposure to French prior to attending school. Unfortunately, we do not have data on language-use habits of the restricted speakers during their early childhood. However, given that 65% of restricted speakers are from homes where only one parent is Francophone, we surmise that the restricted speakers have received minimal exposure to French prior to attending school, since linguistic exogamy rarely results in the transmission of the minority language (cf. Castonguay, 1981).
61. The present discussion will exclude the distinction between the inflected and periphrastic future since neither has been the object of study according to restriction in the use of Ontario French.
62. The presence of *so* in Ontario French is not unlike that of *job* in Quebec and Ontario French in that it is integrated into the lexicon of Ontario French, it is discursively frequent and it is associated with working class speech. Thus, it is a *bona fide* marker of the marked informal register.

63. Note that we have not considered the following hyper-formal variants since they are never used by the unrestricted versus restricted students (i.e. *ne...que*) or used only sporadically (i.e. *poste* – two tokens).
64. It is perhaps worth reminding the reader at this point that one of the main reasons why the students focused on in our research have not had extensive opportunities to interact with FL1 speakers is that their parents could not afford the costs of sending their children on extended trips to a Francophone country. Thus, although it may well be that extended stays in countries where the target language is spoken as an L1 are an effective way of improving the learners' (socio)linguistic competence, they are not the most cost-effective and equitable way of achieving this goal.
65. The only neutral variant that is not used in the materials is the futurate present. This probably reflects the fact that it is very infrequent in FL1 speech and is a feature of context-embedded speech.
66. One variant (*ne* non-use) is explicitly acknowledged; however, it is described as a mistake without any qualification.

References

Adamson, H. (1988) *Variation Theory and Second Language Acquisition*. Washington: Georgetown University Press.
Adamson, H. and Regan, V. (1991) The acquisition of community speech norms by Asian immigrants learning English as a second language: A preliminary study. *Studies in Second Language Acquisition* 13 (1), 1–22.
Allen, P., Cummins, J., Harley, B. and Swain, M. (1987) *Development of Bilingual Proficiency Project*. Toronto: OISE, University of Toronto.
Andersen, R.W. (1981) *New Dimensions in Second Language Acquisition Research*. Rowley, MA: Newbury House.
Armstrong, N. (1996) Variable deletion of French /l/: Linguistic, social and stylistic factors. *Journal of French Language Studies* 6, 1–21.
Armstrong, N. (2001) *Social and Stylistic Variation in Spoken French: A Comparative Approach*. Amsterdam: Benjamins.
Ashby, W. (1981) The loss of the negative particle *ne* in French: A syntactic change in progress. *Language* 57 (3), 674–687.
Ashby, W. (1984) The elision of /l/ in French clitic pronouns and articles. In E. Pulgram (ed.) *Romanitas: Studies in Romance Linguistics* (pp. 1–16). Ann Arbor: University of Michigan Press.
Ashby, W. (2001) Un nouveau regard sur la chute du *ne* en français parlé tourangeau: s'agit-il d'un changement en cours? *Journal of French Language Studies* 11 (1), 1–22.
Auger, J. (2002) French immersion in Montreal: Pedagogical norm and functional competence. In S. Gass, K. Bardovi-Harlig, S. Sieloff Magnan and J. Walz (eds) *Pedagogical Norms for Second and Foreign Language Learning and Teaching* (pp. 81–101). Amsterdam: Benjamins.
Bachman, L.F. (1987) *Fundamental Considerations in Language Testing*. Reading, MA: Addison-Wesley.
Barlow, M. (1998) *MonoConc Pro* (Version 1.0) [Computer software]. Houston, TX: Athelstan.
Barron, A. (2003) *Acquisition in Interlanguage Pragmatics. Learning How to Do Things with Words in a Study Abroad Context*. Amsterdam/Philadelphia: Benjamins.
Bartning, I. (1997) L'apprenant dit avancé et son acquisition d'une langue étrangère: tour d'horizon et esquisse d'une caractérisation de la variété avancée. *Acquisition et Interaction en Langue Étrangère* 9, 9–50.
Bayley, R. (1996) Competing constraints on variation in the speech of adult Chinese learners of English. In R. Bayley and D. Preston (eds) *Second Language Acquisition and Linguistic Variation* (pp. 97–120). Amsterdam: Benjamins.
Bayley, R. and Regan, V. (2004) Introduction: The acquisition of sociolinguistic competence. *Journal of Sociolinguistics* 8 (3), 393–338.

Beebe, L. (1988) *Issues in Second Language Acquisition*. New York: Newbury House.
Bienvenue, R. (1983) *French Immersion: Recruitment Factors*. Winnipeg: Institute for social and economic research, University of Manitoba.
Bienvenue, R. (1986) Participation in an educational innovation: Enrollments in French immersion programs. *Canadian Journal of Sociology* 11 (4), 363–377.
Blishen, B., Carroll, W. and Moore, C. (1987) The 1981 socioeconomic index for occupations in Canada. *Canadian Review of Sociology and Anthropology* 24 (4), 465–488.
Blondeau, H. (2001) Real time changes in the paradigm of personal pronouns in Montreal French. *Journal of Sociolinguistics* 5 (4), 453–474.
Blondeau, H. (2006). La trajectoire du futur chez une cohorte de Montréalais francophones entre 1971 et 1995. *Canadian Journal of Applied Linguistics* 9 (2), 73–98.
Blondeau, H. and Nagy, N. (1998) Double marquage du sujet dans le français parlé par les jeunes anglo-montréalais. In J. Jensen and G. Van Herk (eds) *Actes du Congrès Annuel de l'Association Canadienne de Linguistique* (pp. 59–70). Ottawa: Cahiers Linguistiques d'Ottawa.
Blondeau, H., Nagy, N., Sankoff, G. and Thibault, P. (2002) La couleur locale du français L2 des Anglo-Montréalais. *Acquisition et Interaction en Langue Étrangère* 17, 73–100.
Blondeau, H., Fonollosa, M-O., Gagnon, L., Lefevbre, N., Poirier, D. and Thibault, P. (1995) Aspects of L2 competence in a bilingual setting. Paper presented at NWAV 24. Philadelphia: University of Pennsylvania, October 14–18. (Handout and tables).
Bonami, O. (2002) A syntax-semantics interface for tense and aspect in French. In F. Van Eynde, L. Hellan and D. Beerman (eds) *The Proceedings of the HPSG '01 Conference* (pp. 31–50). Stanford: CSLI Publications.
Boutet, J. (1986) La référence à la personne en français parlé: le cas de *on*. *Langage et société* 38, 19–50.
Brown, H.D. (1987) *Principles of Language Learning and Teaching*. Englewood Cliffs, NJ: Prentice Hall.
Calvé, P. (1991) Vingt-cinq ans d'immersion au Canada 1965–1990. *Études de Linguistique Appliquée* 82, 7–23.
Canale, M. (1983) From communicative competence to communicative language pedagogy. In J. Richards and R.W. Schmidt (eds) *Language and Communication* (pp. 2–27). New York: Longman.
Canale, M. and Swain, M. (1980) Theoretical bases of communicative approaches to second language teaching and testing. *Applied Linguistics* 1 (1), 1–47.
Carroll, S. (1999) Input and SLA: Adults' sensitivity to different sorts of cues to French gender. *Language Learning* 49 (1): 37–92.
Celce-Murcia, M.A., Dörnyei, Z. and Thurrell, S. (1995) Communicative competence: A pedagogically motivated model with content specification. *Issues in Applied Linguistics* 6, 5–35.
Chaudenson, R., Mougeon, R. and Beniak, É. (1993) *Vers une approche panlectale de la variation du français*. Paris: Didier Érudition.
Chaudenson, R., Valli, A. and Véronique, D. (1986) The dynamics of linguistic systems and the acquisition of French as a second language. *Studies in Second Language Acquisition* 8, 277–292.
Corder, S.P. (1981) *Error Analysis in Interlanguage*. Oxford: Oxford University Press.
Coveney, A. (1996) *Variability in Spoken French: A Sociolinguistic Study of Interrogation and Negation*. Exeter: Elm Bank.
Coveney, A. (2000) Vestiges of *nous* and the 1st person plural verb in informal spoken French. *Language Sciences* 22 (4), 447–481.

Critchley, S. (1994) Discourse variety in contemporary French language: A pedagogical approach. In J.A. Coleman and R. Crawshaw (eds) *Discourse Variety in Contemporary French: Descriptive and Pedagogical Approaches* (pp. 203–236). London: Association for French Language Studies and Centre for Information on Language Teaching.

Cuq, J-P. (1994) Cadre théorique et modalités d'insertion de la variété linguistique dans l'enseignement du français langue étrangère et seconde. In J.A. Coleman and R. Crawshaw (eds) *Discourse Variety in Contemporary French: Descriptive and Pedagogical Approaches* (pp. 19–34). London: Association for French Language Studies and Centre for Information on Language Teaching.

Day, E. and Shapson, S. (1991) Integrating formal and functional approaches to language teaching in French immersion: An experimental study. *Language Learning* 41 (1), 25–58.

Deshaies, D. (1991) Contribution à l'analyse du français québécois: Étude des pronoms personnels. *Revue québécoise de linguistique théorique et appliquée* 10 (3), 11–40.

Deshaies, D. and Laforge, E. (1981) Le futur simple et le futur périphrastique dans le français parlé dans la ville de Québec. *Langues et linguistique* 7, 23–37.

Deshaies, D., Martin, C. and Noël, D. (1981) Régularisation et analogie dans le système verbal en français parlé dans la ville de Québec. In D. Sankoff (ed.) *Variation Omnibus* (pp. 411–418). Edmonton: Linguistic Research Inc.

Deslauriers, L. and Gagnon, N. (1995) *Capsules. Manuels 5A, 5B*. Montréal: Modulo.

Deslauriers, L. and Gagnon, N. (1997) *Capsules. Manuels 6A, 6B*. Montréal: Modulo.

Dessureault-Dober, D. (1974) Étude sociolinguistique de ça fait que: Coordonnant logique et marqueur d'interaction. Master's thesis, Université de Montréal.

Dewaele, J-M. (1992) L'omission du *ne* dans deux styles oraux d'interlangue française. *Journal of Applied Linguistics* 7 (1), 3–17.

Dewaele, J-M. (1998) Lexical inventions: French interlanguage as L2 versus L3. *Applied Linguistics* 19 (4), 471–490.

Dewaele, J-M. (1999) Word order variation in French interrogatives. *International Review of Applied Linguistics* 125–126, 161–180.

Dewaele, J-M. (2002) Using sociostylistic variants in advanced French interlanguage. *EUROSLA Yearbook* II, 205–226.

Dewaele, J-M. (2004a) The acquisition of sociolinguistic competence in French as a foreign language: An overview. *Journal of French Language Studies* 14 (3), 301–319.

Dewaele, J-M. (2004b) Retention or omission of the *ne* in advanced French interlanguage: The variable effect of extralinguistic factors. *Journal of Sociolinguistics*, 8 (3), 433–450.

Dewaele, J-M. (2004c) Variation, chaos et sytème en interlangue français. *Acquisition et Interaction en Langue Etrangère* 17, 143–167.

Dewaele, J-M. (2004d) Colloquial vocabulary in the speech of native and non-native speakers: The effects of proficiency and personality. In P. Bogaards and B. Laufer (eds) *Learning Vocabulary in a Second Language: Selection, Acquisition and Testing* (pp. 127–153). Amsterdam: Benjamins.

Dewaele, J-M. and Regan, V. (2001) The use of colloquial words in advanced French interlanguage. In S. Foster-Cohen and A. Nizegorodcew (eds) *EUROSLA Yearbook 1* (pp. 51–68). Amsterdam: Benjamins.

Dewaele, J-M. and Regan, V. (2002) Maîtriser la norme sociolinguistique en interlangue française: le cas de l'omission variable de *ne*. *Journal of French Language Studies* 12 (2), 123–148.

DiCesare, D. (in progress) Non acquisition de la préposition *chez* et de sa variante *à la maison* par des élèves ontariens d'immersion française en 9e et 12e année. MA thesis, York University, Toronto.

Dickerson, L. (1974) Internal and external patterning of phonological variability in the speech of Japanese learners of English: Toward a theory of second language acquisition. PhD dissertation, University of Illinois, Urbana-Champaign.

Dicks, J. (2001) *The French Immersion and English Programs in New Brunswick School Districts 17 and 18* (Final Report). Fredericton, NB: Second Language Education Centre, University of New Brunswick.

Dion, N. and Blondeau, H. (2005) Variability and future temporal reference: The French of Anglo-Montrealers. Paper presented at NWAV 32, Pennsylvania, University of Pennsylvania.

Downes, W. (1998) *Language and Society*. Cambridge: Cambridge University Press.

Ellis, R. (1987) Interlanguage variability in narrative discourse: Style shifting in the use of the past tense. *Studies in Second Language Acquisition* 9 (1), 1–20.

Ellis, R. (1999) Item versus system learning: Explaining free variation. *Applied Linguistics* 20 (4), 460–480.

Emirkanian, L. and Sankoff, D. (1985) Le futur simple et le futur périphrastique dans le français parlé. In M. Lemieux and H. Cedergren (eds) *Les tendances dynamiques du français parlé à Montréal* (Vol. 2, pp. 189–204). Quebec City: Government of Quebec.

Gadet, F. (1992) *Le français populaire*. Paris: Presses universitaires de France.

Gass, S. and Selinker, L. (2001) *Second Language Acquisition: An Introductory Course*. London: Erlbaum.

Gatbonton, E. (1978) Patterned phonetic variability in second language speech: A gradual diffusion model. *The Canadian Modern Language Review* 34 (3), 335–347.

Genesee, F. (1987) *Learning through Two Languages: Studies of Immersion and Bilingual Children*. Cambridge, MA: Newbury House.

Genesee, F. (1990) Beyond bilingualism: Sociocultural studies in immersion. In B. Flemming and M. Whitla (eds) *So you Want your Child to Learn French!* (pp. 96–107). Ottawa: Canadian Parents for French.

Genesee, F., Polich, E. and Stanley, M.H. (1977) An experimental French immersion program at the secondary school level – 1969–1974. *The Canadian Modern Language Review* 33 (3), 318–332.

Goldfine, C. (1987) Negation in French L2 learners. *Linguistics* 23 (1), 49–77.

Grevisse, M. (1988) *Le Bon Usage*. Paris-Gembloux: Duculot.

Hallion, S. (2000) Étude du français parlé au manitoba. PhD dissertation: Université de Provence (Aix-Marseille I).

Hansen, A.B. (1994) Étude du E caduc – stabilisation en cours et variation lexicale. *Journal of French Language Studies* 4 (1), 25–54.

Harley, B. (1979) French gender 'rules' in the speech of English-dominant, French-dominant and monolingual French-speaking children. *Working Papers in Bilingualism* 19, 129–156.

Harley, B. (1982) Age-related differences in the acquisition of the French verb system by anglophone students in French immersion programs. PhD dissertation, University of Toronto.

Harley, B. (1984) How good is their French? *Language and Society* 10, 55–60.

Harley, B. (1989a) Transfer in the written composition of French immersion students. In H. Dechert and M. Raupach (eds) *Transfer in Language Production* (pp. 3–19). Norwood: Ablex.

Harley, B. (1989b) Functional grammar in French immersion: A classroom experiment. *Applied Linguistics* 10 (3), 331–359.

Harley, B. (1992) Patterns of second language development in French immersion. *Journal of French Language Studies* 2 (2), 159–183.

Harley, B. and King, M.L. (1989) Verb lexis in the written compositions of young L2 learners. *Studies in Second Language Acquisition* 11 (4), 415–436.

Hart, D. and Lapkin, S. (1998) Issues of social-class bias in access to French immersion education. In S. Lapkin (ed.) *French Second Language Education in Canada: Empirical Studies* (pp. 324–350). Toronto: University of Toronto Press.

Hart, D., Lapkin, S. and Swain, M. (1989) *Final Report to the Calgary Board of Education: The Evaluation of Continuing Bilingual and Late Immersion Programs at the Secondary Level.* Toronto: Modern Language Centre, OISE.

Hart, D., Lapkin, S., Swain, M. and Howard, J. (1991) *French Immersion at the Secondary/Post-Secondary Interface: Toward a National Study* (Report submitted to the Department of the Secretary of State). Toronto: Modern Language Centre, OISE.

Hart, D., Lapkin, S. and Howard, J. (1994) *Attrition from French Immersion Programs in a Northern Ontario City: 'Push' and 'Pull' Factors in Two Area Boards.* Report to Canadian Heritage. Toronto: Modern Language Centre, OISE.

Hashimoto, H. (1994) Language acquisition of an exchange student within the homestay environment. *Journal of Asian Pacific Communication* 4 (4), 209–224.

Hickey, T. (2001). Mixing beginners and native speakers in minority language immersion: Who is immersing whom? *The Canadian Modern Language Review* 57 (3), 443–474.

Houston, A. (1985) Continuity and change in English morphology: The variable (-ing). PhD dissertation, University of Pennsylvania.

Howard, M. (2005) L'acquisition de la liaison en français langue seconde: Une analyse quantitative d'apprenants avancés en milieu guidé et en milieu naturel. *Corela*, Numéros spéciaux, Colloque AFLS.

Howard, M., Lemée, I. and Regan, V. (2006) The L2 acquisition of a phonological variable: The case of /l/ deletion in French. *Journal of French Language Studies* 16 (1), 1–24.

Huebner, T. (1983) *Longitudinal Analysis of the Acquisition of English.* Ann Arbor, MI: Karoma.

Huebner, T. (1985) System and variability in interlanguage syntax. *Language Learning* 35 (1), 141–163.

Jeanjean, C. (1988) Le futur simple et le futur périphrastique. Étude distributionnelle. In C. Blanche-Benveniste, A. Cheurel and M. Gross (eds) *Grammaire et histoire de la grammaire, hommage à la mémoire de Jean Stéfanini* (pp. 235–257). Aix en Provence: Presses de l'Université de Provence.

Kenemer, V. (1982) *Le français populaire and French as a Second Language: A Comparative Study of Language Simplification.* Quebec City: CIRB.

King, R. and Nadasdi, T. (2003) Back to the future in Acadian French. *Journal of French Language Studies* 13 (3), 23–337.

King, R., Martineau, F. and Mougeon, R. (2009) First person plural pronominal reference in urban varieties of European French: A diachronic sociolinguistic study. York University: Unpublished manuscript.

Kinginger, C. (2008) Language learning in study abroad: Case studies of Americans in France. *Modern Language Journal* 92 (1), 1–124.

Knaus, V. and Nadasdi, T. (2001) Être ou ne pas être en immersion. *The Canadian Modern Language Review* 58 (2), 287–306.

Laberge, S. (1977) Étude de la variation des pronoms définis et indéfinis dans la français parlé à Montréal. PhD dissertation, Université de Montréal.

Labov, W. (1966) *The Social Stratification of English in New York City.* Washington, DC: Center for Applied Linguistics.

Labov, W. (1972) *Sociolinguistic Patterns.* Philadelphia: University of Pennsylvania Press.

Labov, W. (1990) The intersection of gender and social class in the course of linguistic change. *Language Variation and Change* 11 (2), 205–254.

Lambert, W.E. and Tucker, G.R. (1972) *Bilingual Education of Children*. Rowley, MA: Newbury House.
Lapkin, S. and Swain, M. (2000) Task outcomes: A focus on immersion students' use of pronominal verbs in their writing. *Canadian Journal of Applied Linguistics* 3 (1–2), 7–22.
Lapkin, S., Hart, D. and Swain, M. (1995) A Canadian interprovincial exchange: Evaluating the linguistic impact of a three-month stay in Quebec. In B.F. Freed (ed.) *Second Language Acquisition in a Study Abroad Context* (pp. 67–94). Amsterdam: Benjamins.
Le Dorze, P. and Morin, N. (1994) *Portes ouvertes sur notre pays. Manuel 3A, 3B*. Montreal: Guérin.
Le Goffic, P. and Lab, F. (2001) Le présent <pro futuro>. *Cahiers Chronos* 7, 77–98.
Le Nouveau Petit Robert (1996) *Dictionnaire de la langue française*. Paris: Dictionnaires le Robert.
Le Petit Larousse (1993) *Dictionnaire encyclopédique*. Paris: Larousse.
Lealess, A. (2005) En français, il faut qu'on parle bien: Assessing native-like proficiency in L2 French. MA thesis, University of Ottawa.
Lesage, R. and Gagnon, S. (1992) Futur simple et futur périphrastique dans la presse québécoise. In A. Crochetière, J-C. Boulanger and C. Ouellon (eds) *Actes du XVème Congrès international des linguistes* (pp. 367–370). Quebec city: Les Presses de l'Université Laval.
Lindholm-Leary, K. (2001) *Dual Language Education*. Clevedon: Multilingual Matters.
Lynch, A. (2002) On the notion of 'nativeness': Incomplete acquisition and linguistic variation in a bilingual city. Paper presented at NWAV 31, Stanford University, California, October 10–13.
Lyster, R. (1994a) The effect of functional-analytic teaching on aspects of French immersion students' sociolinguistic competence. *Applied Linguistics* 15 (3), 263–287.
Lyster, R. (1994b) La négociation de la forme: stratégie analytique en classe d'immersion. *The Canadian Modern Language Review* 50 (3), 446–465.
Lyster, R. (1996) Question forms, conditionals, and second-person pronouns used by adolescent native speakers across two levels of formality in written and spoken French. *Modern Language Journal* 80 (2), 165–182.
Lyster, R. (1998) Form in immersion classroom: in and out of focus. *Canadian Journal of Applied Linguistics* 1 (1–2), 53–82.
Lyster, R. (2007) *Learning and Teaching Languages through Content: A Counterbalanced Approach*. Amsterdam: Benjamins.
Lyster, R. and Rebuffot, J. (2002) Acquisition des pronoms d'allocution en classe de français immersif. *Acquisition et Interaction en Langue Étrangère* 17, 51–72.
MacFarlane, A. and Wesche, M. (1995) Immersion outcomes: Beyond language proficiency. *The Canadian Modern Language Review* 51 (2), 250–274.
Major, R.C. (1999) Gender marking in second language phonology. Paper presented at NWAV 28, University of Toronto and York University, October.
Major, R.C. (2004) Gender and stylistic variation in second language phonology. *Language Variation and Change* 16 (2), 169–188.
Mannesy, G. and Wald, P. (1984) *Le français en Afrique Noire: tel qu'on le parle, tel qu'on le dit*. Paris: L'Harmattan.
Marriott, H. (1995) The acquisition of politeness patterns by exchange students in Japan. In B. Freed (ed.) *Second Language Acquisition in a Study Abroad Context* (pp. 197–227). Amsterdam: Benjamins.
Martel, P. (1984) Les variantes lexicales sont-elles sociolinguistiquement intéressantes? *Sociolinguistique des langues romanes*. In *Actes du XVIIe Congrès*

international de linguistique et philologie romanes (pp. 183–193). Aix-en-Provence: Presses de l'Université de Provence.

Martineau, F. and Mougeon, R. (2005) *Vais, vas, m'as in spoken Quebec and Metropolitan French: A Diachronic and Dialectal Perspective*. Paper presented at the Linguistics Symposium on Romance Languages, University of Texas at Austin, February 24–27.

Massicotte, F. (1986) Les expressions de la restriction en français de Montréal. In D. Sankoff (ed.) *Diversity and Diachrony* (pp. 325–332). Amsterdam: Benjamins.

Matsumara, S. (2001) Learning the rules for offering advice: A quantitative approach to second language socialisation. *Language Learning* 51, 635–679.

McLaughlin, D. and Niedre, J. (1998) *Pont vers le futur. Manuel de français 2*. Montreal: Guérin.

Morin, Y.Ch. (1978) The status of mute 'e'. *Studies in French Linguistics* 1 (2), 29–40.

Mougeon, R. (1996) Recherche sur les origines de la variation *vas, m'as, vais* en français québécois. In T. Lavoie (ed.) *Français du Canada – Français de France* (pp. 60–77). Tübingen: Niemeyer.

Mougeon, R. (1998) French outside New Brunswick and Quebec. In J. Edwards (ed.) *Language in Canada* (pp. 226–251). Cambridge: Cambridge University Press.

Mougeon, R. and Beniak, E. (1991) *Linguistic Consequences of Language Contact and Restriction: The Case of French in Ontario*. Oxford: Oxford University Press.

Mougeon, R. and Beniak, E. (1995) Le non-accord en nombre entre sujet et verbe en français ontarien: Un cas de simplification? *Présence Francophone* 46, 53–65.

Mougeon, R. and Rehner, K. (1997) *Sociolinguistic Variation in French Immersion Students' Speech*. Paper presented at the 28th annual conference of the Canadian Association of Applied Linguistics, Memorial University, St. John's, NF, 2–4 June.

Mougeon, R. and Nadasdi, T. (1998) Sociolinguistic discontinuity in minority language communities. *Language* 74 (1), 40–55.

Mougeon, R. and Rehner, K. (2001) Variation in the spoken French of Ontario French immersion students: The case of *juste* versus *seulement* versus *rien que*. *Modern Language Journal* 85 (3), 398–415.

Mougeon, R., Beniak, É. and Coté, N. (1981) Variation géographique en français ontarien: Rôle du maintien de la langue maternelle. *Journal of the Atlantic Provinces Linguistic Association* 3, 64–82.

Mougeon, R., Nadasdi, T., Rehner, K. and Uritescu, D. (2002) *The sharing of Constraints in Minority Speech Communities*. Paper presented at NWAV 31, Stanford University, October 10–13.

Mougeon, R., Haillon-Bres, S., Papen, R. and Bigot, D. (2008) M'as tout vous dire comment ça se passe à l'ouest du Québec. Paper presented at the international conference, *Les français d'ici II*, University of Ottawa, May 22–25.

Mougeon, R., Nadasdi, T. and Rehner, K. (2009) Évolution de l'usage des conjonctions et locutions de conséquence par les adolescents franco-ontariens de Hawkesbury et Pembroke (1978–2005). In F. Martineau, R. Mougeon, T. Nadasdi and M. Tremblay (eds) *Les français d'ici: etudes linguistiques et sociolinguistiques sur la variation du français au Québec et en Ontario* (pp. 145–184). Toronto: Éditions du GREF.

Nadasdi, T. (2001) Agreeing to disagree: Variable subject-verb agreement in immersion French. *Canadian Journal of Applied Linguistics* 4 (1), 78–101.

Nadasdi, T. and McKinnie, M. (2003) Living and working in immersion French. *Journal of French Language Studies* 13 (1), 47–61.

Nadasdi, T., Uritescu, D., Mougeon, R. and Rehner, K. (2001) A sociolinguistic analysis of phonetic variation in the spoken French of Franco-Ontarian and immersion students. Paper presented at the annual meeting of the Canadian Association of Applied Linguistics, Laval University, May 24–26.

Nadasdi, T., Mougeon, R. and Rehner, K. (2003) Emploi du futur dans le français parlé des élèves d'immersion française. *Journal of French Language Studies* 13 (2), 195–219.
Nadasdi, T., Mougeon, R. and Rehner, K. (2004) Expression de la notion de 'véhicule automobile' dans le parler des adolescents francophones de l'Ontario. *Francophonies d'Amérique* 17, 91–106.
Nadasdi, T., Mougeon, R. and Rehner, K. (2005) Learning to speak everyday (Canadian) French. *The Canadian Modern Language Review* 61 (4), 543–563.
Nagy, N. and Blondeau, H. (1998) Double subject marking in L2 Montreal French. *University of Pennsylvania Working Papers in Linguistics* 6, 93–108.
Nagy, N., Moisset, C. and Sankoff, G. (1996) On the acquisition of variable phonology in L2. *University of Pennsylvania Working Papers in Linguistics* 3 (1), 111–126.
Nagy, N., Blondeau, H. and Auger, J. (2003) Second language acquisition and 'real' French: An investigation of subject doubling in the French of Montreal Anglophones. *Language Variation and Change* 15 (1), 73–103.
North York Board of Education (1986) *Report to the Director's Committee on French as a Second Language Programs*. North York: North York Board of Education.
O'Connor Di Vito, N. (1991) Incorporating native speaker norms in second language materials. *Applied Linguistics* 12 (4), 383–396.
Offord, M. (1994) Teaching varieties and register. In J.A. Coleman and R. Crawshaw (eds) *Discourse Variety in Contemporary French: Descriptive and Pedagogical Approaches* (pp. 185–202). London: Association for French Language Studies and Centre for Information on Language Teaching.
Olson, P. and Burns, G. (1983) Politics, class, and happenstance: French immersion in a Canadian context. *Interchange* 14 (3), 1–16.
Ontario Ministry of Education (2000) *The Ontario Curriculum Grades 11 and 12: French as a Second Language – Core, Extended, and Immersion French*. Toronto: Queen's Printer.
Parkin, M., Morrison, F. and Watkin, G. (1987) French immersion research relevant to decisions in Ontario. *Review and Evaluation Bulletins, No. 1*. (ERIC Document Reproduction Service No. ED 295 473).
Picard, M. (1991) La loi des trois consonnes et la chute du cheva en québécois. *Revue québécoise de linguistique* 20 (2), 35–49.
Poplack, S. (1989) The care and handling of a megacorpus: The Ottawa–Hull French project. In R. Fasold and D. Schiffrin (eds) *Language Change and Variation* (pp. 411–451). Amsterdam: Benjamins.
Poplack, S. and Walker, D. (1986) Going through (L) in Canadian French. In D. Sankoff (ed.) *Diversity and Diachrony* (pp. 173–198). Amsterdam: Benjamins.
Poplack, S. and Turpin, D. (1999) Does the FUTUR have a future in (Canadian) French? *Probus* 11 (1), 134–164.
Poplack, S. and St-Amand, A. (2007) A real-time window on 19th-century vernacular French: The Récits du français québécois d'autrefois. *Language in Society* 36 (5), 707–734.
Rand, D. and Sankoff, D. (1990) *Goldvarb Version 2: A Variable Rule Application for the Macintosh*. Montreal: Centre de Recherches Mathématiques, Université de Montréal.
Rebuffot, J. (1993) *Le point sur l'immersion au Canada*. Anjou, QC: Centre Educatif et Culturel Inc.
Regan, V. (1995) The acquisition of sociolinguistic native speech norms: Effects of a year abroad on second language learners of French. In B.F. Freed (ed.) *Second Language Acquisition in a Study Abroad Context* (pp. 245–267). Amsterdam: Benjamins.

Regan, V. (1996) Variation in French interlanguage: A longitudinal study of sociolinguistic competence. In R. Bayley and D.R. Preston (eds) *Second Language Acquisition and Linguistic Variation* (pp. 177–201). Amsterdam: Benjamins.

Regan, V. (2004) The relationship between the group and the individual and the acquisition of native speaker variation patterns: A preliminary study. *IRAL – International Review of Applied Linguistics in Language Teaching* 42 (4), 335–348.

Regan, V. (2005) From speech community back to classroom: What variation analysis can tell us about the role of context in the acquisition of French as a foreign language. In J-M. Dewaele (ed.) *Focus on French as a Foreign Language. Multidisciplinary Perspectives* (pp. 191–209). Clevedon: Multilingual Matters.

Regan, V., Howard, M. and Lemee, I. (2009) *The Acquisition of Sociolinguistic Competence in a Study Abroad Context.* Clevedon: Multilingual Matters.

Rehner, K. (1998) Variation in the spoken French of grade 9 and 12 students from extended French programs in the greater Toronto area: Negative particle *ne*, expressions of restriction and markers of consequence. MA thesis, York University, Toronto.

Rehner, K. (2002) The development of aspects of linguistic and discourse competence by advanced second language learners of French. PhD dissertation, OISE/University of Toronto.

Rehner, K. (2004) *Developing Aspects of Second Language Discourse Competence.* Munich: Lincom Europa.

Rehner, K. and Mougeon, R. (1999) Variation in the spoken French of immersion students: To *ne* or not to *ne*, that is the sociolinguistic question. *The Canadian Modern Language Review* 56 (1), 124–154.

Rehner, K. and Mougeon, R. (2003) The effect of educational input on the development of sociolinguistic competence by French immersion students: The case of expressions of consequence in spoken French. *Journal of Educational Thought* 37 (3), 259–281.

Rehner, K., Mougeon, R. and Nadasdi, T. (2003) The learning of sociolinguistic variation by advanced FSL learners: The case of *nous* versus *on* in immersion French. *Studies in Second Language Acquisition* 25 (1), 127–156.

Rhodes, N., Christian, D. and Barfield. S. (1997) Innovations in immersion: The Key School two-way model. In R.K. Johnson and M. Swain (eds) *Immersion Education: International Perspectives* (pp. 265–283). Cambridge: Cambridge University Press.

Roy Nicolet, L. and Jean-Côté, M. (1994) *Portes ouvertes sur notre pays. Manuel 1A, 1B.* Montreal: Guérin.

Sandy, S. (1997) L'emploi variable de la particule négative ne dans le parler des Franco-Ontariens adolescents. MA thesis, York University, Toronto.

Sankoff, G. (1997) Deux champs sémantiques chez les anglophones et les francophones de Montréal. In J. Auger and Y. Rose (eds) *Exploration du lexique* (pp. 133–146). Quebec City: CIRAL.

Sankoff, G. and Cedergren, H. (1976) Les contraintes linguistiques et sociales de l'élision de /l/ chez les Montréalais. In M. Boudreault and F. Mohren (eds) *Actes du XIIIe congrès international de linguistique et philologie romanes* (pp. 1101–1117). Quebec City: Les Presses de l'Université Laval.

Sankoff, G. and Vincent, D. (1977) L'emploi productif du *ne* dans le français parlé à Montréal. *Le Français Moderne* 45, 243–256.

Sankoff, G. and Thibault, P. (1980) The alternation between the auxiliaries *avoir* and *être* in Montreal French. In G. Sankoff (ed.) *The Social Life of Language* (pp. 311–345). Philadelphia: University of Pennyslvania Press.

Sankoff, G. and Vincent, D. (1980) The productive use of *ne* in spoken Montreal French. In G. Sankoff (ed.) *The Social Life of Language* (pp. 295–310). Philadelphia: University of Pennyslvania Press.

Sankoff, D., Sankoff, G., Laberge, S. and Topham, M. (1976) Méthodes d'échantillonnage et utilization de l'ordinateur dans l'étude de la variation grammaticale. *Cahier de linguistique* 6, 85–125.

Sankoff, D., Thibault, P. and Bérubé, H. (1978) Semantic field variablity. In D. Sankoff (ed.) *Linguistic Variation: Models and Methods* (pp. 23–43). New York: Academic Press.

Sankoff, G., Thibault, P., Nagy, N., Blondeau, H., Fonollosa, M-O. and Gagnon, L. (1997) Variation in the use of discourse markers in a language contact situation. *Language Variation and Change* 9 (2), 191–217.

Savignon, S.J. (1983) *Communicative Competence: Theory and Classroom Practice. Texts and Contexts in Second Language Learning.* Reading, MA: Addison-Wesley.

Savignon, S.J. (1997) *Communicative Competence: Theory and Classroom Practice. Texts and Contexts in Second Language Learning* (2nd edn). New York: McGraw-Hill.

Sax, K. (2003) Acquisition of stylistic variation by American learners of French. PhD dissertation, University of Indiana, Ann Arbor, MI, UMI Dissertation Services.

Segalowitz, N. (1976) Communicative incompetence and the non-fluent bilingual. *Canadian Journal of Behavioural Science* 8 (2), 121–131.

Segalowitz, N. (1977) Bilingualism and social behaviour. In W.H. Coons, D. Taylor and M-A. Tremblay (eds) *The Individual, Language and Society in Canada* (pp. 179–195). Ottawa: The Canada Council.

Siegal, M. (1995) Individual differences and study abroad: Women learning Japanese in Japan. In B. Freed (ed.) *Second Language Acquisition in a Study Abroad Context* (pp. 225–244). Amsterdam: Benjamins.

Söll, L. (1969) Zur Konkurrenz von 'Futur simple' und 'Futur proche' im modernen Französisch. *Vox Romanica* 28 (2), 274–284.

Swain, M. and Lapkin, S. (1990) Aspects of the sociolinguistic performance of early and later French Immersion students. In R.C. Scarcella, E.S. Anderson and S.D. Krashen (eds) *Developing Communicative Competence in a Second Language* (pp. 41–54). New York: Newbury House.

Swain, M. and Lapkin, S. (2005) The evolving sociopolitical context of immersion education in Canada: Some implications for program development. *International Journal of Applied Linguistics* 15 (1), 169–186.

Tarone, E. (1988) *Variation in Interlanguage.* London: Edward Arnold.

Tarone, E. (1990) On variation in interlanguage: A response to Gregg. *Applied Linguistics* 11 (4), 392–400.

Tarone, E. and Swain, M. (1995) A sociolinguistic perspective on second language use in immersion classrooms. *Modern Language Journal* 79 (2), 166–178.

Tennant, J. (1995) Variation morphophonologique dans le français parlé des adolescents de North Bay (Ontario). PhD dissertation: University of Toronto.

Thibault, P. and Daveluy, M. (1989) Quelques traces du passage du temps dans le parler des Montréalais, 1971–1984. *Language Variation and Change* 1 (1), 19–45.

Thibault, P. and Vincent, D. (1990) *Un corpus de français parlé. Montréal 84: historique, méthodes et perspectives de recherche.* Quebec City: Department of Languages and Linguistics, Laval University.

Thomas, A. (2000) Étudiants de FLS, français familier: Influence sur la prononciation. Paper presented at the meeting of Association for French Language Studies, Laval University, Quebec City, August 24–27.

Thomas, A. (2002a) L'acquisition du morphème *ne* au niveau avancé du FLS. In C. Tatillon and A. Baudot (eds) *La linguistique fonctionnelle au tournant du* siècle: actes du 24ᵉ colloque international de linguistique fonctionnelle (pp. 327–334). Toronto: GREF.

Thomas, A. (2002b) La variation phonétique en français langue seconde au niveau universitaire avancé. *Acquisition et Interaction en Langue Étrangère* 17, 101–122.

Trévise, A. and Noyau, C. (1984) Adult Spanish speakers and the acquisition of French negation forms: Individual variation and linguistic awareness. In R. Andersen (ed.) *Second Languages: A Cross-Linguistic Perspective* (pp 165–189). Rowley: Newbury House.

Trudgill, P. (1974) *The Social Differentiation of English in Norwich*. Cambridge: Cambridge University Press.

Uritescu, D., Mougeon, R. and Handouleh, Y. (2002) Le comportement du schwa dans le français parlé par les élèves des programs d'immersion française. In C. Tatilon and A. Baudot (eds) *La linguistique fonctionnelle au tournant du siècle: actes du vingt-quatrième Colloque international de linguistique fonctionnelle* (pp. 335–346). Toronto: GREF.

Uritescu, D., Mougeon, R., Rehner, K. and Nadasdi, T. (2004) Acquisition of the internal and external constraints of variable schwa deletion by French immersion students. *International Review of Applied Linguistics* 42 (4), 349–364.

Valdman, A. (1998) La notion de norme pédagogique dans l'enseignement du français langue étrangère. In M. Bilger, K. van den Eynde and F. Gadet (eds) *analyse linguistique et approches de l'oral: recueil d'études offert en hommage à Claire Blanche-Benveniste* (Vol. 10, pp. 177–188). Paris: Peeters Leuven.

Valdman, A. (2003) The acquisition of sociostylistic and sociopragmatic variation by instructed second language learners: The elaboration of pedagogical norms. In C. Blyth (ed.) *The Sociolinguistics of Foreign Language Classrooms: Contributions of the Native, Near-Native, and Non-Native Speaker* (pp. 57–78). Boston: Thomson/Heinle.

Valdman, A., Pons, C., Scullen, M. and Jourdain, S. (2002) *Chez nous. Branché sur le monde francophone*. Upper Saddle River, NJ: Prentice Hall.

Van der Keilen, M. (1995) Use of French, attitudes and motivations of French immersion students. *The Canadian Modern Language Review* 51 (2), 287–304.

Vincent, D., Laforest, M. and Martel, G. (1995) Le corpus de Montréal 1995: Adaptation de la méthode d'enquête sociolinguistique pour l'analyse conversationnelle. *Dialangue* 6, 29–46.

Walter, H. (1977) *La phonologie du Français*. Paris: PUF.

Walter, H. (1990) Une voyelle qui ne veut pas mourir. In J.N. Green and W. Ayres-Bennett (eds) *Variation and Change in French. Essays Presented to Rebecca Posner on the Occasion of her 60th Birthday* (pp. 27–36). London: Routledge.

Wesche, M., Morrison, F., Pawley, C. and Ready, D. (1986) *Post-Secondary Follow-Up of Former Immersion Students in the Ottawa Area*. Ottawa: Centre for Second Language Learning, University of Ottawa.

Wolfram, W., Carter, P. and Moriello, B. (2004) Emerging Hispanic English: New dialect formation in the American South. *Journal of Sociolinguistics* 8 (3), 339–358.

Willis, L. (2000) Etre ou ne plus être: Auxiliary alternation in Ottawa–Hull French. MA thesis, University of Ottawa.

Young, R. (1988) Variation and the interlanguage hypothesis. *Studies in Second Language Acquisition* 10 (3), 281–302.

Young, R. and Bayley, R. (1996) VARBRUL analysis for second language acquisition research. In R. Bayley and D.R. Preston (eds) *Second Language Acquisition and Linguistic Variation* (pp. 253–306). Amsterdam: Benjamins.

For Product Safety Concerns and Information please contact our EU Authorised Representative:

Easy Access System Europe

Mustamäe tee 50

10621 Tallinn

Estonia

gpsr.requests@easproject.com